# JESUS'S AUDIENCE

# JESUS'S
# AUDIENCE

*The Social and Psychological
Environment in which He Worked*

Prolegomena to a Restatement
of the Teaching of Jesus

LECTURES AT NEWQUAY 1971

## J. DUNCAN M. DERRETT

*With a Foreword by*
THE BISHOP OF TRURO

A CROSSROAD BOOK
THE SEABURY PRESS · NEW YORK

First published in Great Britain in 1973
by Darton, Longman & Todd Limited
85 Gloucester Road, London sw7 4su

© 1973 by J. Duncan M. Derrett

The Seabury Press
815 Second Avenue
New York, N.Y. 10017

Printed in the United States of America

*Library of Congress Cataloging in Publication Data*

Derrett, John Duncan Martin, 1922-
Jesus's audience.

"A Crossroad book."
1. Jews—Social life and customs.
2. Jesus Christ. I. Title.

DS112.D4 1974 225.9 73-17893
ISBN 0-8164-1148-4

# Contents

# 6      CONTENTS

# *Foreword*

Dr. Derrett's three lectures on 'Jesus and his Audience' certainly
kept nearly two hundred clergy, at school for three days in Newquay,
alert and interested. If, as he himself asserts, mere book-learning
cannot make people come alive, he managed to contrive this both
with the audience he addressed and the audience of which he was
speaking.

Here was a teacher who could speak with practised detachment
both of things properly familiar to his hearers and of things surprisingly to them unfamiliar. He took us back on his imaginary
journey in space and time to visit Jesus and his audience in their
own bizarre setting—and brought us back perhaps after a few
shocks, but certainly not unhinged.

We enjoyed surprising him at times with speedy answers to some
of his questions. He did not, however detached, always disguise his
delight at being able to bring out of his peculiar treasures things
new to us as well as old.

This Diocesan Bishop does have baths and does get his hair cut,
but then I hope he is not one who would seek to show superior
holiness.[1] I can, however, say that I am better informed about
Jesus's audience, and the better able to rid myself of Western
prejudices and understand the Gospels, since hearing how Dr.
Derrett sees the teaching of Jesus.

I would commend his book most warmly and do so, I believe,
with the support of many clergy who, with me, are most grateful
for the lectures on which it is based.

*Lis Escop, Truro:* December, 1971          MAURICE TRURON:

1. A reference to the typical Asian association of asceticism with holiness,
   mentioned at p. 19 below.

# Preface and Introduction

Canon H. A. Blair asked me to give some lectures to the Truro Diocesan Clergy School, which took place from the 27th to the 29th September, 1971. They were well received, which pleased me since though it was not my first contact with clergymen (for I had met some at conferences before) it was my first confrontation with them in numbers. Like all professional men they have an atmosphere of their own; and since, when I was a child, I had received unfavourable impressions of long since deceased men of their calling, it was quite a revelation to be treated by clergy in what may fairly be called an affectionate manner.

Canon Blair went further and most kindly agreed to read through the first draft of this book. It differed from the published version in that it contained, as an additional appendix, a treatment of the Virgin Birth, a splendid example of ancient piety and poetry (and at the same time a bone in the throat of would-be believers). The subject, indeed, deserves no handling but an exhaustive one, which cannot even be said of my existing treatment of Jesus's conception (*Man*, vol. 6, no. 2, 1971, pp. 289–93). That would-be appendix can eventually develop into something more substantial, and the loss to this volume is minimal. Canon Blair did not pretend to exercise any censorship; but his comments on style and some points of substance throughout the draft were most valuable. I lost the natural use of my mother tongue during the Second World War and I could have used such careful 'reading' many times before. I am most grateful to him for the care he took.

If my work, here and in an earlier book, has any value, this is not, in fact, due to clerical encouragement; but encouragement from men and women who feel that my researches could be useful has certainly meant much to me. This is worth enlarging upon,[1] since by far the majority of religious authors (I mean within Christianity) are clergymen, or laymen given to enthusiasm for religion. It is unusual to pick up a book written by one who regards religious research as another piece of intellectual effort, one who is not concerned in the saving of souls (and is not too sure what is meant by that expression), and is detached, if not from the interests of the Church then at least from its pursuits. Indeed, I am far detached from the former . . .

A man's attitude to his work—what he sees as his function—has a great subconscious effect on his productivity, and his products. The fact that his neighbours might laugh at his notions on the subject is neither here nor there. If they *accept* his products, and use them, and he knows this, he may well lean over to provide for them what *they* really want, not the best he can give. So an author's circle of acquaintances is most decidedly relevant to his academic activity, and the pretence that it is not has never impressed me. Now my efforts in the stony field of New Testament research have been received by theologians with curiosity, surprise, and a good deal of nose-wrinkling. They judge the work, as most of us that are not better than human do, by the results. Not a few of them have found that my efforts tend (quite unexpectedly, and irrespective of any intention on my part) to weaken propositions once taken for granted in a powerful school of New Testament scholarship. I shall never forget the horrified whisper of a very senior man (a household name amongst the adepts), who, struggling to cloak indignation with a modicum of compassion, pointed to a page of which I was

1. In these and other personal remarks, consistent, I think, with our age, which rejects the pose of 'scientific objectivity' (for every 'scientific' writer is the child of his environment and the prisoner of his personality and experience) I follow the sage, and overdue advice tendered by Fr. X. Léon-Dufour at *The Gospels and the Jesus of History* (London, Collins, 1968 (Fontana paperback)), 271, but not in the sense in which he offered it. In his view no one should write about Jesus without openly admitting his faith (or want of it), because the presence or want of faith must influence his judgment and his technique. But there is a third position. A man may have faith due to conviction (see below, p. 152, for the contrasting Hebrew notion), and if he is open to conviction his faith is moulded, and emerges. His readers may well share his experience, since many of them are (or ought to be?) in a similar position. Léon-Dufour's book is a remarkably well balanced production and has excellent bibliographies to each chapter; but it is centred (quite naturally) in the New Testament, and not in the New Testament's world.

the innocent author (annotated in the vernacular with a clearly legible *Was soll dies?*) and said 'My dear friend [always an ominous beginning], you have cut across half a century of critical scholarship!' My reply, being tempered with prudence for once, did not represent my thoughts, which were 'So much the worse for critical scholarship.' I had raised a question which I was incompetent to answer myself, and which has not yet been answered in print, to the best of my knowledge. On the other hand, many, whose own training and temperament (so much more important in the last resort than academic qualifications) lead them in opposite directions to the 'household name', find some of my efforts a source of glee: yet I am as shy of praise from the wrong source as I am indifferent to the alarm of those who are too old to start thinking again. And what circle of friends does all this bring me? None.

For all my perilous adventures I am (in January 1972) no more an intimate of theologians than I am of the clergy. Not that I have avoided clerical contacts: it is simply a fact that my everyday activities do not call for their participation, while my theological doings have, by and large, not endeared me to any of them. It does not follow that one who rummages through the gospels and ferrets out traces of their beginnings is automatically qualified to commune with those who function in the ministry; and the clerics who have actually invited me to stretch my legs under their tables are remarkable chiefly for this, that they know, by instinct and experience, where kindness is properly bestowed. These somewhat unexpected comments are enough to assure, or reassure, my reader that I am indeed in a position to do what few have done before, namely to tackle the topic of the teaching of Jesus without bias, preconceived aims, or subconscious allegiances. What was given to me was not given by the Church, and what I have it cannot take away from me.

I am a teacher, which, in my corner of the academic world means automatically a researcher. I have not had to eat my hat yet, but men of my kind see nothing shameful in admitting that they have made a mistake and that they are now better informed. A teacher of this sort is automatically a learner, and he likes nothing better than helping other people to learn. That does not mean cramming things down their throats. I was asked to do a piece of teaching at Truro. I was received, as I have said, kindly. I came away. The thing might well have ended there, but for a question which that Clergy School posed in an acute form. The diocese appeared in the guise of learners—and what was it they were really keen to learn? That the text of the gospels really called out, loud and clear, the authentic voice of Jesus (properly 'the Lord Jesus'), capable of being translated by the clergy into words meaningful to the average person in any dilemma of his, acute or trivial. They were keen to learn this, but they did not know how to set about it; and they were sensitive lest their predetermined object bias their judgment and interfere with the process they wanted to undergo. What could a professional teacher do for them, since he was not an intimate of theirs, did not speak their language, and, by definition, eschewed their declared object? The respective positions had to be defined. Irrespective of what they wanted to hear, their speaker's notion of how they should begin to listen to their sources was the first unfamiliar concept which they were asked, for the sake of argument, to accept. And other speakers on the same occasion proceeded upon similar lines, if in other contexts. The School was intended not so much to convey information as to induce in the participants readiness to listen to new sorts of tunes, to pick up harmonies which had previously been ignored or rejected. And on that basis I felt that the teacher's function was properly exercised.

In our day teachers do not recite material for their students to learn by heart. Our teachers (unlike those of Jesus's time) actually encourage dissent and discussion. True, in Jesus's day, this could go on in the closely circumscribed limits of loyal personal solidarity between teacher and taught: but dissent which threatened that bond was not offered or tolerated. A purely dogmatic tone was normal, and offended no one. It is not surprising that clerics brought up on biblical style should expect to use a dogmatic style themselves, and should react firmly against any dogmatic proposition that is inconsistent with their own. But the virtue of our educational system is that it regards dogmatic methods as historically understandable, but intellectually inferior and gross: and I found that my audience was prepared (as I hope my reader now is prepared) to accept in the spirit in which it is offered a teacher's researches, to be used by them as best they can, given their own capacities, their own experience, and (are they aware of them?) their own prejudices and limitations.

It was a fairly recent discovery for me that Jesus, that exotic person, is too easily overrated as well as underrated, like other exotics, in an environment (e.g. ours) which is totally foreign to him. By 'overrated' I mean what is now believed or said of him in liturgy does not correspond to what he is represented as proposing and propounding in our authoritative texts, the gospels. The church has added, for its own purposes, many coats of varnish to what was once a wholly credible picture. It makes me think of stones I have often seen in India. These were once beautifully carved with lively little scenes of heroism and human virtue. The silly villagers have, in their minds, turned their ancestors of seven centuries or so ago into deities. The stones are smothered with oil and coloured powder (that being the style of offering worship), until they look quite disgusting and no trace of the beautiful sculpture can be made out. The ancient Hebrews had a highly sophisticated style of speaking of 'unseen' things; they threaded symbol upon symbol, and spun elaborate patterns of allusive, evocative thought, prose music. Their Greek neighbours sometimes understood what they were 'going on about'; more often they did not. Hebraic poetry induced semi-hypnotic psychic states in those who did not grasp the religious history and linguistic, literary richness that was conveyed by the texts, and it was not long before spurious intellectualisation and bogus research piled imaginative speculation on top of materials which had ceased to have an easy life of their own, but were on the way to being mummified. The gospel is bound in boards studded with jewels, and is kissed reverently; but the contents are dimly understood, if understood at all. And nonsense creeps in while no one is looking. I am not sure that the position is improved when the gospels are translated into 'stockbroker English', and bound in red cloth. More than that is needed. Jesus would not have wanted to be 'overrated'. A statement such as 'Jesus is God', can be very puzzling to modern man, whose instinct to question it is by no means to be despised. What would Jesus himself have said about it? Odd as it struck me when I discovered the fact, it remains a vexed problem for the theologians (who ought to know) what Jesus *did* suppose he was.

Similarly, Jesus is dreadfully *underrated*. Since, whatever else he was (and he was a man of superb courage, courageous beyond the limits of the most courageous in a courageous age), he was evidently a Master in my own Faculty, I am alarmed at a want of interest in his teaching generally, and at lack of interest in what seems to me a vital question, namely, how far has the teaching of Jesus been swallowed up in the teaching of the churches? Acres of paper are covered by discussions as to the methodology by which one determines whether a particular account, like the Walking on the Water, or even the Sermon on the Mount, can be traced back to the historical Jesus. But I have, for all my travels through the theologians' writings, never come across a treatment of what I should regard as essential: how far do the theologians' subconscious desires to please their students, their desire to be 'with it', influence their judgment as well as their mode of presentation? And how many of the clergy give way to what might be called 'weak-mindedness' by those who are not in their precise dilemma, so that they represent the teaching of Jesus as if it were not far above what the congregation can achieve with a modicum of gentlemanly effort?

Leo Tolstoy did a good deal of New Testament research. In spite of his extensive library and correspondence he could not, indeed, arrive at an understanding of the precise situation of Jesus as a Jewish teacher in an oriental environment. I do not have the pen of a Tolstoy, and vivid attempts to satirise the effect of 'with it' theology would never be forgiven. I must confess that I feel sure Tolstoy was right in his main contention, that, assuming that intellectual effort can recover the teaching of Jesus, this, and this alone, must be the criterion for determining whether one is a student of Jesus. He who decides that he is, knows that he has a permanent and unchanging standard by which his life must be guided. A teaching such as 'You must not kill, unless the government of the day tells you that you are at war' is in perpetual danger of being stigmatised as compromise with the devil. The Prince of this World[2] may be an unfashionable entity at the moment, but, after my adventures in the theologians' field, I feel sure that no honest man can offer himself as a teacher of *Jesus's* teachings and still live his life as if the devil were the true and effective ruler so far as he is concerned.

I made this point once, and the reply I received was that the usages and customs of the Church, not to speak of the laws by which it is established in this country, sanction, permit, and encourage friendly, indeed affectionate, relations between theologians, clergy and laity. If the clergy were to live in ivory towers (a quip at my

---

2. If readers find my comment odd, that tells them something about themselves. They would approve of swimming-coaches who have never entered water. On the Devil see Mt. 4: 8–9; Jn. 8:44, 12:31, 16:11; 2 Co. 4:4; Ep. 6:12; 1 QS ii. 19–25a; Mart. Is. 2:4.

expense?) and holy righteousness, and abstain from defiling contact with 'this world' they would be like the Pharisee in the Temple, and unfit for their calling. My comment was also gently reproved, as being unnecessarily aggressive (was this a defensive attitude on my part?), and in bad taste. A man like I, it was suggested, should not be guilty of bad taste. Moreover, since the teaching of Jesus was not finally and indisputably established, any example I might care to choose might turn out to be unfortunate. The Church's teaching permits Christians to go to war, however much war is abhorrent, as is all brutality (now called in some quarters 'ill treatment'). It might be that further research would prove that the Church was right and Tolstoy and those who share his views wrong. The Church's willingness to allow divorced persons, whose former spouses were still alive, to remarry in church vowing perpetual faithfulness to the third party, is, to my mind, highly anomalous: but I am, it is said, too ready to accuse men of hypocrisy and 'with it' theology when the truth of Jesus's teaching in this particular is none too clear, and if it were its relevance to modern conditions remains (so they say) to be proved.

I hope I have shown that I have, and reserve, complete independence of all teachers. But I must, of course, except those teachers who, in the first century A.D. (or, in the case of St. John the Evangelist, *conceivably* a little later), put together with immense artistry and skill the surviving traditions of Jesus, their Master. Their works were the respective culminations of many years of meditation, research (into the Hebrew Bible), and pastoral experience. When the gospels were first chanted aloud—slowly with the sounds rising, falling, and warbling on the syllables of words meticulously placed in the key positions of the lines—the audiences (now called 'congregations') will have shrieked aloud, and numbers will have fainted. The beauty of the stories and sayings, with their multiple allusions to well-known tales in the Hebrew scriptures, to maxims of the Jewish faith, to well-established symbols of Jewish religious hope; the intelligence with which stories about Jesus were chosen to tell the believer intimate things about his *own* psychological position; the awful clarity of the warnings and judgments pronounced upon those who, knowing the message to be true, did not live in accordance with it—all these made the experience of listening to the reading of the gospel a gruelling affair, gruelling, and, no doubt, uplifting as no other contemporary literature was. I am not independent of those teachers, and, like others, I cannot go behind them except by using indications, hints, allusions, and signs which they have planted there for us to notice. My research is based upon no predisposition of mine, except to do justice to those masterly composers, those musicians of words, and so to do justice to their own Master, in whose relevance even for the non-Jewish world they utterly believed. If what I say, and the way I say it, offends any section of our population, it is just too bad! I know that there are many that recognise that the academic reconstruction of Jesus's teaching will have only a place within the rich life of the Church, which itself determines the function of Scripture—while at the same time asserting, as I do, that unless the Master is understood the labourer labours in vain.

I am not trying to suggest that non-Christian authors have been any more successful than conventionally minded Christians in depicting the story of Jesus. I have not encountered one who did not have serious biasses of his own.

Then, for whom am I writing? I know exactly who he is. He is a young person, or young in heart and mind, who has no opinions about Christianity, and, at the same time, no traumatic prejudices against it. He is curious, but not so overwhelmed by curiosity that he would ransack libraries for information. He also suspects that most writers he would encounter would be either very obscure or sceptical (and he himself has scepticism to sell), or profound believers of the 'I believe from the bottom of my heart' type, whose objectivity is suspect. I want him to have a chance to hear how an uncommitted person sees the teaching of Jesus. The parables can now be understood as Jesus's own hearers understood them. I want him to prepare his mind to read the gospels and epistles *as if he were a first-century man*, a pagan, say, who lived within the ambit of Jewish religious ideas and practice; he would then be like the Syro-Phoenician woman—ready to argue with Jesus, and actually convince him (Mk. 7:26–30)! To convince him, that is to say, and in turn be convinced by him! I want Jesus to have a chance to communicate with my imaginary student, and the first step must be to rid that student of his Western prejudices, the limitations of his 'cynical materialist' world, so that, even if he never likes first-century man he can at least understand him.

I do not know how clergy and theologians will welcome my scheme in its entirety. My reception at Newquay related to 'stage one' of a triple-decker enterprise. I fear stage two might have been a harder one for them to digest. For it is a natural tendency to assimilate someone you love and respect into your own world; while my effort is to disengage Jesus from our world in order to return to our world with an authentic image of him and his teaching.

My attempt to make a contribution to Christian theology would, thus, come in three stages: (1) a description of Jesus's audience, (2) a restatement of Jesus's teaching as his contempories heard it, and (3) a restatement of that teaching in terms which should be valid and intelligible today, intelligible to people who do not, for example, believe in the devil and in eternal fires. This book is 'stage one'. I tremble at the thought of the third, but if it is to be done, done it will be. And whatever help is necessary for it will be forthcoming. My isolation from people is no problem for Him 'who spoke, and the world was'. That I should actually lecture to an entire diocesan clergy is a fact which, in my mind, has an element of awesome incongruity (it reveals the enterprise of the organiser); something even more unexpected may well be in store for me. My reader will surely have the courage to study what, he may be sure, took a lot of courage to compile.

Scholars may well object. 'He is', they may say, 'about to fall headlong into a trap!' Even if, they say, one can depict Jesus's audience from relevant materials, notably from the gospels themselves (which reveal most when their authors were off their guard), Jesus's teaching will not be easy to recover, since, as I have admitted, the first Church retold it in a fashion pleasing to itself. We did not, indeed, have to wait for a Hellenic Church, in which contact with the Jewish world had worn thin, to sophisticate Jesus's teaching. That process was already at work before the gospels were compiled, including those of Matthew, Luke and even Mark. That is a hurdle I shall try to get over when the opportunity for 'stage two' comes up. Meanwhile let us concentrate on stage one.

An incredulous reader may ask, surely qualified people have attempted this before? They have not. Since the fathers of the Church of the second century, the leading minds in theology have been Hellenic, Western. If we are to leave aside the theme of asceticism, the contribution of the Syrian orient has not been distinguished sufficiently from its Western counterpart, and there is no easy means of finding out whether it occurred to a Greek-speaking theologian, even in ancient times, to depict the contemporaries of Jesus, in all their Asian peculiarities, as an anthropologist would require. Modern works by actual Syrians are of ambiguous quality.[3] Often they give an excellent insight into material conditions and social manners in the Near East: but there is no check upon what proportion of their information is valid for Jesus's time. It has, rather, been natural enough that those who preached the faith should assume that their congregations would more readily accept Christ and his teachings if Christ were brought to them, than if they were to be brought to Christ. Christ became, in the process, a Greek, or a half-Hebrew, a character out of a comparative-religion romance, a mystery, a figure calling for awe rather than attention. The same transfer is still being made. Professor C. H Dodd, in his most recent book (perhaps unfairly criticised for its old-fashioned concept of historicity),[4] repeatedly, to judge from tell-tale expressions, projects Jesus in terms appropriate to a contemporary of ours, and speaks of his world as if it were (barring

3. The works of Abraham Mitrie Rihbany (e.g. *The Syrian Christ*, London, 1919) and George M. Lamsa (e.g. *Gospel Light*, Philadelphia, 1939) are of absorbing interest, but the authors themselves could not sift the wheat from the chaff.
4. *The Founder of Christianity* (London, Collins, 1971). Passages to which attention might be drawn occur at pp. 31 ('traffic of two worlds' is a distinctly non-oriental notion, since to the Asian the two worlds overlap and coexist); 43 ('perennial factors in history' characteristically retells past events in current language); 36 (some accounts of Jesus's doings are 'not in character', an idea dependent on the European notion of consistency); 77 (Judaism had no 'integrity' in this sense); 87 (what could contemporaries have understood by 'real religion'?); 97 (forgiveness, and 'forfeited by their disloyalty' are sentimental notions out of keeping with the situation); 101 ('you have said it' is a euphemism to avoid a tabooed utterance, not an 'accepted form of affimation' only, which in any case it certainly was: Mt. 26:25); 127 ('yoke' is, in spite of the words, not 'his', but Yahweh's as he interpreted it, and it was not a paradox); and 127-8. At the last place Dodd says 'In the pursuit of his mission he found himself obliged not merely to neglect some of the finer points of current religious practice (such as fasting on the proper days) but also to break some of the rules which were thought necessary to safeguard the religion of the Law (such as those of sabbath observance)'. This suggests a British itinerant preacher forced to put up at places where the beds were not aired. The 'last appeal to the Galileans' (p. 134) also sounds rather like Winston Churchill speaking on the state of the Navy. I trust my Newquay lectures will show that Hebrews had no such expectations of each other, nor such attitudes towards each other. Consequently they could not have 'assessed situations' in the sense Dodd implies at p. 139.

a few oddities) like ours, which it was not. This is an understandable method, and one which, unless he is warned of the dangers, the average reader would unhesitatingly (and unconsciously) accept. Yet, if we are to understand Jesus we must commence by visiting him in his own setting, however bizarre the experience. I have no doubt but that such an imaginary journey back in space and time would be a shock, such as might temporarily unhinge many of us. And few modern teachers would, as a matter of course, require their students to realise that fact.

There are excellent books written by Western man for Western man about Ancient Israel. Their habits, their beliefs, their theories, their fantasies, and their hopes, are described fully, coolly, and ineffectually. Their authors are like men who have learnt a foreign language from books, and never had the inestimable advantage of learning from a native speaker on the spot. The writers have never lived in an Asian society, and when they hear of the lives and attitudes of Asians who live amongst us here in Britain[5] they are astounded. Jesus's contemporaries were like that, only more so. No Acts of Parliament, no Race Relations Board would compel a public-house keeper to serve one of them if he turned up, by some miracle, and made it known that he wanted a glass of wine. The odd garments, the wild facial expressions, normal to those to whom the unseen world is as real as the phenomenal world, the exaggerated and loud demeanour, the absence of anything recognisable as culture (in our definition of it): all these would be very bad for business if they were encouraged. John the Baptist will have worn enveloping robes (against the heat) and after a while the want of a daily bath will have made itself noticeable, except, no doubt, on the days when he went into the river (and how deep did he go?). Those enthusiasts who believed in ritual dips did so for holiness's sake, not hygiene, and they could over-do it wildly[6]—and there were those still more holy who never washed at all. Imagine a diocesan bishop who showed his superior holiness relative to the diocesan clergy by never taking a bath on principle! Or not cutting his hair!

Teachers who have studied Latin and Greek, and trained their

5. Ursula Sharma, *Rampal and his Family. The Story of an Immigrant* (London, Collins, 1971). At many points the Asian speakers actually confirm what I say below in their own words.
6. Jos., *Life*, 11.

minds in western sciences, perhaps added a certain amount of Hebrew, and then capped all with a gentlemanly stay in the Holy Land, looking at the Arab inhabitants much as we look at animals in the Zoo, are (despite their best efforts) somewhat less than competent, if well-meaning guides. Their studies of rabbinical thought, or Jewish theology in the time of Jesus, or kindred subjects[7] are splendid so far as they go. It is all sound book-learning. But it does not make *those people* come alive. Nor is the matter improved if one prepares studies of the material culture from books and archaeology. There are excellent books on Life and Times in the environment in which Jesus worked:[8] but they tell us little or nothing of the psychology of the people, which is all-important. And yet the materials lie, as they have always lain, ready to the hand. Jesus himself, adjusting his speech to his hearers' levels, tells us what they could understand and what their prejudices were.

Leslie D. Weatherhead's books[9] do not approach my theme historically. Nor does Daniel-Rops' *Jesus en son temps* (which has gone into two editions). William Barclay's *Jesus as They Saw Him*[10] does not scrutinise Jesus's audience at all. J. G. Davies' *Daily Life in the Early Church*[11] does not deal with Palestinian life in the first century, nor does his *Social Life of Early Christians*[12]—these are books of imaginative reconstruction of episodes in the third to fifth centuries inclusive. His *Making of the Church*[13] is in a similar style. His *Early Christian Church*[14] deals with the background to the apostolic age in the first 35 pages. Though in a more scholarly style, it is not a study of Jesus's audience from within. On the other

---

7. I have in mind Fr J. Bonsirven's *Palestinian Judaism in the Time of Christ* (New York, McGraw-Hill, 1965) and R. N. Longenecker, *The Christology of Early Jewish Christianity* (London, S.C.M., 1970).

8. The works of K. E. Wilken (1953) and A. C. Bouquet (1954) and the series of works on the History of New Testament Times up to that by Werner Foerster (1959), translated as *Palestinian Judaism in New Testament Times* (Edinburgh, 1964). There is the work of Joachim Jeremias, including his collected essays, *Abba*, and his *Jerusalem in the Time of Jesus. An Investigation into Economic and Social Conditions during the New Testament Period* (London, S.C.M., 1969). I should commend for its scope and brevity and simplicity of style J. L. McKenzie's chapter in *A Catholic Commentary on Holy Scripture* (1953), but for a slight tendentious aroma (appropriate there).

9. *It Happened in Palestine* (London, 1936). *Holy Land* (London, 1948).

10. S.C.M. Paperback, 1962.                                    11. London, 1952.

12. London, 1954.            13. London, 1960.            14. London, 1965.

hand Roy A. Stewart's *Rabbinic Theology* (Edinburgh/London, Oliver & Boyd, 1961), which was not received with great enthusiasm by the learned, does in fact contain numerous particulars about, references to, and comments upon the mentality, prejudices, and assumptions of the Hebrews who contributed to, made up, and inspired the Talmuds and ancient *midrashim*; apart from the fact that the materials come from centuries long after the first century *as well as that century*, I should strongly recommend it, and indeed I view it with a much more appreciative eye than did its specialist reviewers. F. F. Bruce's *New Testament History* (London, 1969) is also commendable.

There *is* a work on Jesus's audience, but it is, though most interesting, of no help in understanding what that audience was like.[15] There are books entitled Men and Manners, the Living World of the New Testament, and even the New Testament in its Environment.[16] But they tend to be surveys using history as a mouthpiece for the authors' theology: theologians speaking 'God-

15. J. Arthur Baird, *Audience Criticism* (Philadelphia, 1969). The same remark may be made about A. W. Mosley's article at *New Testament Studies*, vol. 10 (1963–4), 139–49.
16. J. P. Arendzen, *Men and Manners in the Days of Christ* (London, 1928); H. C. Kee and F. W. Young, *The Living World of the New Testament* (London, D.L.T., 1960); G. B. Caird, *The Apostolic Age* (London, Duckworth, 1966); Floyd V. Filson, *The New Testament against its Environment* (London, S.C.M., 1950) (the attitude to magic, pp. 94–6, betrays the standpoint). The works of Eric F. F. Bishop (e.g. *Jesus of Palestine, The Local Background to the Gospel Documents*) belong to a genre essentially deriving from the literature of pilgrim guides. They are an aid to the pious, and not seldom illuminate the biblical text. But they tell us nothing of the mentality of Jesus's audience, and no more does that enormous encyclopedia of Palestinian life, G. Dalman's *Arbeit und Sitte*. The works of converted Jews would have been of immense value had they not come from minds unsympathetic to Judaism (see n. 19 below), approaching the gospels more or less uncritically. Nevertheless A. Edersheim's *Life and Times of Jesus the Messiah* (1883 and reprinted many times subsequently) and his *History of the Jewish Nation* (revised edn., London, 1896), and the work of N. Levison (especially his *Parables*, 1926) have quantities of valuable information within them. Edersheim's *Temple, its Ministry and Services* and his *Sketches of Jewish Social Life in the Days of Christ* were both written in order to give readers an idea of the scene 'on which, and the persons among whom the events recorded in New Testament history had taken place'. Both were most useful, but to modern taste the want of a sense of humour towards the Jews, whom Edersheim approaches with typical Victorian sanctimoniousness, is as fatal as the uncritical pro-Christian and anti-Jewish slant

talk', presuming in their own readers knowledge and leanings of which the audience of Jesus was completely innocent. I have complained before of the habit of turning Jesus into a Man for All Seasons, a person not different in quality from the prestige figure in each society (e.g. once a public-school boy, now a left-wing revolutionary?). Small wonder that his teachings are not taken seriously, and that the groups that meet to listen to his Word wonder why they themselves are not more numerous, more united, or more confident!

Theologians will recognise in what I have been saying something reminiscent of Henry J. Cadbury's *Peril of Modernising Jesus*,[17] a book which satirises most effectively the tendency of preachers and other experts to translate Jesus into the modern world. I do not agree with some of his detailed notions, for Cadbury, too, had no personal intimacy with the ancient and oriental world: but he was, in local idiom, 'dead right' in his main contention. Cadbury ranks as a respectable theologian, but his attitude, though treated with deference, is ignored in practice for want of the appropriate means to react to it positively.

Glimpses of Asian and African societies of today can shock, and a most sympathetic exponent of life there will agree that their standards and ours differ fundamentally. Their criticisms of us would not be less sharp than ours of them. I shall not go into details, for there is no point in wounding a sensitive person. Scally-wags in our own civilisation(s) can give no clue to the mentality of the men to whom collectively Josephus attributed (no doubt rightly) the fall of the Jewish state. One must go to the East to understand *why* they are (*a*) so 'backward' politically, and (*b*) so 'advanced' in religious disposition: the two go together—quite appropriately in sociological terms. In trying to understand them we must jettison our own standards, our sanctimoniousness, our affectation of cultural superiority, our sentimentality, and, in particular that self-deception which enables us to pride ourselves (in spite of evidence

which he gives to his work wherever, as often, New Testament history impinges upon his 'scene'. There is a further handicap, of which his contemporaries were as little aware as himself, lurking behind the unconscious assumption that the theories of the Pharisees to be found in the Talmuds would serve, without qualification, to depict the 'Jewish' outlook in the time of Jesus. The Dead Sea Scrolls have cured us of that.

17. New York, Macmillan, 1937. Happily reprinted as an S.P.C.K. paperback in 1962.

to the contrary) upon consistency, a quality Asians will never understand.

At this point, readers sensing that, if I were to describe the ancient East frankly, I should use unparliamentary language will interrupt me. Mankind is basically the same the world over. We have seen on television likeable adolescents from the forests of South America, and from nomadic tribes of East Africa, who obviously have a lot in common with our own adolescents. And babies, whatever the colour of their skins, are obviously babies everywhere. But the Romans who crucified Jesus were not babies, and the various sections of Hebrew society which cooperated to have Jesus destroyed by the Romans were not 'likeable adolescents'. They were products of a complex society, an old civilisation, much older than ours, which we can learn to understand only if we get up very early in the morning. In my own view only life amongst Asians can teach one their prejudices, their superstitions, their strengths and their weaknesses, and if one cannot spend, as I did, the sensitive part of one's youth with them one must be prepared for the shock I have spoken of, or one will have learnt nothing at all.

This way of putting things will not please the 'Gentlemanly Jews', as I call them. These are the partly-assimilated Jews long settled amidst our nominally Christian communities, *with* Europe, but not yet *of* Europe. Intermarriage here and there, long absence from Eastern climes, a fair complexion, the abandonment of occupations requiring the ultimate in thrift and cunning, and the ready assumption of gentile manners, as well as their inevitable prominence in any professional or artistic activity, have made them look like Europeans, and behave like them. Inbreeding is essential if Jews are to remain Jews, but the Asian characteristics, for the most part, are wearing thin. The Arabs do indeed identify them as Europeans, and no wonder. Meanwhile Christians have long been keen to have their assistance in unravelling the background to the Christian faith. Whilst finding Jews *en masse* repugnant culturally (as is likely, for they flouted all the rules of social cohesion by immigrating in the first place) they invited individuals to take part in biblical research, and I am sure little progress could have been made without them. In due course Jews, having learnt (and eventually taught) the techniques of Western scholarship, pursued biblical studies on their own and independent of Christian stimulus.

A number of Jews made contributions specifically to New Testament studies.[18] Many of them were teachers by training, profession, or inclination. It is not surprising that they attempted to make the Jewish world of the first century seem homely, easy to understand, not so very different from Victorian England. The Gentlemanly Jews made a 'gentlemanly' story out of the New Testament record, and as much harm has flowed from this as good. The world of the New Testament was not a gentlemanly world. Some Western Jews of today will probably regard my present effort as unfortunate, since it represents their ancestors in a disagreeable light.[19] I am not

18. I have in mind C. G. Montefiore and I. Abrahams. The late Paul Winter promised to be a more critical counterpart, but his untimely death left his work incomplete. The function of the 'gentlemanly Jews' was to represent Judaism and the character of the Hebrews in a light favourable to nineteenth-century liberal ideas. This was automatically hostile to any objective historical approach, and still more inconsistent with any investigation which would now be recognised as anthropological or sociological. Their 'market' was all too ready for these aberrations. A splendid example is to be found in J. W. Etheridge, *The Targums* (London, 1862), I, 13–14. The traditional approach to the book of Genesis allegorised Esau and Laban, transforming them into symbols of evil; their dealings with Jacob, therefore, illustrated (to the mind of Hebrews contemporary with Jesus) the hazards to which the righteous (and the Hebrew nation!) are subject in life. Etheridge is indignant at these apparently gratuitous departures from the Masoretic text of the first book of Moses. He is, conversely, delighted with the *Historical and Critical Commentary on the Old Testament* of M. M. Kalisch, which deals with Gn. 33: 4–11 in a tone of syrup, typical of Victorian sentimentality, abandoning traditional interpretation for something which the promulgators of the Masoretic text can never have contemplated.

19. Many acute Jewish minds, trained in Hebrew and rabbinics, have been drawn to Christianity, and conversion has, in some cases, brought them to high positions in the Church. The case of H. L. Pass (1875-1938) was most interesting (see C. S. Gillett, *Herman Leonard Pass. A Memoir* (London/ Oxford, Mowbray, 1939). I am obliged to a pupil of his, the Rev. Donald Young, for further information. Obtaining distinction at Cambridge for his semitic studies (with articles to his credit: he published in the *Jewish Quarterly Review* for 1899), he became, on conversion, outstanding for his work as a teacher of ordinands. He became a great churchman, outstanding too for his lack of interest in, and deprecation of, the Old Testament and of all traditional Jewish learning. His *Divine Commonwealth* (London/ Oxford, 1936), which is about the Beatitudes, makes no use of Jewish sources, even of the Mishnah! Here the Victorian, pre-sociological, emotional rejection of the mentality inside which Jesus, as teacher, was bound to function, could not but vitiate his intellectual endeavour: and he was a great intellectual, as his works, and reminiscences of him, confirm!

deterred by this. No one hesitates to study Tudor England because many of its worthies would not be given house-room now.

Someone may ask, 'But surely the works of Josephus, in the famous but not too accurate translation of Whiston, have been available quite cheaply for a very long time, and the true nature of the Hebrews' civilization at the relevant period has had the widest publicity?' I think the answer is that readers of Whiston's *Josephus*, like the readers of old John Lightfoot in the seventeenth century, were more or less compelled to make a simple mental equation: 'the Jews were wicked people; they had Jesus crucified; he condemned them for their disobedience to God: anything we hear about them tending to show that they were victims of a well-merited punishment only serves to bear him out: and the less we learn about them (except to illustrate his Word) the better'. Typical of Hebrew and rabbinical studies in that and the next century (cf. J. Cocceius) were endeavours to prove that the Hebrew writings already showed the Jews that Jesus was their Messiah, and that their blindness was wicked as well as incredible. But the world has moved on, and we shall understand a great deal more about Jesus if we get to know his world sympathetically. I have hinted that one can indeed know sympathetically a society which is culturally repugnant.

I want to describe the contemporaries of Jesus without praise or blame. My readers must never again seek mentally to bring them home, to naturalise them, or make them into Britons for the time being. In France the works of R. Aron and J. Isaac have tried to produce a cosy, homely attitude, as a result of which Christians can recognise Jews as their—almost—co-religionists. From the point of view of the twentieth (or should I say twenty-first?) century's social needs the less discomfort one feels in thinking of one's Jewish, or gentile, neighbours the better. But to pretend that the ancient Jewish world was a cosy one into which we could fit easily is unintellectual, and the concentration upon such features of ancient Judaism as happen to coincide with modern Christian tastes and spirituality (neglecting the beastly aspects) is a disservice to scholarship. One might well ask whether there was, amongst the Hebrews, any correspondence with *any* section of our own society. If there were it would make my 'stage three' immeasurably easier. I am not sure that there was *no* correspondence. However, if the hat fits occasionally that is pure coincidence.

My scheme is to divide into sections the information I have been able to gather. It is a rather condensed treatment, and I have deliberately stayed clear of dictionaries and encyclopedias, picking up my few illustrations from original sources alone. The references have been given so that a reader may look up the sources for himself, and I take it for granted that specimens will be more informative for him than any attempt at exhaustive treatment. Many citations will be quite familiar to people who read their bible or hear it read out regularly. Some extremely familiar allusions I have left unreferenced: the reader will see the point for himself. Many will be surprised from time to time to see in what contexts passages are cited.

A feature of lecturing style might irritate some readers. When the lecturer wishes to ram a few points home, especially aspects of his subject new to his audience and neglected generally, he tends to repeat himself and revert to favourite themes more frequently than is usual in print. Topics such as 'solidarity', 'consumption', 'prestige' are emphasised in this way here, with the intention of leaving the hearer in no doubt that if he neglects them for the future his understanding of the New Testament will be defective.

Our material tells us, not surprisingly, more about religious matters, and about the relations between teachers and pupils, and their competitors, than about other aspects of life. This spoils the balance. But the gospels are about teaching, and without it they themselves would not exist. They are highly sophisticated and clever teaching programmes, the depth of which we have hardly begun to probe. Since most scholars are Western, the pupils ultimately of Hellenes, the admirers of sharp, logical, precise minds, few have realised that the gospels say a very great deal more than their surface suggests, and those that have realised this (apart from the too easily despised practitioners of the pulpit) have made it known fitfully and unsystematically. Gospel irony, which is one of the gems of world literature, is almost entirely unrecognised for what it is.

An instinctive dislike of Asian ways of thought and expression have induced scholars to shut their eyes to techniques which no Greek would use. 'But the texts are in Greek', they protest, 'and we are', they say, 'rather good at Greek'. But this is the Greek of the international, cosmopolitan sect that purported to worship the deity of the Hebrews, called Yahweh, *alias* 'the Lord', under the direction of a thoroughly Jewish teacher, called Jesus, who acquired (we are not quite sure how) the designation Messiah (*alias* Christ). That was not ordinary Greek, or to the extent that it was it barely concealed a very un-Greek activity and mode of thought. How foreign the Jews and Greeks felt to each other is eloquently shown by a curious passage in Josephus's *Against Apion* (§§.176–182).[20] It reads exactly like some Brahmin from New Delhi describing how Swami Vivekananda was received in America. Josephus quotes Clearchus, who is himself quoting no less a personage than Aristotle giving details of his (very naïve) astonishment at the intelligence, adaptability, and other merits of a certain Jew from, it would seem, Jerusalem, as far back as about 345 B.C. The key phrase in which Aristotle is made to express his approbation of this Hebrew philosopher is this: 'he was Hellenic not merely in speech but even in soul'. In other words the Jew had managed not only to be fluent in Greek (as Hindus are all too fluent in English) but also to think, and feel, like a Greek—which was a marvel. Josephus, of all people, would have suppressed such a comment if he had not thought it highly complimentary to his people; and it is obvious that that is exactly how he saw it.

After depicting the mental furniture of Jesus's contemporaries as best I can, I add some scattered fragments in a different tone and with a different, but parallel, purpose. Here I shall go into some detail, and the reader not acquainted with theological pedantry will, I hope, have patience with me while I explain some passages of very different levels of difficulty. These explanations have not been given before. I wish to impress upon the reader that there is *still* a very great deal to be found out. The Christian story is not all 'tied up and done with'. Neither the pious nor the agnostic nor the anti-Christian knows enough about it. No one can dismiss the subject until he is better informed. And no one who is not a model of patience can say that he has applied his mind to it at all.

No bibliography could possibly satisfy the really curious. I offer a bibliographical note to help a reader of this book who is more or less confined to the English language, and whom I imagine to be in a certain position having read my survey of Jesus's audience. I imagine that the people were, virtually, what the less educated of our compatriots call 'a bunch of wogs', and that my reader has

20. H. Lewy, at *Harvard Theological Review*, vol. 31 (1938), 222, suggests the figure of the Jew may be an invention of Josephus. Even if this is so (and it strikes me as unlikely) my point remains equally valid (if not more so).

accepted this, and is not offended by it. He places this together with another piece of information which he obtained independently, and he wants to go further and acquaint himself with what really went on. That piece of information is that Jesus's teaching (without which the Crucifixion and Resurrection would have been meaningless) has never been equalled, let alone surpassed.

# Abbreviations

The reader for whom especially I have written is not in the habit of handling the Bible. A table of abbreviations, therefore, needs to be set up, so far as the Bible is concerned, not in alphabetical order but in the order of the books. In the *Jerusalem Bible* the Apocrypha also appears, and the order is as shown below. It is perhaps convenient to note at this point that the book usually called 'Ecclesiastes' is shown as Qo and 'Ecclesiasticus' as Si (for Ben Sirach, Sirachides). For apocryphal material not in the *Jerusalem Bible* or the *New English Bible* (*Apocrypha*) reference must be made to R. H. Charles' compilation (below).

| | | | | | |
|---|---|---|---|---|---|
| Gn | Genesis | Pr | Proverbs | Zp | Zephaniah |
| Ex | Exodus | Qo | Ecclesiastes | Hg | Haggai |
| Lv | Leviticus | | (Qohelet) | Zc | Zechariah |
| Nb | Numbers | Sg | Song of Songs | Ml | Malachi |
| Dt | Deuteronomy | | (Canticles) | Mt | Matthew |
| Jos | Joshua | Ws | Wisdom | Mk | Mark |
| Jg | Judges | Si | Ecclesiasticus | Lk | Luke |
| Rt | Ruth | | (Sirachides) | Jn | John |
| 1 S | 1 Samuel | Is | Isaiah | Ac | Acts |
| 2 S | 2 Samuel | Jr | Jeremiah | Rm | Romans |
| 1 K | 1 Kings | Lm | Lamentations | 1 Co | 1 Corinthians |
| 2 K | 2 Kings | Ba | Baruch | 2 Co | 2 Corinthians |
| 1 Ch | 1 Chronicles | Ezk | Ezekiel | Ga | Galatians |
| Ezr | Ezra | Dn | Daniel | Ep | Ephesians |
| Ne | Nehemiah | Ho | Hosea | Ph | Philippians |
| Tb | Tobit | Jl | Joel | Col | Colossians |
| Jdt | Judith | Am | Amos | 1 Th | 1 Thessalonians |
| Est | Esther | Ob | Obadiah | 2 Th | 2 Thessalonians |
| 1 M | 1 Maccabees | Jon | Jonah | 1 Tm | 1 Timothy |
| 2 M | 2 Maccabees | Mi | Micah | 2 Tm | 2 Timothy |
| Jb | Job | Na | Nahum | Tt | Titus |
| Ps | Psalms | Hab | Habakkuk | Phm | Philemon |

| Heb | Hebrews | 2 P | 2 Peter | 3 Jn | 3 John |
|-----|---------|-----|---------|------|--------|
| Jm | James | 1 Jn | 1 John | Jude | Jude |
| 1 P | 1 Peter | 2 Jn | 2 John | Rv | Revelation |

The following works will be found in R. H. Charles, *Apocrypha and Pseudepigrapha of the Old Testament*, 2 vols. (Oxford, 1913, reprinted 1968).

| Ass. Mos. | Assumption of Moses | Jub. | Book of Jubilees |
|-----------|---------------------|------|------------------|
| 2 Bar. | 2 Baruch | 3 M. | 3 Maccabees |
| 3 Bar. | 3 Baruch | 4 M. | 4 Maccabees |
| 1 En. | 1 Enoch | Mart. Is. | Martyrdom of Isaiah |
| 2 En. | 2 Enoch | Ps. Sol. | Psalms of Solomon |
| 1 Esd. | 1 Esdras | Secr. En. | (see 2 En.) |
| 2 Esd. | 2 Esdras or 4 Ezra | Sus. | Susanna |
| Ep. Jer. | Epistle of Jeremy | Test. | Testaments of the XII Patriarchs |

## MISCELLANEOUS REFERENCES

| Bab. Tal. | The *Babylonian Talmud*, cited by page and side of the page, tractate by tractate, may be consulted in the English translation edited by I. Epstein, London, the Soncino Press. |
|-----------|-----------|
| Jos. | Flavius Josephus, whose works may conveniently be consulted in the Loeb edition of the classics, a series of nine volumes edited successively by H. S. Thackeray, R. Marcus, and L. H. Feldman. |
| Jos., *Ant.* | The *Antiquities* of Josephus. |
| Jos., *BJ.* | The *Bellum Judaicum* ('Jewish War') of Josephus. |
| *LNT.* | Derrett, *Law in the New Testament* (London, Darton, Longman & Todd, 1970). |
| Mishnah | The Mishnah, cited by tractate and paragraph. It may be consulted in the Bab. Tal., or, more conveniently, in H. Danby, *The Mishnah* (Oxford, 1933, reprinted often). |
| Pal. Tal. | The *Palestinian Talmud*, often called the Talmud of Jerusalem, which may be consulted in the French translation of Moïse Schwab. |
| 1 Q | This sign stands for 'Qumran Cave 1' and is the initial abbreviation for Dead Sea Scrolls works available in translation in treatises on the Dead Sea Scrolls mentioned in the Bibliographical Note below. |

# FIRST LECTURE

# The Social Scene

## §1. GENDER

Life is a tension between opposites and, unpleasing as the contemporaries of Jesus would be to us if we could visit them, they too were human beings and were held between opposing forces as we are—though more obviously so in all contexts, so that a balance was more difficult for them to maintain. The difference between male and female was more pronounced. Jewish lawyers, in their fussy way, said a great deal about people of neuter or indeterminate gender, but they cannot have been more common than they are now. Many of them were absolved by nature from the tedious and worrying urges towards sex-enjoyment, which were called the 'evil inclination' (p. 32 below), and to that extent they and castrated males were to be congratulated; but they were otherwise despised unless, as sometimes happened, heathen princelings could employ them: they were marginally more loyal than people with many relations to look after.[1]

The Jews felt, as Asians still do, that to be born female was a disadvantage, the sign, perhaps, that an expectant mother's or father's prayers were not answered.[2] When one counts people one does not count their women and children.[3] If the husband has a righteous motive he can divorce his wife without thinking twice about her reactions, or her merits.[4] A woman was supposed to be willing to accept any offer of matrimony that anyone might care to

1. Jos., *BJ*, i. 488.
2. During the first forty days of pregnancy the parents pray that the child may be a son.
3. Mt. 14:21. Neither Mt. nor Lk. take seriously Mk's. pregnant hint that the men were organized like an army (Mk. 6:40, 44) (presumably finding it too far-fetched).
4. 1 Esd. 9:9, 12.

make to her.[5] While the birth of sons meant more hands to work for the family,[6] and more arms to fight for it, avengers to pay off inherited scores,[7] the reappearance of a father's self in other bodies,[8] the proof of a father's goodness (for a good father is honoured in his sons who imitate him),[9] the birth of a daughter brought sadness.[10] Unlike a son she would leave the home at her marriage, and her behaviour might keep in turn her parents' and her husband's families in suspense.[11] An unchaste male might break the commandments against adultery or against allowing a woman to become a harlot;[12] the latter offence might be condoned and he might escape the penalty for the former. But an unchaste girl ruined her family's reputation and the vagaries of teenagers were a constant source of alarm.[13] Women could work in the fields but all the heavy labour was men's and if the housework could be done with existing pairs of hands another daughter was simply another more or less useless mouth to feed. We do not come across the contemporary expression known amongst the Greeks ('Dear wife, if the child you are expecting is a healthy male keep it, if a female expose it'), but the attitude was not altogether different.

Since women, until they were past the age of childbearing, were an anxiety to themselves and others,[14] they were usually confined to the home, and, apart from the more public parts of the village, did not move about without escort, and behaved themselves decorously in the presence of strangers. Amongst the lower orders a boldness of speech was not unthinkable, granted some show of justification.[15] The head was covered as an aid to modesty.[15a] But coquetry cannot have been unknown, since the rigid separation of the sexes always increases sexual curiosity as well as sexual appetite. At home women read little; perhaps few were literate. But songs and superstitions, stories, old wives' tales, and medical magic, and everything appertaining to religion which did not require detailed scriptural knowledge was their domain; the culture, though nominally controlled

5. Si. 36:21 (26).                       6. Tb. 5:17; Si. 16:1–2, 30:2.
7. Si. 30:6.                             8. Si. 30:4.
9. Mt. 5:4; Jn. 8:41–44; cf. Jn. 13:35 (not ironical).        10. Si. 22:3.
11. Si. 22:5. Bold glances amount to 'fornication': Si. 26:9, 42:9–14. Sus. 63.
12. Ex. 20:14; Dt. 5:18; Lv. 19:29; Dt. 23:17.
13. 4 M. 18:7. Ass. Mos. 11:12.
14. Si. 7:25, 22:4, 26:10–12. To have kept one's virginity before marriage was meritorious, but not rare (indeed it was normal): Tb. 3:14.
15. Mk. 14:67.          15a. Misnah, B. K. VIII. 6. See below, p. 140 n. 209.

and propagated by males, who alone took to book-learning, was actually carried in the mores and the uneducated traditions of the females. The religious aspirations of women were accordingly encouraged, and were only marginally subject to their guardians' control (cf. §10, p. 69).[16] Public entertainments in which men and women participated (in groups segregated by gender) were rare.[17] Only in religious contexts, particularly prayer, listening to religious discourses, and the like were men and women to be found regularly together, though once again not mixed promiscuously.[18] Female students of religious teachers could hardly have existed in the proper sense of that term, for studentship (§28) implied bible-study —but female admirers and hearers were a recognised anomaly,[19] and religious teachers had to watch their step, lest their familiarity with women throw doubt on their motives and reputation for holiness.[20]

There must have existed business women, apart from petty traders such as those who sold their families' produce or artefacts in the market. They will have functioned through agents. But they were rare. The typical life for a woman was this: she was given (betrothed) in marriage by her father or nearest male relative when she was about the age of puberty (between 12 and 13); until that time she was watched carefully,[21] for if signs of virginity were missing on the marriage night her bridegroom would accuse her parents of fraud, and the financial provision made for her in the marriage settlement (*ketubah*) would be less (perhaps up to 50%) if she were a non-virgin than if she were a virgin. As a married woman her task was to please her husband,[22] to look at no other man (excepting blood-relations and the privileged people mentioned above), and to bear sons, especially in her youth.[23] A barren woman was a financial liability in the sense that she had failed to provide the means whereby the family prospered, and barrenness led to social as well as financial insecurity and even disgrace.[24] Infertility was

---

16. Lk. 1:38. *LNT*, 350, n. 3.
17. Mk. 6:24. *LNT*, 345–6. A lascivious occasion was different: Jdt. 12:12; Si. 9:9.
18. Ac. 1:14.
19. Mk. 15:41; Lk. 8:2, 10:42. Women partial to Pharisees: Jos., *Ant.* xvii. 41, *BJ*, i. 107. 'Enrolled widows': 1 Tm. 5:9. No female student could be a teacher: 1 Tm. 2:11–12.
20. Jn. 4:27.                                                      21. 3 M. 1:18.
22. Est. 5:14 (sycophantic attitude); Si. 26:13ff. (extravagant praise).
23. 2 Esd. 5:50–55.                              24. Lk. 1:7; 2 Esd. 9:43; Si. 42:10.

not blamed on the husband, though he might attribute want of issue to sins that he had committed or that had been committed by the group to which he belonged (§4). The typical married woman was economically minded, home-centred, narrow-horizoned, and incapable of self-development on what we call 'her own two feet'. If a woman recovered from a serious illness she was not expected to go away for convalescence, but to continue with housework.[25] To suggest that housework was not the best thing a woman could do was a paradox.[26] Women seldom figure in Jewish history, except as factors in political intrigue or otherwise doubtful contexts.[27] Even the pious Alexandra (78–69 B.C.) had fatal weaknesses.[28] Female leadership existed in myth and legend (Judith and Esther), as an example of how even the least important element in society could do wonders if Yahweh willed. It was not that women were nonentities, but considerations of etiquette, domestic requirements, and frequent underemployment among males, kept them in the background in which they could be and no doubt were a force for good of a somewhat narrow and conventional kind. It was not a progressive society: 'progress' meant nothing to them. Stability, security, perpetuity were their goals and female energy was directed to those ends. In theory an adulteress could be executed by stoning, and still more theoretically so could an adulterer.[29] That indicates society's attitude to female misbehaviour, rather than actual practice. To questions of sex and life we shall return in the last lecture (§24). The role they played is well illustrated by the status of the widow. A chaste widow who remained unmarried though she could have remarried was regarded as an ascetic and so worthy of high esteem,[30] and widows who fasted often were esteemed holy.[31]

## §2. PARENTAL AUTHORITY

After a child reached the age of 5 he began to learn that the society was duty-orientated, not right-orientated.[32] Except in commercial contexts (where rights dominated) no one was concerned about his rights; everyone wanted to know his duties and wished to be thought 'worthy to fulfil them'. No one questioned the right of parents to their sons' earnings, nor the duty of the latter to obey and support

25. Mt. 8:14–15; Mk. 1:29–31.    26. Lk. 10:42.
27. Jos., *BJ*, i. 76, 168, 174, 262, 568, 571.    28. Jos., *BJ*, i. 107.
29. *LNT*, 163–4.    30. Lk. 2:36.
31. Jdt. 8:4–7.    32. 2 Esd. 8:12.

their parents indefinitely.[33] This could be difficult if the mother was divorced, when the sons might have to support both parents separately. Obedience was so taken for granted that the biblical provisions for the stoning of a stubborn and rebellious son were virtually a dead letter.[34] Even if one were to desert a father with his consent one would be disobeying the commandment to obey.[35] A son was always inferior to his father.[36] 'My father' was a commonplace form of respectful address.[37] Society's requirement of obedience was stricter than the scriptural text.[38] A pleasing counterpart to this was the father's care and discretion in handling his sons. Strict, even rough upbringing was the norm.[39] A father knew what was best for his son.[40] But on that basis a father could be proud of his sons' rectitude[41]—his sons would be severe with their own, and a man could be proud of his grandsons.[42] Unquestioning obedience being the norm, a father could afford to be affectionate and generous. His patience with well-meaning but ineffective sons would be a virtue about which he could be complacent.[43] Elder sons, as their fathers' right hands, would rule over younger sons and would enforce, if necessary,[44] respect from them. Silence became younger people.[45] The elder brother, particularly the eldest, was often disinclined to be generous and compassionate, and younger brothers had a reputation for rebelliousness and ill-concealed resentment, both against their elder brother and against their father.[46] When a father had an only son he naturally treated him circumspectly: he would require obedience, but he would couple it with consideration.[47] Obedience, no matter how achieved, was what mattered.[48] The son would be like a junior partner. It was always in the father's and his wife's interest that the sons, and particularly the eldest son, should stay at home and manage the farm economically and prudently. It was stupid to distribute one's estate in one's lifetime, though one was tempted to do that in old age.[49] A wise father

33. LNT, 109–11.
34. Dt. 21:18–20. LNT, 119, n. 5.
35. Mk. 1:20; Lk. 9:61. Si. 3:12–16.
36. Mt. 22:43; Jn. 14:28.
37. Mt. 23:9.
38. Si. 3:7.
39. Si. 7:23, 30:1, 12.
40. Lk. 11:13.
41. 2 Esd. 9:45.
42. Si. 3:3, 5, 14.
43. Test. Gad 6:3.
44. Test. Jos. 10:6, 17:1.
45. Si. 32:7.
46. Mt. 21:28–32, Lk. 15:11–32.
47. Si. 36:12 (17); Ps. Sol. 13:8 (9), 18:4.
48. Mt. 21:28–32. The parable of the Prodigal Son (Lk. 15) is based on this assumption (it would be ludicrous otherwise).
49. Si. 33:19–23; 1 M. 9:55. LNT, 107–8. Philo, Q. Gen. 3:60.

intended to remain in control indefinitely, and therefore he was
ready with forgiveness, since an unrelenting attitude would ultimately damage his own security and future. After the father's death
the sons often worked the farm jointly and avoided separation.[50]
Joint living was cheaper, more efficient, and better for the widowed
mother's comfort and the care of other dependants. A family always
had dependants, members who earned less than their keep (and
were called with the frankness of the period 'unprofitable'). To be a
good son was to carry on the father's responsibilities, and thus to
inherit his prestige. Yahweh was related, they thought, to Israel as
a father to a son, and the father–son relationship typified the ideal
relationship between the Jew and the national deity,[51] who naturally
preferred his sons to strangers.[52]

In a traditional society, one which acquired new skills seldom and
slowly, age was not a source of embarrassment to others nor shame
to its sufferer. The older one was the more experience one had,
experience of the relations between the seen world and its unseen
concomitant (§23), and experience, if not expertise, in the policies
and practices of successful living. Thus age and wisdom were
readily associated and the relatively small proportion that reached
their 60s could live on in affection and respect contributing to
their family's prestige.[53] It was readily assumed that a man who
watched his great-grandson at play was a man of exceptional virtue.
For his line to continue so far was thought sure proof of his own
worthiness. All his descendants, whatever their own age, viewed
him and his advice with awe. And 'younger', 'junior', was synonymous with 'inferior'.[54]

## §3. MARRIAGE

The extent of parental authority was shown in arranged marriages.
A widower, or a man who had divorced his wife, could indeed get
himself betrothed, if necessary, personally. But first marriages, the
psychologically and socially crucial unions of a virgin with the
'husband of her youth', were always arranged.[55] In the more old-
fashioned areas it was not permitted for the young betrothed couple
to meet before the wedding night (which was usually within a year

50. The grandnephews of Jesus: Hippolytus at Eusebius, *Hist. Eccl.* iii. 20.
51. Mt. 7:11, 11:25–27, 23:9; Lk. 1:17, 12:32; Jn. 8:41; Ws. 5:5.
52. Mt. 10:5–6, 15:22–24.                    53. Mt. 27:1; Si. 32:3.
54. 1 Tm. 4:12.                              55. 2 Esd. 9:47; Si. 15:2.

of the betrothal)[56] when the bridegroom acquired his bride by inter-course, or was presumed to do so by the very fact of seclusion with her in the wedding chamber.[57] This system, which seems barbaric to the Western mind, is still in use in Asia and parts of Africa and works very well. To *desire* a woman other than one's wife was con-sidered evil.[58] The first intercourse must take place not out of desire for *her* but of desire for issue *from* her.[59] The young couple in fact become devoted to each other in no time, and the absence of court-ship and of 'courting' seems to be a help rather than a hindrance. The parents arrange marriages for their own convenience, so as to be linked to families of good repute, good financial prospects,[60] and helpful political influence. There is a mystery of nature, as puzzling then as it is still. A daughter's attachment to her parents undergoes no change on her marriage. But a son's loyalty to his parents is modified by marriage, and even scripture took note of this fact and authorised a husband to regard his wife as nearer to him than they. Small wonder they insisted on choosing her for him.[61]

It is clear from the behaviour of the Herodian family that poly-gamy (strictly 'polygyny'), which survived as a theoretical part of the traditional customary law, was a privilege reserved for rulers. Even princes were forced to divorce their wives before they could marry afresh in the lifetime of the first.

Divorce was in theory a perpetual possibility. It could take place at the husband's option.[62] It sometimes occurred with the wife's own concurrence or connivance, but it was a traumatic possibility which in theory kept the wife subordinate to her husband's whims. There were judicial divorces in the sense that the community knew ways in which a woman could get freedom from a husband who suffered from a revolting disability or other grave defects: but even so it was he who gave, though under pressure, the letter of divorce which freed her to marry any other Jew. But when marriages were

56. Test. Jud. 10:4.
57. Seclusion, as in modern India, implies intercourse: Jdt. 13:16 (oath taken to rebut the presumption). Test. Reub. 3:10b; Si. 9:9.
58. Mt. 5:28-29.
59. Tb. 8:7. Essenes included a sect who married but abstained from inter-course with their wives when the latter were pregnant: Jos., *BJ*, ii. 161.
60. Marriage might secure an inheritance: Tb. 6:11-12.
61. Gn. 2:24. 1 Esd. 4:25.
62. Si. 7:26. Jos., *BJ*, i. 578. Jews were aware that some other peoples allowed the parent to divorce the daughter from her husband: Jos., *BJ*, i. 508-9.

contracted the representatives of each family[63] bargained over the *ketubah*, the amount payable to the wife in the event of the husband's death or his divorcing her, and in that way many an unhappy husband was virtually prevented from ridding himself of a nagging or disrespectful wife. Cases are known in which a man's friends looked in their purses and found the necessary amount so that they could rid him of an unsatisfactory companion and themselves of a disagreeable hostess. In order not to bring respectable people to shame a fastidious husband who could find the *ketubah* amount, or who could show that the betrothal contract was vitiated (e.g. for want of virginity), would sign the deed of divorce and hand it to the bride or her representatives in the presence of discreet witnesses, incurring no publicity in the usual sense, or shame—which was a sensation which was greatly feared.[64]

Young brides would live in the homes of their 'in-laws'. Hence mothers-in-law were careful in choosing daughters-in-law, and unity between them and their unmarried sisters-in-law was something which everyone desired,[65] but which, we can be sure, was not always attained. Daughters-in-law were of course subordinate to their mothers-in-law and one day they would occupy the same position in their own homes if their husbands pulled their weight, saved money, and acquired homes of their own. Separation, as such, was not the goal, but harmony.

## §4. RELATIONSHIP AND PRESTIGE

An eminent man, with us, need never receive his commonplace brothers and sisters. He may not know his cousins' names, let alone their whereabouts. Hebrew society was patrilineal as well as patriarchal, and the advance of one member of an agnatic family would advantage all his kindred through males, and even, though to a lesser extent, his relations by blood and marriage (his cognates and affines). The loss endured by one member, or one branch, would redound to the loss of all. To have powerful and important relations was to be, potentially, powerful oneself. Sharing and reciprocity were the signs of relationship, which was taken very seriously. If some of a group proposed a course of action naturally they expected others to follow suit.[66] A kinsman stood by one.[67] He was presumed

63. Jn. 3:29.                    64. Mt. 1:19.                    65. Mt. 10:35.
66. Mt. 11:16–19. Jn. 7:2–10 (brothers at least must believe, or their society is meaningless).
67. Sus. 30. One must provide for one's own kin: 1 Tm. 5:4, 8.

trustworthy and was the obvious person to choose if one wanted to deposit valuables.[68] Even friends were so trusted.[69] To fail to respond to the demand of near kindred one must have a really good excuse.[70] A friend was sentimentally bound to grant any request.[71] Union of blood, the blood-tie, was valued very highly. The blood-feud still existed and every member was responsible for avenging injuries to his blood kindred,[72] to redeem any of them from slavery, or otherwise.[73]

Those with whom one automatically shared food and services, and who rendered reciprocal benefits and conferred reciprocal favours were like brothers and were referred to as such. Sharing a meal symbolised unity of mind, in a way quite foreign to the modern Western outlook, but not necessarily to the modern Orient.[74] Sharing demonstrated brotherhood.[75] The gift of no more than cold water could confer an unending obligation.[76] Brother, cousin, fellow-villager, fellow-faction-member, and friend were all degrees of 'brotherhood'.[77] Even a fellow villager was presumed to be sympathetic to one's cause.[78] To refuse a friend a loan to feed *his* friend was to lose prestige oneself and at one remove, because the man who is refused would also lose face; one's failure to meet *his* needs would be to disgrace oneself. No importunity would be needed to extract such a loan.[79]

Individualism was unknown, except in the world of prayer. But whatever advantages were obtained from Yahweh by praying to him would accrue to the group and prayer by and on behalf of groups was as normal as private prayer. What a householder did he did

68. Tb. 5:13, 10:6; 1:14.                      69. Tb. 9:1, 2.
70. Mt. 12:48–49 (better Mk. 3:31); Lk. 14:26; Mt. 7:7.      71. Mk. 10:35.
72. Mt. 23:35; Mk. 12:7; Lk. 11:47–51; Ac. 5:28; 2 Esd. 1:32 (cf. Sus. 46); 1 M. 9:42; 1 En. 47:4. Jos., *BJ*, i. 235, 236, 342.
73. Jn. 15:13. Note Ba. 4:6; Ep. Jer. 6:2.
74. Mt. 26:23; Mk. 14:18; Lk. 13:26 (a claim to recognition), 15:15 (fellow-diner with swine!), 22:29; Ac. 11:3; Rv. 3:20; 2 Esd. 1:38; Tb. 1:11; 1 En. 62:14. If *A* ate with *B*, with whom *C* would not eat, but *C* would eat with *A*, *A* would desert *B* on the arrival of *C*: Ga. 2:12–13.
75. Ac. 2:44, 4:34; 1 M. 12:20–23.
76. Jos., *Ant.* xviii. 192–4 (a kind slave gets his freedom and becomes an administrator!).
77. Tb. 6:17.
78. Mt. 11:1; Jn. 7:52 (local solidarity); 2 Esd. 15:19.
79. Lk. 11:6. Derrett at C. K. Barrett and others, edd., *D. Daube Comm. Vol.* (forthcoming).

'with all his house'.[80] Sinful citizens made sinful cities.[81] A leader detected in error implicated all his followers automatically.[82] It is easy to understand how, though an evil king could no longer corrupt the Hebrews, they would resent him furiously.

In an un-individualistic world shame was corporate. If one became ashamed of one's comrade one suffered acutely. He behaved so as to make one ashamed and one would seek to rid oneself of this comradeship. If he deliberately put one to shame one knew this as a hostile act. One felt shame at the thought of the former relationship and turned away one's face from him when he came near.[83] He was no longer *worthy* of one.[84]

One cannot overemphasise the significance of this characteristic. Standing 'on one's own two feet' was unknown. It would be difficult to find any occupation, even that of a king's minister, which fulfilled that requirement. People propped one another up and if a member of a group fell, his group fell with him. The prestige of a group depended on that of its members. A senior member could by forethought, adaptability, and sheer ability raise his family and associates to political prominence and social eminence. A junior member's thoughtless escapade might ruin a whole group.[85] Vendettas, revenge, though reprehensible in religious terms (since the objects or victims were also children of Yahweh) were a normal part of thought and not a rare feature of practice, and there was no better way of starting a vendetta than conveying an insult to a leading member of another group. For prestige was an entity of far greater value than money, and its relationship to it is worth describing.

In the oriental world to this day prestige is more important than any other factor and people will commit suicide rather than forfeit it. Human dignity as understood in that environment is utterly different from 'human dignity' as we understand it. To them human worth was recognised in being in Yahweh's care, in simply remaining alive and well.[86] Unseemly behaviour in private, mean motives, and sharp practices are not inconsistent with human dignity in our vocabulary, provided the offender pleases influential people. Since in the ancient world, as in the East still, pecuniary security was fleeting and undependable, while society's demands were pervasive

80. Jn. 4:53. *LNT*, p. xxxiii, n.1. Lk. 22:32; Est. 16:18; Mart. Is. 5:9.
81. Mt. 11:20–24.                                      82. Mk. 14:66–70.
83. Mk. 8:38 (cf. Is. 1:28–29); Lk. 9:26; Test. Reub. 4:2–3.
84. Mt. 10:37–38.          85. Jos., *BJ*, ii. 303.          86. Mt. 6:26, 28.

and searching (there being no secrecy and little private life), a man might have dignity if he was in rags and never visited anyone.[87] Prestige depended most commonly on the ability to confer services which were highly valued and could not be remunerated.[88] Remuneration meant a relationship of superior (the payer) and inferior (the payee). Reciprocity was the cement of, and witness to, equality, brotherhood.[89] The more reciprocity between equals the better. An unreciprocal, unremunerated service placed people in the very undesirable position of a debtor: and this feeling was worked off freely by showing respect for the benefactor. It is a natural outcome of this that it was universally believed that if a benefit was conferred on $X$, even without $X$'s knowledge and without $X$'s specific request, $X$ was indebted to the benefactor and must pay off his debt[90] in any way of which he was capable, unless he was to be considered as one of the 'poor', for whom Yahweh makes recompense (since a recompense there must be).[91] And in view of the concept of solidarity, one who did any benefit for an agent, dependant, or junior of $X$ had a claim on $X$'s favour, for he had benefited $X$.[92] This is the chief reason for the Asian's great concern to be hospitable and to make his guest stay long and consume much.[93] The more hospitality, the more gifts one had given, the greater the prestige.[94] One would be ashamed to give absolutely nothing.[95] Those that refuse to offer hospitality are fit objects for sarcasm.[96] Of course people could entertain for ulterior motives, and one could accept invitations in the same spirit;[97] but it was good form to transact business before relaxing at table, and by keeping one's host from his meal encourage him not to postpone dealing with your request longer than absolutely necessary![98]

87. Secr. En. 43:2–3.
88. Paul at Ac. 20:33–34, and see below, p. 171. This explains the topsy-turvy notion at Mk. 9:35.
89. *LNT*, 138–40.
90. A tip was expected for a trifling service: Mt. 25:1–13.
91. Lk. 14:12–14; Tb. 2:2 (*faithful* poor).
92. Mt. 10:40–42, 18:5, 25:35–46; Mk. 9:37, 41; Lk. 7:4–5, 10:16; Jn. 5:23, 12:26, 21:15–17.
93. Ws. 5:14. Receipt of hospitality confers a long-lasting obligation: Jos., *BJ*, i. 516 (and see above, p. 39 n. 76). Mt. 15:22–23 looks back to 1 K. 17:8–15!
94. Mt. 10:11; Mk. 9:5, 12:41; Jn. 21:15–17; Si. 20:14–16 (!), 29.
95. Mk. 12:42.                                                96. Lk. 10:11.
97. Est. 5; Si. 13:7.                                         98. Tb. 7:11, 15.

In a society in which norms were more or less settled by at least seven centuries of consolidation and tradition, heightened by the essential difference between Hebrew and non-Hebrew, the man who commanded respect was one who demanded least, offered most, and thus furthered, by his own personality and conduct, the aims of society. Piety, thrift, almsgiving, and concern for the welfare of those who could not repay a kindness: these were the roads to prestige. Wealth of course facilitated this, but it was not a necessary precondition of it. The *wise* man, whose life personified the ideals of the nation, and who gave what he could in charity, was the prestige-holder. People were proud to be related to him and to be recognised by him.

To understand how important prestige was one must note how sensitive the Hebrews were to ridicule.[99] Signs of contempt upset them emotionally. In our world, indeed, contempt, hostility, and indifference act, if they act at all, as a stimulus, or we may retaliate effectively. One feels for those who cannot (they value human opinion too highly). Amongst the Hebrews, as in Asia still, contempt from superiors is tolerable, even expected! Contempt from equals is so scorching as to make life impossible and survival doubtful. Honour and respect, and the visible and recognisable signs of it, are necessary to daily life. The Dead Sea Scroll community (perhaps the same as the Essenes, p. 136 below) subjected to a penalty a member who gesticulated with the left hand—what, I wonder, would happen to one who was deliberately rude to one of that community? Not only the requirements of formal politeness, the elaborate etiquette of an unhurried world, but also constant recognition of status and of personal worth, was required and emotional reactions could be expected if one fell short in that regard. It was essential therefore that in behaviour and personal performance every member of the unit, large or small, must live up to what was required of him.

We have noticed how failure to perform the unremunerated service implied want of prestige. To be compromised, to lose the freedom of action which was left to one after one's duty of obedience was performed, was death to one's status. For a woman to wink at a stranger or for an official to take bribes or fail to give justice to a person unable to offer a bribe[100] was a loss of prestige not only to them personally, but much more important, to those whose own prestige depended on their performance. The husband and his

99. Si. 1:30, 2:5.                                              100. Si. 35:14 (17).

agnatic family in her case, and the ruler or his ministers in the case of the official, would have their faces blackened, as the phrase went, if the balance of prestige did not always incline the right way.[101]

To signalise prestige and to tap, as it were, its barometer, one entertained. Entertainments, feasts, great and small, were not held simply to give the hosts company. The world was so well supplied with people that company was never lacking. Thus the main object of the expense was to enable people to rejoice: but by accepting hospitality one recognised the status of the host, and by giving him exactly equal hospitality later one took from him a pledge of continued equality. On special occasions, such as weddings, gifts were given in the same way, to pledge and to show reciprocation. To give too lavish a feast was to embarrass people whose co-operation would be needed; to omit to invite important people would be to slight their status and question their future; to ignore an invitation would be to assert superior or 'independent' status[102]—and in giving and accepting invitations great care and deliberation was needed, for a potential host needed guests at least as much as they welcomed his hospitality.[103] A man was humiliated if he was treated as a beggar; and to rejoice without calling one's neighbours to share in one's rejoicing was nothing less than advertising one's indifference to their co-operation—unthinkable![104]

Most towns—all villages, and *a fortiori* all hamlets—were open to armed attack from the king's enemies or robbers. The thief was a delinquent Israelite, a mistaker of his place in rural economy, to whom economic deterrents applied; the robber was an outcast, a stranger, one who had temporarily or permanently put himself out of society, its constraints, and its self-sufficient system of self-discipline. A man needed sons, brothers, cousins, and friends to defend him and his womenfolk against these attacks. Every town and village had its feuds, and every family its hereditary enemies.[105] All of them were 'sinners'! Naturally: one should not dislike any fellow Hebrew unless he were a 'sinner', and if a man or group were hostile and could be expected to take an opposed line on any controversial matter of national, guild, or agricultural policy, it was

---

101. Lk. 18:5. *New Test. St.* Vol. 18 (1972), 178–191.
102. Mt. 22:2–14; Lk. 14:24.    103. Lk. 14:23, 24:29.    104. Lk. 15:4–10.
105. Lk. 1:71–73; 2 Esd. 5:9, 6:24; Mt. 13:25, 39 (capable of sowing weeds in one's field). The Hebrew's capacity for faction was phenomenal even by Asian standards: Jos., *BJ*, i. 150 and throughout.

obvious that they or some of them were or had been 'sinners'.[106]
For the 'righteous' would, naturally, be our friends! But when the
village was under attack, unless (as not seldom) there was a group
of partisans inside the camp, friends and enemies would join in a
common defence, and lessen, temporarily, their poor opinion of
each other.

Prestige is related to earning, but, as we have seen, by no means
necessarily earning of money. The balance of indebtedness was by
no means a merely financial one. Prestige could be acquired by
frequent entertaining and giving in charity, the latter naturally
being a greater prestige-earner than the former. Whatever was
earned, by 'wisdom', 'teaching', meritorious conduct, right living,
politic ways, being a father of a well-conducted family, was regarded,
not as the personal acquisition of the earner, but as an asset of the
group. Consequently it was taken for granted that faith (i.e. unquestioning expectation of a benefit from Yahweh) shown by one
or several members could operate to the advantage of another
member who might be devoid of it.[107] The merits earned by ancestors
could be relied on by their descendants.[108] Vicarious merit, vicarious
faith, vicarious sin were all commonplace notions, part of popular
thought.[109] There was a solidarity between the generations.[110] A
sacrifice by *A* could atone for the sins of *B*.[111] People shared food
from one pot or dish,[112] and they shared the merit or demerit of
good and bad deeds. A man naturally relied on his friends' or
associates' standing as he relied on his own garnered harvest.[113]
Morally this *could* be, at times, a demoralising doctrine, as some
teachers pointed out.[114] The corporate claims of 'Israel' as if

106. Mt. 5:43, 26:45; Jn. 7:7. Essenes swore to hate sinners (Jos., *BJ*, ii.
     139), on the pattern, perhaps, of Ps. 26:5; 139:21-2.
107. Mk. 2:5, 5:36, 7:29 (even amongst non-Hebrews!).
108. *Zekhut avot* on which see Roy A. Stewart, *Rabbinic Theology* (Edinburgh/
     London, Oliver and Boyd, 1961), 127-33. Mishnah, Avot II. 2.
109. Jn. 9:2, 34; Ass. Mos. 3:5. The notion of baptism for the dead (to which
     St. Paul objects at 1 Co. 15:29) must be derived from this Jewish concept
     of vicarious merit. The concept of sharing merit is well at home in the
     East: R. Gombrich, 'Merit transference in Sinhalese Buddhism: a case
     study of the interaction between doctrine and practice', *History of Religions*,
     vol. 11, no. 2 (1971), 203-19.
110. *Genea* as at Mk. 8:38, 9:19; Lk. 11:50. Heb. 11:40; 2 M. 12: 40-45.
111. Test. Benj. 3:8; 2 M. 7:38. Jos., *BJ*, i. 73.          112. Mk. 14:20.
113. Lk. 12:18 (comic-ironic; a passage never properly understood).
114. Mt. 25:1-13; 2 Esd. 7:102-45 (115); Ba. 2:19.

'Israel' were a man, a corporate personality, are often encountered in the New Testament. Yet, not surprisingly, a teacher's dissatisfaction with individual specimens of the category 'Israelite' would lead at one and the same time to a denial of the validity of ancestral or any other vicarious merit, and to a denial that there was any real 'Israel' except in the quite hypothetical body of descendants of Abraham, Isaac, and Jacob who happened to be obedient to the requirements of Yahweh—the deity to whom those patriarchs were related as pledgers, and (*sc*. Isaac) pledges, of faith.

## §5. TRIBE, RACE, AND NATION

Jews have always immigrated into other nations the more readily for their intending not to become assimilated with them. The 'nations', the 'heathen' were always in a collective sense opposed, even in their quality as hosts, to that immigrant, industrious, thrifty, talented, and prosperous community. Viewed from outside the Hebrews seem concrete, unified, solid, perpetual. The refusal of hospitality (due to strict dietary laws) and the horror of intermarriage with non-Jews kept them pure in the ritual sense, and unembarrassed by the reciprocity which would, sooner or later, have meant co-operation, adhesion, and loss of identity amongst the heathen. The 'host' nation was host only in a sense, perhaps not in the senses which mattered most. The Hebrews, because of their self-discipline, made excellent businessmen and administrators (exactly like the Brahmins of India and for the same reasons), and the hard training of youth produced over many generations of endogamy a kind of hereditary aptitude for book-work, for study and for serious concern with affairs.

They took themselves and their nation very seriously, and identified it as a common descent from ancestors who had, actually or notionally, pledged themselves to a divine being who was, because he was almighty, more powerful than, and in every sense more real than the gods of the heathen. This automatically stated, in terms the ancient world understood, the superiority of the Hebrews over the heathen. A god was a subconscious projection of a society's self-image, and the god of the Hebrews was greater than other gods. Needless to say the majority of the heathen were in doubt about this, though many of them must have been polite enough to smother the fact. But the want of comradely exchange between the host nation and the Jews whom it regarded, unfairly, as parasitic upon it was very irritating and from time to time anti-Hebrew movements broke out in Persia, Egypt, Palestine, and elsewhere.[115] The Hebrews attributed this exclusively to the malice of their idolatrous neighbours and were always on the look-out for such pogroms and took, it would seem, too little care to avoid precipitating them. For example, it was dangerous as well as tactless to encourage so many Greek girls to be converted to Judaism in order to marry their boys.

In their homeland the Hebrews were not undivided. The tribes that returned from the Babylonian captivity were virtually united; the prospect of complete 'reunion' was conventionally yearned for. The descendants of Israel-Jacob were theoretically equal, yet they were conscious of separate functions and separate destinies as symbolised by Jacob's cryptic blessings upon his issue.[116] The race, 'nation', was Hebrew. But every man knew the tribe to which he belonged (unless he was a proselyte or a descendant of such) and was proud of his ancestry. It is clear that pedigrees and records were kept, no doubt inefficiency as to the higher branches of the family tree. We know from our own experience that people ponder on their ancestry when they have nothing else to boast of. The poor, highly taxed, and insecure Hebrew peasantry were concerned to keep, and if possible to improve, the reputation of their tribe, though its reality was more in their thoughts than in any actual manifestation. Levites and Cohens (priests) on the other hand had a genuine reason for preserving and consulting their pedigrees. The priests could not marry any and every girl and though they could marry Israelites (non-Levites and non-Cohens) they forfeited their right to be High Priests thereby. This loss was fictional, but not insignificant for that. Priestly families normally intermarried with priestly families and so formed a caste.[117] They were respected as such.[118] Membership of priestly families was financially valuable, as priests, their wives, and children, ate (as it were) at Yahweh's table, and, provided they were ritually pure in terms of the purity required for each kind of food, they could live on the offerings made in the Temple, and where this was impracticable (due to living far from Jerusalem), they could live on tithes paid to them by Israelites. The right to tithes was a valuable right, and one could live well on it without performing any productive function. Levites were no longer in actual receipt of tithes[119] but they had hereditary assets in lieu of payment for the

115. Jos., *BJ*, ii, 266ff., 285ff., 457ff., 487ff., 559ff., vii. 361ff.    116. Gn. 49.
117. Lk. 1:5.         118. Si. 7:29.              119. *LNT*, 216–17.

Temple service they collectively performed, and the Levite caste, as we can conveniently call them, regarded itself as superior to the common Israelite, as normal rules of precedence acknowledged.[120] Pedigrees interested everyone, and public registers existed.[121]

Offspring of unions between Hebrews and non-Hebrews were despised. Offspring of adultery were base morally, bad in quality as well as socially disadvantaged.[122] Offspring of a mixed marriage were regarded as little better than those. Proselytes were a special class of person, and these were by no means incorporated into the body of Israelites rapidly and effectively. A convert to Judaism was expected to be inferior socially as well as economically.[123] An important proselyte was a cause for pride,[124] and the motives of proselytism were not always scrutinised closely.[125] Heathen admirers of Judaism were many, and numerous non-Jews were sympathisers of the Temple and its cult.[126] But many were content with a kind of half-proselyte status, retaining their uncircumcised condition (circumcision was a national identity-symbol), but accepting the truth of the religion of Yahweh and respecting the observances which most Jews were brought up to perform. It was up to the Hebrews to act so as to enhance the standing of their god in the eyes of the nations,[127] and leading personalities must have realized from time to time that too ready an acceptance of proselytes would enlarge the number of those whose behaviour could not be predicted to 'glorify the Name' of Yahweh. The religion, the race, and the nation were, in theory, one.

## §6. THE FOREIGNER

No period of Hebrew history is devoid of the foreigner. Schoolboys learning English history not so long ago were able to visualise England as if she lived independent of nations other than her own. The arrival of foreigners was for centuries an embarrassment for

120. Mt. 1:1; 1 Esd. 4:37, 39. 1 Tm. 1:4.
121. Josephus (born A.D. 37–38!) calls them *demosiai deltoi* (*Life*, 6) and appears to rely on them for his own pedigree for seven generations.
122. 1 Co. 7:14; Ws. 3:16, 4:4–6. 'Money purifies bastards', i.e. if they acquire wealth—they can intermarry with Jews of pedigree and their issue are true Hebrews! (Bab. Tal., Kidd. 71*a*—a rabbi cites Ml. 3:3).
123. Tb. 1:8; Mishnah, Hor. III. 8. He must beware of being too pleased with his new status: 1 Tm. 3:6.
124. Jdt. 14:10; 2 M. 9:17.                                       125. Est. 8:16.
126. Jos., *BJ*, i. 354, 357, ii. 409–10.
127. *LNT*, 203, n.1. Pal. Tal., B.M. 8a.

which social life made no provision. Hebrews were in a different position. They had always lived cheek-by-jowl with non-Hebrews and they regarded them with dislike, a dislike readily returned. They avoided, and were avoided, by deliberate choice on both sides. If you found pigs being herded you knew you were out of Hebrew territory and among the 'nations'.[128] This dislike was not based on individual preference, individual estimates, or individual experience.[129] I have explained that the Jews, like most ancient and traditional societies (the so-called 'developing' societies), had corporate attitudes and joint opinions. The father's enemy was the son's enemy, and *vice versa*.[130] Individual opinions were seldom held, let alone expressed.[131] Younger, inferior people would not dare to express an opinion differing from that of their seniors, or could do so only with great tact.[132] And the society was hostile to the 'nations', the 'heathen', who were, by definition, 'unrighteous',[133] and proud.[134] It comes as a shock to us to learn that the Hebrews, who disdained contact with foreigners, accused them at the same time of pride: but what they meant by it was that the foreigners ridiculed them, and I have explained how pained they were by ridicule, which, again by definition, could hardly be merited in the eyes of its victims. Characteristically, they enjoyed ridiculing others, who of course merited it![135]

Foreigners had their own gods, their loose ways, and stood for a way of life negating all the Hebrews held dear. They would marry anyone, and took no care of their personal purity (if they had any) or their moral reputation. They were ignorant of life's secrets,[136] and one day the light of Yahweh's worship would enlighten them.[137] They were led by impulse, unreflective appetite, or mercenary motives.[138] If they were Persians they might even have sexual intercourse with their own mother. . . . No one, except themselves, minded very much if their assets were destroyed.[139] Since they did not accept that there was one god, one Super-father, they did not realise that all human beings, however racially and facially dissimilar from themselves, were entitled to their care and consideration. In

128. Mt. 8:28–32.    129. Mk. 13:13.    130. Jn. 15:23; cf. 1 En. 56–57.
131. Mk. 13:12 (reversal of the solidarity of society).
132. Mt. 10:17–18; Si. 32:7.    133. Mt. 5:47.    134. Si. 32:18.
135. Their own self-important and self-righteous manner simply asked for ridicule: Jos., *BJ*, ii. 224; Horace, *Satires* i. 9, 69.
136. Mt. 6:32.    137. Mt. 24:14.
138. Mt. 6:32–33; Lk. 12:29–30; Mt. 8:34, 28:15.    139. Mk. 5:13.

short there was a cultural clash of a violent character, which the Hebrews' failure to 'assimilate' and to be absorbed, their cultural and social solidity and impermeability prevented their mitigating or mollifying. Like the Ibo of Nigeria or the Asians in East Africa in our own day the Jew's diligence, application, and success in business made him the object of envy and distrust.

The Jew meanwhile was not entirely self-sufficient. His religious poetry and folk-lore was not entirely satisfying. The profound scholarship and 'wisdom' (including magical proficiency) of Eastern nations (i.e. not, in general, the Greeks) impressed him.[140] The plastic arts and intellectual subtlety even of the Greeks attracted him. If he could insulate himself from the deleterious effects of some of their myths and legends he could enjoy their poetry and certainly appreciated their language with its great vocabulary and subtlety of expression. Hellenic ways of thought were alien to him, they were too individualistic, too mobile, too facile, too superficial. But the Greek language was better in every way than his own and he borrowed vastly from it. Moreover since Greek-speaking rulers were in charge of the Land of Israel the language had a snob value. Like French in pre-revolutionary Russia, Greek in Palestine was the language of the realms of higher education and fashion. A twin-minded approach developed amongst leisured classes, as we find in India today. Males spoke a smattering, or more than a smattering of Greek, if they moved in international or big commercial circles; or were confined to Aramaic if they remained bound to the village and traditional ways. Women seldom learnt Greek unless they belonged to rich families and were sent to be 'finished' in the households of friendly foreigners. People were bilingual for much the same reasons and with much the same limitations as the rural people of modern mid-Wales. They resented the ubiquity of Greek culture, they thought it basically wrong-headed (shameless Greek mores repelled them), but they admired some of its products. And nations which were stronger financially, and better organised politically, marched up and down Palestine and their officials spoke Greek. One must protect our culture, thought the Hebrews, from contamination from their alien ways, but one may safely learn their tongue and deal with them (as far as our Law permits) in order to prosper from their prosperity. It is interesting, however, that Agrippa II, king of Chalcis (Lebanon) A.D. 48–53 and ruler of the tetrarchies which

140. Mt. 2:1.

had belonged to Philip and Lysanias A.D. 53–93, brought up at the Court of Claudius, lacking no educational opportunities—the same King Agrippa that figures at Ac. 25:13–26:32—wrote ungrammatical and unidiomatic Greek which Josephus was naïve (or malicious?) enough to reproduce verbatim![140a]

True sympathy with foreign ways was never attained, perhaps seldom attempted. Association with foreigners was, on the whole, taboo;[141] intermarriage out of the question.[142] The principles and practices of idolatry were ridiculed in a naïve fashion, showing an utter lack of cross-cultural comprehension, a limited degree of communication.[143] The 'nations' only utilised the Hebrews, exacting tolls and tribute from them, ignoring, or painfully obviously recognising their prejudices and customs, and taking credit for forbearance in so doing. One day the desire for vengeance which burned low in every Hebrew breast, the urge to requite and to even the balance,[144] would become realised, and Yahweh would judge and punish the heathen and make them pay, as only he could, for their 'unjust' treatment of Israel, one of the many sins which they had continued to commit against him.[145] The feeling that this would happen, that such a day of reckoning would come, must have helped the Jew in a tricky situation to hold his tongue, swallow his resentment, and turn to as good an account as tact could make it, the insolence of the heathen 'host' who was no host, 'neighbour' who was no neighbour. Hebrews learnt to have a well-governed tongue in such company, at least, handy in international business. The reed bowed before the storm, only to rise when it had passed.

Not a few foreigners were curious about Judaism.[146] Personally they were ritually unclean, and their taste for pork made them even more repellent than their lack of circumcision. Though one hesitated

---

140a. Jos., *Life*, 365–6 (cf. 359!).
141. Ac. 10:28–29, 11:3; 3 M. 7:14–15.
142. 1 M. 1:15. The rigour of the principle was modified in favour of female proselytes.
143. Ws. 13:13–19, 14:15–21, 15:7–13; Ep. Jer. 6:5, 73. Jos., *Against Apion*, ii. 236–49 (Loeb edn., ed. Thackeray, i, 387ff.) Josephus's tact does not conceal his ignorance.
144. 1 M. 2:68. Josephus shows this spirit at work incessantly after the death of Herod the Great.
145. 2 Esd. 1:34; Si. 36:3; 1 En. 46:4–8, 90:20; 2 Bar. 40:1, 72:1–6; Ps. Sol. 17:32.
146. Mk. 7:24–26.

to enter their dwellings one could stretch a point and conceivably invite them to one's own,[147] thus keeping one's prestige intact. But the Roman emperor, unclean or not, paid for sacrifices to be offered for him to Yahweh, a formal admission that if Yahweh was real the heathen too were capable of showing him respect, and the Hebrews accepted the reasonableness of this position,[148] which most of us would think rather strange. Heathen sovereigns thought it a small price to pay for the Hebrews' acquiescence in their rule.[149] On much the same basis the East India Company attempted to endear itself to its Hindu subjects by making offerings to the goddess Kali (to the discomfiture of its Muslim subjects). Foreigners, i.e. non-Hebrews, moved here and there throughout the Jewish homeland and settled in villages and towns in enclaves inside it. Many of them developed a respect for the Jewish religion in the broadest sense, and recognised that aspects of it were true, whatever they may have thought about its exclusiveness.[150] Sentimental antiquarianism or pseudo-mysticism of the 'wonders-of-the-East' type will have brought not a few foreigners to enquire into and to admire Hebrew lore and law—and we know that there were exchanges of traditional learning and legend with Persia, Egypt, and India.[151] Rootless Hellenism needed something which it could obtain from the dug-into-the-soil traditionalism of an archaic, non-progressive, hierarchical society, and the exclusive Jew (perhaps his exclusiveness was an added attraction) was rather gratified than impressed by this fact.

The movement which began under the Seleucid kingdom, after Alexander the Great's empire had fallen to pieces, and ended with the Maccabean wars, a movement to Hellenise the Hebrews from within, had provoked so violent a counter-reaction from the villager, the natural traditionalist, and the educated religious teacher, that no one, in the time of Jesus, seriously suggested that Judaism was

147. Ac. 10:23. One reason for avoiding pagans' villas was the suspicion that their female servants' abortions got stuck in the drains or were buried under the floor!

148. 1 Esd. 6:31; 1 M. 7:33. Philo, *Leg. Gai.* 157, 317 (ed. Colson, vol. 10, 80, 158). Until the War of A.D. 70 the position was not questioned: Jos., *BJ*, ii. 409–10.

149. Jos., *BJ*, ii. 341.

150. Lk. 7:4–5; Ac. 10:1–7.

151. The example of suicide at Masada recommended on the analogy of Indian suicides is related by Jos., *BJ*, vii. 351, 357.

compatible with any cultural compromise.[152] If individual Jews, like Alexander the brother of Philo and Tiberius Alexander, his nephew, gave up observances[153] and sided with the Romans against their co-religionists, this could be a (regrettable) feature of the cosmopolitan world. In the Land of Israel and for practical purposes throughout the dispersion the Hebrew identity was preserved with zeal and sincerity. Jews speaking many tongues more fluently than their traditional Aramaic[154] came to Jerusalem for the greater feasts, especially Passover. If they could not come (as was more often the case) they sent their 'first fruits' and their Temple Tax in the month before Passover, just as if they would benefit from the Temple services personally.[155] Martyrdom, they thought, was preferable to compromise with other faiths, and since observances and faith were inseparable, observances too must be cherished, if necessary, at the cost of life itself.[156] And all this strengthened solidarity still further.

## §7. HIGH AND LOW

Yet, when one looked more closely, these 'brothers' were not as 'solid' in weal and woe as descendants of Abraham could have been expected to be if tribal unity had been maintained.[157] The tighter the ties the harder the stresses.[158] The links that bound high and low, traditionally 'brothers' in so far as they were all sons of the patriarchs, were well recognised in theory, but the concern with prestige (§4) tended automatically to undermine the duty of comradeship, especially in the face of foreign cultures and, still more, foreign rule. How everyone wished to be 'great' in his group, and how bitter the conflicts, internal and external, this involved![159] One's own group is the last to be impressed.[160] And the public's censure is hateful.[161] The only method devised to overcome this all too natural tendency was that of using prestige to mitigate eminence, in a characteristic way which may take a moment to explain. Men

---

152. Note the attitude at Jos., *BJ*, i. 108.
153. 1 M. 10:14. Tib. Alexander was none the less successful at his task of governing the Jews: *BJ*, ii. 220.
154. Ac. 2:5–11; Ba. 4:36, 5:5.
155. Philo, *Leg. Gai.* 156, 317 (ed. Colson, vol. 10, 78–80, 156).
156. Jos., *BJ*, ii. 174, 197–8, vii. 323ff.        157. Mt. 3:8.        158. Mt. 15:5.
159. Mt. 20:26; Si. 10:20; 2 M. 5:6. No individual of rank could tolerate subjection to his peers: Jos., *BJ*, i. 31. On envy see *BJ*, i. 67, 77, 208.
160. Mk. 6:4–6; Jn. 7:5.                                                    161. Si. 26:5.

could acquire greatness, accumulating property by manipulating the ruling power. The latter needed native interpreters, agents, spies, accountants, and factotums, and would make it financially desirable for any native notable to sympathise with its cause and policies. The natural leaders were those to whom prestige accrued by the means I have mentioned already. Serving the public with their example, wisdom, and means they could be relied upon to voice the public's needs and to project, as we say, the correct image of the Hebrews. Those who were dependable in business, i.e. those whose power prevented their relations and friends from interfering with their contracts without at the same time forfeiting their loyalty, were also religious, i.e. abstained from fraud and overreaching because of the 'will of Heaven' and not because they might be detected. The religious, dependable, and efficient automatically accumulated huge fortunes,[162] much of these, no doubt, consisting in deposits entrusted to them by optimistic and confident members of the public, especially their own relations. In course of time business contacts and political networks overlapped; revenue responsibilities and even police duties came to be added to a popular as well as knowledgeable merchant, though, if his business was to flourish it would be altogether better for these undertakings to be shared within a single family: one brother might be an official and another a merchant, and they could pool their information. Business and piety, business and scholarship, and business and administration were by no means incompatible occupations. In course of time certain families would develop networks of connections that tended to monopolise all prestige-producing activities.

Prestige could, as I have said, be held by a sage who did not own anything. But conspicuous wealth advertised success in business and suggested to the average person that its owner had no need to cheat others, irrespective of professed integrity. A notably wealthy man was, if he stayed so for any time, in a position to placate or serve the ruler. He was therefore within the mesh of political power. He was in a position to confer favours and thus accumulate more prestige. People came to him for favours, sat near him while he was at home and hoped for some crumb from his table, some sign of recognition of their devotion to him. One did not approach the great empty-handed, at least on the first visit; if he accepted the gift (described as homage) he accepted the obligation thus thrust upon

162. Religious converts might well think in terms of money-making: 1 Tm. 6:5.

him.[163] The petitioner hoped to steal a march on his competitors and to acquire prestige by association on the basis that these latter would be excluded. But their indignation might reach the patron over his head.[164] And people were indignant when prestige was assumed by the apparently unqualified.[165]

The great accepted these 'clients' complacently, and this was one way of becoming great within Israel—one was a father to the orphan and the widow and the poor, and on that footing every unemployed person within reach who had the slightest shred of claim on the footing of relationship or a past service rendered, claimed to be a client and was happy in the thought that he was one of the 'poor', after whose needs the great man would be sure to look. No doubt he would try to obtain some service from this unpromising client, or the latter's self-respect would give way and he would incur blame as a mere parasite.[166] He would 'lift up his countenance' upon the unfortunate, but not necessarily undignified petitioner, and not turn his face (we should say his nose) disdainfully away. And if they met in a public place the great one might not be too proud to return a salutation (the lowly greeted the great first).[167]

The low and the lowly: many were low in the sense that they were poor in financial terms. There were a great many poor who had no chance to emigrate. Many crazed and deranged, many diseased and burdensome to their unfortunate relations provided a standing problem to the latter, who would take every conceivable step to make them income-producers again. One who was born crippled could earn for his relations as a beggar at some place where people were bound to pass in numbers.[168] How much more would others be in need of a cure whose earning capacity had been lost! Besides the sick and injured, the dispossessed and others low in the monetary sense, possibly proud of some important ancestor, even if he was as far back as Reuben, there were those who, without being paupers or physically or mentally afflicted, were lowly in the sense that they humbly depended upon their 'great' neighbours to attend to their

163. Mt. 2:11; Si. 20:27–29.
164. Mt. 20:21, 24; Mk. 10:41. Slander and backbiting were all too easy: Jos., *BJ*, i. 72.
165. Mk. 6:3.                                            166. Si. 40:28–30.
167. Mt. 10:13, 23:6. To fail to return a greeting was an outrage: Jos., *BJ*, ii. 319, 326.
168. Ac. 3:2.

needs. The attitude of mind that was conventionally associated with the 'poor' was not mendicancy or pauperism, but a faithful dependence upon the sense of responsibility of the other party to this unequal relationship. In this way they helped *him*: they conferred upon him the prestige which comes from doing things for others. And in that way rich and poor, high and low, could find a special kind of reciprocity and save each other's reputation. The great needed their dependants, their clients, to give them a sense of their own function. This state of affairs is an essential feature of the Eastern scene to this day and has no counterpart in Western life. It explains why the occidental traveller, meeting an oriental official, is surprised to discover that the latter expects to be thanked personally, as if he were conferring a favour, when he is only doing his legal duty, for which presumably he is paid.

The 'clients' could easily figure as sycophants, flatterers. One treats the great with elaborate courtesy, indistinguishable from flattery to our ears. Tale-bearing, intrigues, even acts of would-be vengeance, spring up in this context, where the hanger-on seeks desperately to do some unasked 'favour' for the great one, hoping it will not also be unwanted. If he is true to the relationship he will not do an act which necessarily redounds to his patron's disadvantage, revealing the ulterior motive and want of true knowledge of the relationship (which implies true insight into the patron's best interests).[169] If a mistake is made the client, who claims to be, but is not, a servant, will be treated as if he were no better than one, and a bad one at that.

The rich and politically eminent were not the only 'high' ones in Israel. A distinct category of great was the *rabbi*.[170] The word 'rabbi' means 'my great one', 'my master', and is a term of respect which, with various grammatical and dialectical variations, figures several times in the gospels. In course of time this word has become associated with licensed teachers of the Pharisaic persuasion (§26), but in the time of Jesus it could be applied to any notable, provided he was notable by traditional, native standards. The characteristic of greatness in its specially Jewish sense (not unknown in India when Brahmins ruled the roost) was knowledge of the Law and the power to teach it effectively. The political aristocracy included, we can be

169. *LNT*, 40–43. Si. 28:2–6.
170. Mt. 23:6, 8. Rabbis, experts in law, were held in the highest esteem: Jos., *BJ*, i. 648; *Life*, 191–2. Mt. 5:19 c–d.

sure,[171] the High Priestly families who were hereditary custodians of the most prized ritual observances of the nation. The priests as a class were trained in ritual observances, especially the law relating to offerings and to the fitness of these for their purposes, the nature of sins (whether or not they were also crimes, §22), the calendar, and requirements of ritual purification from the most common (§24) to the most rarefied kinds.

Not all priests could be called rabbis, since not all had progressed beyond the stage of mere imitation and thoughtless repetition of rules in action (though they would be oracles to that extent). But anyone who learnt his bible by heart and could expound the commandments, and did so for the instruction of his fellow-countrymen was a rabbi, a great one.[172] He was regarded as performing a divine function, since Yahweh himself taught and told, so scripture said, Moses how to teach the children of Israel; and the mass of laws and customs to be found in the written law and in traditional glosses deriving from it and attaching themselves more or less loosely to it (§22) must be made available to the public for its guidance by those only who had immersed themselves thoroughly in the subject. They alone could remove the curse that lay upon the ignorant.[173] The rabbi, in these terms, taught by example and practice, and by answering questions posed to him. He could also take the initiative and give public lectures, exceptionally in the Temple courts and in synagogues up and down the country. And if the public listened eagerly and did not tire of his expositions he was certainly a rabbi without any licence or ordination. A learned and responsible man often acted as reconciler, advocate, intermediary, helping to unite conflicting interests and to modify extreme attitudes.[174] One who performed this function often would soon become 'great' in the sense I explained above, for the disputing parties would decline in prestige so as to become his 'clients'. We shall not be surprised to learn that men were eager to acquire a smattering of esoteric learning, a superficial knowledge of the Law, to be called 'rabbi'.[175]

Since the concentration and memory needed to learn the Law was itself a prime mental training, it is not surprising that rabbis found themselves very good at business or administration. But one would

171. Josephus constantly refers to the 'chief priests and notables': *BJ*, ii. 301, 316, 331 (chief priests and council), 336, 411, 422, 428 (cf. 322, 342).
172. Lk. 2:47; Test. Levi 12:3.                          173. Jn. 7:49.
174. Jn. 14:16, 26, 16:7,13.                             175. 1 Tm. 1:7.

not expect them to be full-time artisans.[176] Another sign of high prestige was their being appointed trustees for widows and orphans.[177] A childless widow was in a hard plight.[178] The trustees' 'expenses' will certainly have been met from the trust funds and without realising it even a man with a reputation for piety and 'fear of Heaven' would find himself enjoying life: he could seem to be rich, not so much by obviously earning the appropriate means, but by living on 'expenses' incurred by travelling up and down on the affairs of his many wards.[179] His equals and seniors would hesitate to remove him from such a pleasant position, because lowering the prestige or 'honour' of one's 'neighbour' was regarded as a very reprehensible thing in itself[180] and fraud must be proved against a man before he can be treated as untrustworthy.

Since religious knowledge overlapped with secular knowledge a teacher could be a judge. Yahweh himself was a judge, the Hebrews believed. He judged mankind daily, and would judge them finally at the End of Days. Teaching and judgment were equally divine functions. And judgment was traditionally regarded as a governmental activity. Long ago judges had been the equivalent of kings in a society too primitive and incoherent to recognise the value of kingship. A man good enough to teach duties to the Israelites was fit to be their judge, and was applied to for an opinion or a decision, and where decisions were out of the question because of the *de facto* Romano-Hebraic condominium (§8) the public normally agreed to abide by a rabbi's award as if it were a legal decision. True, recalcitrant or greedy people took other steps (p. 91) but traditionally the native chiefs (i.e. the rabbis) had a right to assert their opinion unasked and were greeted and treated with devotion and humility fit only for unquestioned interpreters of the will of Yahweh. People looked to the rabbi-judge to 'justify' them, i.e. to hear their case, to hear their opponents', to see their point of view, and to hold them in the right. Ideally he was no respecter of persons, but this will only have been a fact when his prestige was so high and his honour so free from all possibility of compromise, that he need fear no one's resentment and no one's interference behind his back. In their palmy days the rabbis gave decisions *ex cathedra*, and never ex-

---

176. Mk. 6:3 (gospel irony).     177. 2 Esd. 1:20–21.     178. Lk. 7:12.
179. Mk. 12:40; Lk. 20:47; Ass. Mos. 7:6–7; Ps. Sol. 4:11–15. *Novum Testamentum* vol. 14 (1972), 1–9.
180. Elders must in no case be rebuked (as such): 1 Tm. 5:5.

plained their reasons (except to their pupils, or irate colleagues). They never had to justify themselves before the public, unless they gathered that they were suspected of corruption.

We have noticed the proselyte and his low position (§5). Other elements could surely be called low, though their position would not necessarily be humble in our estimation. Servants were unquestionably inferiors, and were frankly treated as such.[181] Slaves were even more so. The difference between a son, who was an unpaid servant, and a servant was that the latter was remunerated and might, or might not, earn his keep; whereas the son would inherit the father's capital or a share therein, and thus had a direct interest in its size and liquidity. The slave was of course maintained by his master and received no remuneration. Most Jewish slaves were only temporarily in that status, until, in fact, their labour had paid off the debt in respect of which they had become enslaved. Servants and slaves were allowed to maintain themselves at their master's expense and they often took full advantage of this and unless they were held in check they could fare a good deal better than self-employed free men who had others dependent upon them.[182] But no servant or slave could determine the destination of the capital estate, however much he might 'eat and drink' of the income.[183] A son, however poorly kept, was his father's representative and would be owner or master in due time: he, at least, would be respected, if a servant or agent was not.[184]

We come at last to the anomalous status of the Samaritans. This now fast-dying sect is the remnant of a populous and proud people who were indeed Hebrews by religion and to some degree even by descent but due to accidents of history were not recognised by the Hebrews as part of the true Israel. The cult of the Hebrews was eventually settled at Jerusalem, where it had been for centuries before Jesus's time. The Samaritans regarded the Jerusalem cult as improper[185] and wrongheaded, and they believed it their religious duty to ignore or hamper it, and to belittle the Jewish rabbis and their Law. The oral element of that Law was totally rejected by the Samaritans. Their own copies of the five books of Moses differed slightly from the rabbis' and they refused to regard as canonical all the historical and prophetic books which the Hebrews reverently

---

181. Lk. 12:47–48, 17:7–10, 22:27; Jn. 13:16, 15:20.
182. Mk. 13:35; Lk. 12:37, 15:1.          183. Lk. 15:19; Mt. 24:45–51.
184. Mk. 1:20, 12:1–9.          185. Lk. 9:53. Jos., *Ant.* xviii. 30, *BJ*, ii. 232.

gathered as evidence of the communication to them of the holy spirit. The Samaritans had Mt. Gerizim as their holy mountain, as they still do, and under foreign rule they at times sought with success the favour of the common foe, the emperor. Their hostility to the religion observed by the Hebrews meant, as ever in ancient Asian societies, nothing less than hostility to the Hebrews as a nation[186] and the Samaritans, who should have been the Jews' allies in all conflicts with the heathen, were on terms of relentless hatred with them. They were, we may be sure, distinguished by their dress and doubtless by their accent, situated as they were between the Jews of Galilee and those of Judaea. Jesus actually referred (or was made out to refer) to them as 'foreigners', for so they must often have seemed.[187]

Regional differences were easily noticed. No doubt the privileged position of Jerusalem gave its inhabitants mighty ideas of themselves, and they were 'lifted up', a dangerous moral situation. Places were thought important because they were the birthplaces of famous people, as was Bethlehem because of David. Some regions were evidently slightly regarded, of which Nazareth would seem to have been one.[188] Each region, especially in the hilly tracts, of which Palestine has so many, had its own accent, its own variety of Aramaic.[189]

We cannot leave the topic of social status and relative esteem without referring to the subject of ostentatious burial in the ancient world. It is an accepted Jewish belief that to bury the dead is a charitable act (see the book of Tobit)[190] and to accompany the corpse of any Jew to the grave is meritorious, especially because the deceased cannot reciprocate (therefore Yahweh will). A superstition which might pass without notice, the habit of providing new, rock-cut tombs for important people, and the habit of loudly bewailing the dead, the custom of swathing the corpse in bandages soaked in quantities of costly spices and oils was an instance of what anthropologists call 'conspicuous consumption'[191] tending to honour the deceased and so to distinguish him and his relations (secular or, if he had none, then spiritual) from the common man. The grave of the latter was unmarked and his burial perfunctory. The preservation of the corpse as long as possible was considered a sign of

186. Jn. 4:9.  187. Lk. 17:16.  188. Jn. 1:46, 7:52 (cf. Is. 9:1, 2).
189. Mt. 26:32, 73, 28:7, 10; Mk. 14:28 (cf. Dt. 10:11), 70.
190. 2 Esd. 1:23; Si. 7:33; Ps. Sol. 2:31 (27).  191. Jos., *BJ*, i. 184.

holiness (Ps. 16:10, cf. Jb 17:14).[192] In death the beggar lies, we say, by the side of kings. But the ancient Hebrews regarded such expenditure as I have mentioned as by no means improper and the great had expensive funerals. His brother's head could be worth 50 talents to a prince who wanted to bury the corpse intact.[193] Every mourning family was expected to give expensive funeral feasts to the public (as in modern Gujarat), even if it broke them.[194] Even the Hellenistic practice of making grandiose tombs (though anathema to the pious Jew) was adopted by so nationalistic a Jewish family as that of Simon Maccabeus.[195] The popular cult of visiting the tombs of saints did not readily extend the honour to nationalist heroes. Those whose words and deeds are no memorial cannot be honoured by a costly tomb. Moreover those who have glorified Yahweh's name, i.e. the martyrs, could not be honoured by any except such as were prepared to follow their example.[196]

No study of high and low in Judaism is complete without noting the uncomfortable fact that no one could be counted happy till his death (Si. 11:28). The Hebrews frankly gloated over the thought that fortune might be reversed at any moment.[197] Riches were a prelude to poverty, as the water-wheel turns round. The poor can rise up and the rich fall empty, and it was Yahweh's will. Since the righteous were also 'poor' (§8) it is not surprising that the discomfiture of the 'rich' was a hope of which the pious were never ashamed. One could go so far as to say that at the End of the Age the mean shall rule the honourable, and the poor the strong and rich—as if this were both chaotic, and, ultimately, desirable.[198] The only persons not subject to this law of impredictability of fortune were the great whose greatness was known in Heaven: these even had stars that in some sense belonged to them, as the sons of Jacob had.[199] In the contexts of daily life the fear of shame and desire for honour led to concern that in public ceremonies no mistake should be made as to one's relative status (§10). But one could live to see dramatic variations, or so one thought. Was this, like the 'righteous' man's assumption that riches meant sin, or if not sin, then sleepless

192. Jn. 11:17 (marvellous irony).          193. Jos., *BJ*, i. 325 (38 B.C.).
194. Jos., *BJ*, ii. 1.                      195. 1 M. 13:25–30.
196. Lk. 11:47–51; Mt. 23:29–31. Derrett, at F. L. Cross, ed., *Studia Evangelica IV* (Berlin, 1968), 187ff.
197. Lk. 1:51–3; Si. 10:14–15, 25, 11:21, 21:4. Jos., *Ant.* xviii. 267.
198. 2 Bar. 70:3–4.                          199. Mt. 2:2; cf. Mk. 10:40.

nights(!), an opiate for the unfortunate (for whom brigandage was an alternative to unemployment)?[199a]

## §8. THE SINNER

We have reviewed Jewish society rapidly, noted its outstanding characteristics and remarked on the Hebrews' attitudes towards the heathen and to Samaritans. We must now notice the peculiar status of the 'sinner'. It has been misunderstood, because Western readers of the New Testament have read into it their own attitudes towards deviants. In the West a dichotomy between law and morality has established itself firmly since the end of the Middle Ages. A law-breaker can well be socially acceptable and, on the other hand, one who contravenes the requirements of morality may find the law powerless to punish him. Ostracism is not feared, since society is not monolithic and the law's strength lies in considerations weightier than that mobile factor, public favour. The public itself is diversely made up. Various religions, sects, and fancies, including adherents who deny all super-rational authority, now live side by side protected by the same law. A sinner may be immune, amongst us, from disfavour even at the hands of faithful members of a religious communion to which he belongs or belonged: sin is regarded as, at the worst, an unhappy condition, rather like an illness, from which the sufferer can recover, and will recover more easily if his neighbours are tolerant and friendly towards him. In the ancient world none of these factors existed and the anomalous status of the 'sinner' has to be described with care.

In the eyes of the ruling power a 'sinner' might well be one of the most important amongst the natives. The Alexander I mentioned, and one of his sons (if not both), were most decidedly 'sinners', yet they were amongst the ruling aristocracy. They by no means hoped some rabbi would deign to cast a glance in their direction. On the contrary, they would not admit a rabbi at all. Had the rabbis then had all their legal powers (§17) Alexander and his family would have been made to suffer very severely for their cultural treachery, their moral turpitude in abandoning Jewish observances. They would surely have incurred the death penalty on one ground or another. Thus, if I have chosen my illustration aptly, it will be observed that 'sinner' implies membership of one or more party in opposition to

199a. Jm. 5:1–6; Si. 31:1–8.

the traditional native ethic, and those that upheld it. The notion that Jesus took pity on 'publicans and sinners', much as some Victorian ladies and clergymen used to make expeditions into the slums of East London is wide of the mark.

If the sinners were martyrs to freedom of conscience their martyrdom was exceedingly comfortable. It is generally supposed that they yearned to be reintegrated into Hebrew society, i.e. that of the ordinary villagers and their rabbis: I find no evidence for this, except the bitter references to them in apocryphal literature written by their enemies, who had every reason to hate them. Ancient and traditional societies could not tolerate deviants, and assumed that no one deviated unless he was possessed by an evil spirit, or had been overcome by a lust for women or money or both: and I do not think on the facts this outlook was unreasonable. There is, however, one curious feature of such a situation which is worth bearing in mind. When unorthodox and rebellious sons of a culture have achieved eminence by dubious means, by siding, as it were, with a hostile culture and playing the traitor, they not infrequently wish to be thought patrons of the nation, including those elements which they despised while at all the previous steps on the ladder of their career. Indian politicians who like to be heard quoting Sanskrit *shlokas*, Jewish businessmen who take to Torah-study in their old age, and other examples could be cited of this strange home-coming, which is by no means all hypocrisy. However, it is not a widespread phenomenon, and does not account for the curious relationship which developed between Jesus and the 'sinners', a relationship which unquestionably gave the traditionally minded amongst his contemporaries what is nowadays called 'grave cause for concern'.

The difficulty experienced by 'sinners', for all their advantages, was that they were denied all the networks of reciprocity (except amongst themselves) which came from sharing assets. The 'sinners' we speak of were men who hired assassins in pursuit of gain, professional usurers or extortioners, the men who operated the revenue system, from the highest (e.g. the tetrarchs and their entourages) to the lowest, and women who earned their living by prostitution or had done so.

All these classes were in a difficulty about gifts and tithes. Being Jews they were racially entitled to purify themselves ritually and enter the Temple. But what would make their offerings acceptable? The fact that their acquisitions could not be offered in tithe no doubt increased their available assets. But the same reason prevented them from doing what every Jew loved to do, namely entertain, build up a bank of goodwill, public esteem, precisely on the lines I have explained above. It would have been a different story had the Hellenisation of Judaism gone forward as it showed signs of doing prior to the Maccabean wars, if there had been no doubt but that the Land of Israel would be absorbed into the Roman Empire as Egypt had been, and if the priests had become virtually part of the civil service controlling the natives, as happened in Egypt. But it became more and more evident that this cultural assimilation would not take place, especially in view of the tolerant attitude adopted, from the days of Augustus onwards, towards the Hebrews' religion and customs. They were right. It never did. Consequently, unlike the Brahmins who became Westernised under British and later Anglicised Indian rule (if I can use such a phrase), the Jewish collaborators, and profiteers living on the evils of a non-independent Jewish State, knew, perhaps rather by instinct than by any form of prediction open to them, that it was a political and social necessity for them to be accepted in some form by their non-collaborating fellow-countrymen. Some form of reconciliation was required, but how was it to be done?

Those who disdained the 'sinners' ' company did so undoubtedly to their own cost. The theory was simple enough. Just as a rat needs a hole, and a thief needs a trafficker in stolen goods, so an extortioner or usurer needs people who will accept his hospitality and enter into reciprocal relations with him, or his extortion is to no purpose, granted that he must go on living in their midst. The 'just' did not touch the gains of violence.[200] One must not eat with sinners.[201] Fornication was regarded with horror, and the earnings of prostitutes were tainted. One who ate with them approved their way of life, which was unthinkable for the pious.[202] Unless they rid themselves of their tainted gains[203] they could not enter into normal society even when their practice had collapsed, whether due to natural causes or the protests of zealots. Males could indeed take up honest work. The objection to usurers was not to their taking usury, but to their taking it from fellow Jews. The ideal economy of the Golden Age was still supposed to obtain for this purpose, and no increase was allowed if not by way of commercial investment, and even there

200. *LNT*, 75–76, 281. 1 QS V. 14.    201. 1 Co. 5:11.
202. Test. Levi 14:5. *LNT*, 267–70.    203. Mt. 23:25; Lk. 19:8–9.

it was not permitted except under the cover of a partnership.[204] The theoretical economy still obtained so far as to make it impossible for the pious to eat with a professional usurer.

The Romano-Hebraic condominium made it possible for usurers to escape punishment, for their documents to be acted upon as if valid, and, similarly, for taxgatherers to escape punishment when they exacted taxes and enforced protection and other blackmail-devices under the cover of a legitimate revenue system. The oppressive method was in use of selling by auction the right to exact revenue. The contractors and sub-contractors had the right to manipulate the system, and no doubt the law gave them all the powers they needed. A quantity of money went to Rome and it is not surprising that many Jews, who barely acquiesced in Roman rule, thought that they could very well protect themselves. That taxgatherers were needed for the stability of the area seems certain, and the method they applied was no worse than that in use in Egypt or elsewhere in the empire; but the generality of Hebrews, and certainly the pious, could not accept that anyone who paid revenue to Rome, or to the collaborators of the Romans, was really, under the Torah, obliged to do so, and therefore they regarded all involved in the administration,[205] even the clerks, spies, and soldiers (if any of these were Jews, as no doubt many were),[206] as living upon the fruit of violence.[207]

Various views must have existed upon the question whether the 'mammon of unrighteousness' could ever be accepted by the pious by way of charity.[208] If it could, then part of the way for 'sinners' to acquire merit was paved for them. It would be necessary that the recipients should not feel that their own honesty was compromised by this—a matter of some ingenuity. That some of those who were actually employed in the hated revenue system were conscious of a need to attach themselves to the company of the pious is certain.[209] They may well have realised that the system could not last indefinitely: zealots for the ideal Hebrew self-disciplinary republican system might come into their own at any time and fortunes would be reversed indeed![210]

Meanwhile, until these questions had been solved 'sinners' who wanted to associate with a true Jew had to get him to invite *them*

204. Lk. 19:23.                    205. Mt. 9:9. For Zacchaeus see *LNT*, 278–85.
206. Lk. 3:14.    207. See p. 63, n. 200 above.    208. Lk. 16:9. *LNT*, 82–83.
209. Mk. 2:14.              210. Jos., *Ant*. xviii. 14, *BJ*, ii. 118. Ac. 5:37.

either to his own house if he had one or, if not, to the house of a patron of his. Then he would not eat tainted food and commensality with them would not compromise their temporary associates.[211] It is not impossible that some 'sinners', doubtful of the outcome of the Roman supremacy, advocated the view that the ritual objection, and indeed moral objection to commerce on a social basis between the collaborators and the pious, was anachronistic, and it remained only for an acceptable method to be devised under the religious Law whereby the taboo might be lifted. But there is no proof of this. All we have is the assurance of the gospels that such approaches towards reconciliation occurred, and that Jesus favoured them.

## §9. CONTRACT AND EQUITY

Because all Jews were theoretically brothers the ethics of the Golden Age persisted in socio-economic theory. No law of contract, indeed, was ever so scrupulously worked out as the Jewish law. Those who offered and those who accepted offers chose their words with care and uttered them before witnesses. Solemn speech, the three-fold utterance, became the weighty and the grave citizen.[212] In the Golden Age there had been no need, they thought, of documents to keep a record, to trip up hope by sudden reference to unexpected technicalities.[213] But documents were necessary aids to memory. Memories were copious and exact, but a multiplicity of business and extreme particularity and fastidiousness required skilled draftsmanship and a careful retention of archives. If one went to court and proved one's case and the witnesses acknowledged their signatures one would be sure to obtain judgment, unless the judge had been given a bribe. But this was not the end of the matter from the Jewish standpoint. Knowing the behaviour of the typical patriarch, they assumed without question that *ideally* 'mercy' must be blended with 'judgment'. Neither could exist without the other.

In reality insolvent debtors would be taken off to a filthy prison where their sufferings would extract payment from their relatives, who would be ashamed of their having left one of their own in prison. If this was not possible a stranger might show compassion (i.e. 'mercy') on the debtor. Otherwise he would be sold for what his labour was worth. Within their notions of status, high and low, Hebrews were markedly compassionate to their fellow-Jews. The

211. Mt. 9:10; Mk. 2:16.          212. Mt. 26:34; Ac. 10:16.
213. 1 En. 69:9–10. Debtors hated documents (!): Jos., *BJ*, ii. 427.

notion of 'loving one another' was by no means foreign to them.[214] They believed in sharing what they had.[215] They were compassionate at times to non-Jews, when they could thereby 'sanctify the Name', as they put it. For the non-Jew would recognise the supernatural powers of Yahweh, when he saw what a command he had over his worshipper's pocket![216] Not that this prevented the maxim being understood, that 'charity begins at home'.[217] Thus everyone knew that in spite of a written contract and strict terms some time to pay should be allowed. The orphan and the widow should be allowed advantages that strict law would not permit. Consideration must be shown even for the stranger who had no claim of blood kinship, marriage, old friendship, or benefit received. Thus the most legally minded of all ancient nations was safely scrupulous in its law with the knowledge that consideration, compassion, was part and parcel of life as most people (not only debtors) thought it should be lived.

This was not strange. Life, as Asians live it, is unpredictable and to pledge the future is foolish. Since every individual has parents, even grandparents, spouse, siblings, friends, associates, descendants, and others making demands upon him, he can never promise (except as a token of good will) any performance at all.[218] There is no simple future tense in their languages. When a man definitely intends an act he uses the present tense, to convey this idea, 'I do it'. If his wish can be put into action by his own act he puts it in the past, 'I have done it'. But even honest thought can be falsified by events: not that this excuse mollifies the disappointed![219] Lapses were hard to forgive even then, but cannot have been uncommon.[220] Hence to borrow with pathetic cries of need and to be quite unashamedly unable to repay must have been a common occurrence.[221] Compassion was called for, and brotherhood claimed, as a normal part of what would appear to us to be purely commercial life. Suretyship was entered into far too readily by our standards.[222] Naturally there must be limits to this if business is to be efficient, if taxes are to be recovered, if government is to be carried on: and the question

214. Jn. 13:34; Test. Zeb. 2:4. The principle is relied on as axiomatic at Lk. 10:29–37.
215. Lk. 3:11.
216. Mt. 15:31; Mk. 5:19; Ws. 18:13 (naïve notion); Test. Naph. 8:4, 6.
217. Mt. 15: 26–28 (better Mk. 7:27).　　218. Mk. 13:35.　　219. Si. 20:23.
220. Mt. 6:14.　　221. Si. 8:12, 29:1–13; Mt. 5:42.　　222. Si. 29:14–20.

borrowers would often raise would be where these limits should be drawn. If reciprocity is the cement of life, the very breath of society, surely those who recognise the claim of a 'brother' to compassion and to equitable treatment, irrespective of promises to perform a contract, will reasonably figure as 'brothers' when they themselves are squeezed to perform some legal, social, or political obligation. And those who deny brotherhood when it comes to exacting some small debt due to themselves can hardly call upon their debtors' associates or patrons to show forbearance to them when, the wheel of fortune having taken a turn, their own failures attract unfavourable attention.[223]

## §10. BEHAVIOUR IN GENERAL

A list of what we might call the 'gentlemanly' qualities as the educated Hebrew understood them would be very short.[224] 'Good conduct', 'deportment' was conveyed by the characteristic phrase *derek erets*, not quite 'the way of the world', though it sometimes has that vapid meaning (it can also be a euphemism), but rather 'conformity with the ideal norm', 'behaving oneself with propriety'—a complacent concept offering no challenge: good manners rather than good morals. Obsequiously polite to the prestige-worthy,[225] touching their feet,[226] haughty with the unimportant, flowery and circumspect in speech when their balance was good, outspoken and abusive when, as often happened, they lost it, the Jews were quick-tempered amongst themselves, aggressive, overflowing with words.[227] As Josephus repeatedly shows, they could (or at least a notable proportion of them could) be very ready with a knife when faction called. Injuries and insults occurred apparently all too easily, and apologies were seemingly offered without shame.[228] Satire was accepted polemical style.[229] As often happens with societies that have strict patterns of formal politeness, loose talk and vulgar abuse came easily to the tongue.[230] Censoriousness easily overtakes those who are concerned to be righteous themselves.[231] Shamelessly overt in signs

223. Mt. 18:23–35; Mk. 11:25.
224. Si. 21:22–28, 31:16. Mishnah, Avot V. 7.      225. Lk. 7:6–7, 11:27–28.
226. Mt. 28:9; Mk. 1:7; Lk. 17:16; Jn. 13:5 (enacted parable); Ac. 10:26 (revealing).
227. Lk. 6:45; Si. 22:27, 23:1, 7–9, 28:13–26.
228. Mt. 18:21–22; Lk. 17:3–4.
229. Mk. 12:38.                              230. Ac. 23:3, 5; Si. 11:32.
231. Mt. 7:3–5; Jn. 12:6 (naïve accusations); Tb. 2:12–14; Test. Gad 4:3, 6.

of affection, males embraced each other and showed no physical shyness when true or simulated emotion impelled them.[232]

Their attitude to *gratitude* differed utterly from the Western, though it survives in Asia and Africa. Thanks are viewed as a kind of payment. 'Do not thank me', says the Asian, 'for if you do I am paid. I should much prefer you to remain under obligation to me, which can turn out to my advantage some time.' Asians seldom or never say 'thank you'. If gratitude is expressed (cf. Lk. 17:16–18) it is a question of self-humiliation, which is contemplated when there is no possibility of return or reciprocation. The benefactor can obtain only prestige from the useless dependant whom he has helped. Overt gratitude of this type is of course perfectly natural towards Yahweh, whose kindness no one can reciprocate. Those who do not adopt the line of self-humiliation will remain bound to the benefactor, which is easy enough if loyalty has no complications.

Life was hard, serious, and often bitter. Literary illustrations of joy (e.g. the bridegroom leaving his chamber) are pathetically few. The characteristic Jewish sense of humour was keen, sour, and ready—as that of men enured to hardship may well be. Our more sensitive minds find some of their jokes cruel.

Undying affection was sworn very readily.[233] Indeed swearing and casual vows occurred so commonly,[234] as asseverations attempting to attract the attention of ears overloaded with emotional chatter, that religious leaders tried to draw the swearers' and hasty votaries' minds to what they were doing.[235] Yahweh would punish those who took his name in vain and promised him gifts they would forget all too easily, and since solidarity in weal and woe was a tenet of the Hebrews the punishment would visit the innocent as well (even babes unborn)! Everyone had an interest in the total avoidance of blasphemy. But plotters would swear by Yahweh to do what they (alone?) considered righteous.[236] Asseveration was, and still is, an Asian habit which misused the divine, even the divine Name, though the taboo associated with it (it was the Name to conjure with) kept some euphemism or periphrasis on the swearer's lips instead. When one wanted to use a superlative one said 'to death' (as in 'bored to death').[237]

232. Jn. 13:23.                          233. Mk. 14:20; Jn. 11:16.
234. Tb. 9:3, 8:20, 10:7; Si. 18:22–23.
235. Si. 23:9–11; Mt. 5:34, 36–37; Jm. 5:12; Mk. 7:11. *New Test St* 16 (1970),
    364–8.          236. Ac. 23:12; 1 En. 6:4.          237. Mk. 14:34.

More serious was the habit of vowing to Yahweh the good things of life. Particular vows for particular superstitious objects, e.g. to recover from an illness[238] or to prosper in business ventures, were not spiritual or social dangers; and members of society who were not heads of households or legally independent were not allowed to interfere with the family's economy by vows of which its head would disapprove. But if one abstained from enjoyments by vowing to abstain as if they were Temple assets one restricted one's own freedom and also that of those with whom one normally enjoyed table companionship—it could thus be an antisocial act, and under the cover of piety it was often so intended to operate. Still worse were the hasty vows whereby a man fed up with his wife's or parents' behaviour would vow to Heaven the hypothetical value that would otherwise have been spent for their maintenance.[239] This was a hostile act, covering under a show of piety an intention to discard or repudiate a near and dear person who had overstepped the limits of patience. The tighter the ties of the family, the stronger the bonds of friendship, the more demands are made and the sooner the limitations of the individual are explored and exposed. One cannot have it both ways. Real friendship is tested by the ability to quarrel harmlessly. But the associates of a man were not chosen by his heart, but by his parents, his mere descent, his faction, his locality, his age, or his circumstances—and quarrels were as bitter as interdependence was inevitable. Naturally such explosions gave moralists and jurists a problem to think over.

A close mind coupled with extroverted, childlike, sociable behaviour—a strange combination, known to the East where a smiling face and predictable manners go hand-in-hand with thoughts, fears, and plans disclosed only to a few. Unpredictable *bonhomie* alternated with sternness.[240] Enthusiasm could effervesce.[241] They liked to think of themselves as guileless,[242] but crafty,[243] and the kiss of equality like the kiss of respect[244] comes readily from one who is preparing to desert to the enemy's camp.[245] Treachery by a dependant was thrillingly horrible to contemplate,[246] but horror was no stranger to life. Unsqueamishness, indifference to pain, except when it was that of a favourite or associate, was universal.[247] Spiritual

238. Jos., *BJ*, ii. 313.      239. Mk. 7:11. See p. 35, n. 33 above.
240. Lk. 12:37; Si. 10:25.      241. Lk. 14:34.      242. Jn. 1:47.
243. Jdt. 10:19.    244. Tb. 5:16.    245. Si. 12:12.    246. Jn. 13:18.
247. Mt. 14:11. Jos., *Ant.* xiii. 380, *BJ*, vii. 200, 202.

depths, naïvety, and myopic cunning—a combination familiar to every one who has lived long in the East—made that population for ever strange to the modern West.[247a] When the victim was helpless, abuse, open scorn, mockery, and even stones could fly readily enough.[248] Few were ashamed of kicking a man when he was down. 'Happy is he who sees his enemy's downfall!'[249] Not to laugh loudly at or over the unfortunate[250] was to be associated with him and to bear shame oneself. I have already explained that shame was unbearable. All emotions were voiced openly and loudly.[251] One wailed and one gnashed one's teeth.[252] I have seen the latter only once in Britain (when someone learnt of some success I had had) but in the East it is a common experience. So used to dramatising their lives and their feelings they even enact the signs of joy or woe when the circumstances seem to demand them (e.g. a death in the locality) irrespective of any genuine feeling. The Hebrews sorrowed in dust and ashes,[253] and plucked out their hair.[254] Remorse, even if feigned, was indicated by theatrical behaviour.[255] Fasting was not worth undergoing unless everyone saw and appreciated what one was doing. Inauspicious phrases were avoided by circumlocution, and if they were heard the robe was torn dramatically.[256] The great tore their robes to attract the mob's attention to their alarm and fear of the Romans' vengeance if the mob had its way.[257] Mourning was obvious and dramatic.[258] One who had occasion to rejoice, at private success or a public occasion, gave conspicuous attention to his toilet to signalise the fact unmistakeably.[259]

247a. Beautifully explained by Ruth P. Jhabvala, *An Experience of India* (London, Murray, 1966). Long resident in India, Mrs. Jhabvala has every reason to be sympathetic to Asia.

248. Mt. 27:39; Mk. 14:65; Lk. 14:30; Test. Levi 7:2.

249. Si. 25:7; 1 En. 95:3, 96:1. Pr. 24:17. Mishnah, Avot IV. 19.

250. Si. 23:3; Mart. Is. 5:1–2.

251. Mt. 8:12; 1 Esd. 1:32; Tb. 7:7; Si. 38:16–17; 2 M. 13:12.

252. In vexation. Si. 30:10. Extraordinarily frequent in Mt. (8:12, 13:42, 50, etc.) the allusion is to Ps. 112:10 (only).

253. Lk. 10:13; Jdt. 4:11, 13–15; Ba. 4:20; 1 Esd. 9:38; 1 M. 2:14, 3:47. Jos., *BJ*, ii. 237.

254. 1 Esd. 6:71; 2 Esd. 1:8.     255. Jos., *BJ*, i. 506.

256. Mt. 26:65; Test. Jos. 5:2.

257. Jos., *BJ*, ii. 316, 322. Tearing the robe in deprecation: Ac. 14:14.

258. Mt. 9:23; Jos., *BJ*, ii. 6. Prayer could be ostentatiously abject: Est. 14:2.

259. Mt. 6:17, 26:8–9.

Feasting was the typical method of enjoyment,[260] and inhibitions, which restrained the mature members of society, were loosened on the occasions where abundant wine was customarily associated with drunkenness,[261] as at the nationalistic festival called Purim. A Hebrew could think of no better way of symbolising joy or contentment than a feast, when work was over,[262] and the scanty accumulations of the harvest were spent in conspicuous consumption. No joy was like that of a bridegroom (especially the bridegroom of a virgin),[263] and no feast like a wedding feast. The sparse diet and rigidly economical lives of the vast majority[264] made the very thought of a banquet the epitome of happiness. At a banquet a guest's prestige was signalised by the exactly appropriate position in which he reclined at table (or there would be trouble, and the host would be involved in another feud).[265] A society in which there were no degrees was unthinkable,[266] but it must be admitted that no one was served at banquets until all had arrived.[267]

One feasted only with one's near and dear ones, one's reciprocating equals, one's 'brothers' who would, one day, invite one back. And amid the unusual diet of roast meat[268] and abundant wine, first the best and then the less well-flavoured, one gained an extra thrill of satisfaction from the thought that there were others, one's 'enemies', who were excluded,[269] and who could hear the songs and music[270] from far off, and, if one were really lucky, could actually smell what was going on in the kitchen from quite near by! There need only be a gully between the feasters and those whom habit, history, or inclination had absolutely kept out, but it would be enough to make the point.

260. Ass. Mos. 7:8.     261. Jn. 2:9; 1 Esd. 3:18.          262. Ac. 2:15.
263. Jn. 3:29.    264. Lk. 15:29.     265. Mk. 12:39; Lk. 14:7, 10; Si. 29:27.
266. Mt. 18:1.          267. Mk. 10:31.          268. Lk. 15:23; Si. 31:23–24.
269. Lk. 13:28. *Midrash on Psalms*, Ps. 12 (trans. W. Braude, I, 173–4). The
    incident at Jos., *Ant.* xiii. 380, cited at n. 247 above was going rather far,
    but the principle is well illustrated by it. The un-Christian anticipation
    is technically authorised by Is. 65:13.
270. Si. 32:3–6. Hence Lk. 15:25.

SECOND LECTURE

# The Economic and Political Scene

### §11. NATURAL PROCLIVITIES AND THE MOTIVE OF PROFIT

We have already understood how Jews, that is to say the unassimi-
lated Hebrews who still regarded Palestine as their homeland, took
it as axiomatic that their community was a brotherhood, in spite of
tribal differences and what were regarded as only temporary inequalities of wealth and esteem. Yahweh gave and Yahweh could
take away. Instead of hindering the natural urge to acquire, this fact
seems to have stimulated it.[1] If the dominant motive in Hebrew
society was the acquisition and retention of prestige, a second most
important, only marginally less dominant, was the interest in
property. Money, or money's worth, figure in popular tales and
parables to so remarkable an extent that no one can doubt but that
it was normally assumed that the profit motive was unashamedly
ubiquitous. One could even say that one 'gains Christ' if one works
faithfully, even if in so doing one 'loses' in point of comfort or in
pocket. It was no exaggeration to say that for all practical purposes
'money' equalled life.[2]

Yet, characteristically, an opposite tension existed. Assuming that
no family let pass an opportunity to acquire, they all accepted as
part of Judaism that work, particularly valuable work, must cease at
stated intervals and on certain days. Sabbaths and the major festivals
were in different degrees compulsorily freed from work and the
concept of compulsory rest and recreation was deep-rooted. Even
the fictitious residence which enabled the Hebrews to move beyond
the conventional limits of a Sabbath's journey (a fiction the Dead
Sea folk seem to have abhorred) was not used as an analogy to enable

1. Ph. 3:7-11.                              2. Mk. 12:43; Si. 34:21-22.

73

forbidden work to be done, or forbidden acquisitions to be made or enjoyment to be obtained. Where it was most worth their while to stretch the Law they declined to do so. The Sabbath was so strictly observed that, until prudence intervened, even self-defence in time of war was forbidden on that day.[3] During Jesus's lifetime further hindrances to agricultural and commercial gain were in force. The Seventh Year was observed: the land was left fallow compulsorily.[4] 'A dealer in Seventh-year produce' would be a 'sinner' (§8). Debts, too, would be released automatically and bonds would be unenforceable when the Seventh Year set in. To prevent a total lack of credit before the year arrived the jurist Hillel (§26) invented a fiction whereby the effect of the Seventh Year was obviated—and this has remained famous ever since.[5] The Hebrews, left to themselves, systematically limited the right to earn, and those who practised their religion did so literally to their own cost. No one would use the word 'martyrdom' to describe this traditional form of life, but it was certainly a witness.

It would be natural for most peoples who believe in blood sacrifices to offer the worst animals they had (dry cows, etc.). But all the animal offerings, and there were many of them, were subject to stringent rules of fitness, and for our purposes it is enough to say that in their religious dues, voluntary as well as obligatory, the Hebrews paid or provided out of their best. Only beasts without blemish could be offered and the sarcasms of the prophets against an alleged contrary practice could hardly be repeated in Jesus's time, or we should surely have heard of it. Jews thought a great deal of money, mammon,[6] and of earning. But, as we have seen, they were concerned to earn righteously, if possible, and from their earnings they offered tithes to the priests, and offerings to the Temple, and so consecrated their assets and made them fit, as they thought, for their own consumption.

Since the Jew earnt not for himself but for his dependants, comrades, clients, and others whose needs offered him a chance of gaining prestige, the natural proclivity towards acquisition was never selfish in the modern sense of the word and was always tempered by the desire for the end towards which, in their minds, all activity tended,

---

3. 1 M. 2:35–37. Jos., *BJ*, i. 146.
4. Jos., *BJ*, i. 60.                     5. Mishnah, Shev. X.
6. Mt. 6:24. Do not equate *mammon* with 'unrighteous mammon' which is the *anosios kerdos* the Essenes swore to eschew: Jos., *BJ*, ii. 141.

namely a 'good name in Israel'. It is true that we have stories about Sadducees who dined on gold and silver dishes and ridiculed Pharisees (§26) who lived sparely even when they could spend freely: the former said that the latter were misled to suppose that they would fare better in the next life, for, in the Sadducee view, there would be none—hence they made a point of enjoying what they could while they lived. But no one suggests that Sadducees did not look after their own relations, or lived self-sufficient lives, unmoved by their social context.

## §12. ACCUMULATION

It is a trite saying that you cannot take it with you. Desire for wealth, ubiquitous, tempts one into anti-social acts.[7] Those who want their assets to be protected are liable to be compromised in their politics.[8] It was a viable equation to say 'protection = the secular kingdom = evil'.[9] But human nature provides for contingencies.[10] An accumulation of large treasures in the Temple certainly occurred and even caused alarm. But the Temple was a charitable organisation, and its funds were intended for emergencies. The chief objection to accumulation of wealth was that no place, barring the treasury, was really safe. In this, as in other senses,[11] enough is enough. Nocturnal thieves and robbers evidently flourished until drastic action temporarily discouraged them.[12] Since the public liked the thought that the rich would be emptied and the poor filled, the sudden collapse of a rich man would hardly provoke pity except among his kindred, who would, no doubt, tide him over. The religious objection to usury limited direct loans at interest, but did not prevent covert investment of a usurious nature, still less speculation. In fact treasures were coveted ecstatically.[13] The advantage of a hoard, whether of coin (which would not become obsolete) or grain, oil, or wine, was that in time of adversity the rich could 'open their hands' to their poor neighbours and so fulfil their social obligation.[14] If one earned honestly there was no moral objection to accumulation: the more the merrier. Certainly when one's back was

7. Mt. 5:3; Mk. 4:19, 8:36; Si. 26:29, 27:3.
8. Mt. 19:25; Mk. 10:23.  9. Lk. 4:5.
10. Mt. 6:25, 34; Lk. 12:18ff.; Si. 11:18–19, 14:3–5.
11. Ps. Sol. 5:18–20.
12. Mt. 6:19–20, 12:29, 30, 24:43; Mk. 3:27; Jn. 10:8. Jos., *BJ*, i. 204, 304–16, 398–9, ii. 253, 271.
13. Mt. 13:44; 2 Esd. 7:59–60.  14. Secr. En. 51:2.

turned, the steward or bailiff, servants, and hangers-on would do their utmost to reduce the total (p. 58): a peculiar, but genuine interpretation of the principle that charity begins at home. The Jewish law of agency was highly developed and facilitated every enterprise. Of the maxims figuring in this law[15] the most interesting to us was that 'the agent is like the principal', and he represented him, even to the extent of undertaking all such needful acts, delegating to others necessary tasks, as the principal could have done.[16] The principal was bound to trust his agent as long as he acted within the scope of his commission, and this, though it opened the door to fraud, also offered great opportunities for expansion of business, which evidently flourished accordingly.[17] Knowing how far to authorise and how far to trust agents was part of the secret of the Hebrew's business success. He also knew how to test servants and partners and how to reward the efficient in the most appropriate way, i.e. by giving them the opportunity to serve in ampler measure.[18] The royal financier says 'A champion of friendship is to be rewarded by being allowed to rule over many subjects'.[19]

## §13. WAGES AND SOCIAL OBLIGATION

The operation of the laws of supply and demand had unimpeded effect, granted that amongst the Hebrews there was a free market in labour and commodities, subject to tolls. The employer offered the lowest wage which would be accepted by a man having the skills he required, and the labourer could resile from the bargain[20] and, subject to any compensation he might owe his employer, prefer idleness or take up better-paid work elsewhere. The law and custom enabled the labourer to find his own level from hour to hour, as it were, according to the wages and conditions available. When a dispute occurred (as seems not to have been uncommon) as to what the engagement was and what the labourer was entitled to be paid, the labourer was usually believed (on oath) and he was entitled (unless he waived his right) to be paid in cash at the end of the working day. Law and custom favoured the worker and there was

15. *LNT*, 52.
16. Mt. 10:1, 40–42; 28:18–19; Mk. 11:28; Jn. 20:23. An exception appears in Mt. 21:37–41.
17. Mt. 6:24, 7:21, 11:27, 24:45–51.
18. Mt. 24:47, 25:14–30, Lk. 16:11–12, 19:17.
19. Jos., *BJ*, i. 391.                                        20. *LNT*, 10.

no hesitation in viewing the relationship between master and servant as one which, for all its obvious inequalities (§7), reflected the brotherhood of Israelites and recognised the possibility that roles might be reversed in the all-too-near future. Just as few Vietnamese can remember peace, so the contemporaries of Jesus, enured to wars and invasions, had never known political or fiscal stability (and never had a feudal system), so that no class could become entrenched in power.

The contractual wage might be exacted scrupulously, whatever profit the employer might make from the product. But this did not mean that the economic wage was the only wage actually paid. If a wage were paid which reflected the labourer's need for work, it would fall so low, in a period of unemployment and over-population, that subsistence would not be achieved, and the labour force itself would collapse. The Hebrews were unacquainted with combinations between employers to keep wages down and between workers to keep them (and the prices of products) up. Theoretically employers could bring in cheaper labour from other areas. But during our period few had a standard of living above subsistence and the dislocation which would be caused by such an immigration was socially unacceptable. Thus there existed a social value of labour independent of the economic value, and everyone had a notional (i.e. legally calculable) minimum wage.[21] Assume first that work is done for a wage and not as reciprocation amongst equals: then the question arises whether any work shall be done without reward. Amongst the Hebrews this concept did not exist. All services bespoke their reward, even if it was only a nominal tip. Thus where an unemployed workman was ready to do even a few hours' work he was entitled to a notional minimum daily wage, irrespective of the value of his product, and the employer might, in recognition of the solidarity of Israel, pay a full day's wage. This was not only 'righteous' but also economically sound, since other employers on other occasions would benefit from the physical condition of the labour force.

## §14. REACTION AGAINST EXPLOITATION

Even with the reasonable arrangement referred to in our last paragraph it must frequently have happened that sections of the population were discontented. The activities of thieves and robbers

21. Mt. 20:1–16.

show that receivers of stolen property and secret sympathisers with such brigands must have existed.[22] The Temple hierarchy and successful capitalists showed, by their accumulations and conspicuous consumption that the economy, based on a strict application of the law of real property, was not operating in the spirit of the brotherhood of all Israel. The threat of the Jubilee, or Year of Release (or Restitution of property), which seems not actually to have occurred during our period, did nothing to prevent the accumulation of lands in relatively few hands. If the property were earnt righteously, without extortion, the public would accept the fact and look to its owner to give lavishly in alms. No attempt was made to deal with the root cause of financial inequality.

There were large numbers of unemployed and unemployables for whom the overriding obligation to give in charity produced only bare subsistence, and often not even that.[23] The well-to-do regarded their own ability to acquire prestige through them, and otherwise, as whittled away by taxation and the exploitation of the Hebrews by foreigners. It was not the case that Greek and other heathen communities in Phoenicia or the Decapolis, or elsewhere in the Syrian orient, were exempt from taxation which the Jews had to pay. The Jews regarded themselves as notionally a republic led by an absent 'king' (§18) with a High Priest who performed, as best he could, some of the functions of an invisible 'righteous' hegemony.[24] This was a *notional* State (i.e. more real in the imagination than in fact); it had its own *notional* self-taxing system, only part of which (tithes and the Temple tax) was functioning, and the Hebrews simply refused to recognise as lawful, or justified,[25] the *de facto* arrangements under which Seleucids, Ptolemies, and finally Romans had acquired the territories in which they lived and milked them of vast

22. Some Roman officials actually went into partnership with brigands: Jos., *BJ*, ii. 278–9.
23. Lazarus at Lk. 16:20–21. It can be taken as common knowledge that starvation soon destroys appetite (a mercy of nature): *Encycl. Brit.*, 12th ed., vol. 31, 58; 11th ed., vol. 10, 193. Lk. 4:2 signalises something unusual.
24. Being quite practical the native chiefs wanted autonomy under a Hebrew governor appointed by Rome, or at worst a Herodian 'king': Jos., *BJ*, ii. 22, 80. The Roman Gabinius (57–55 B.C.) did indeed do away with monarchy and substituted five circles governed by Hebrew aristocracies (but it did not last): Jos., *BJ*, i. 169–70.
25. Lk. 2:38; Ac. 1:6; 2 Esd. 6:57–58.

revenues which could obviously be much better spent. The Hebrews were, in their own minds, essentially a free people.[26] In consequence large numbers of people openly,[27] and many secretly, aided more or less permanent rebels, who would elsewhere have been condemned as parasites upon society. These included the Zealots, whose opposition to Roman rule took a violent form. Zeal for the Law was widespread, and it could be a convenient cover for paying off old scores.[28] They preyed upon the monied classes and on produce which the ruling power might otherwise have enjoyed, and used a perverse patriotism as an excuse for piracy and brigandage. They weakened the economy without appreciably weakening the foreign regime. Men and boys rushing down an alley trying to escape from a platoon of mercenaries would address as 'saviour' anyone who had the courage to open a door for them; and any general of the government's forces who cleared the district of robber-chiefs would be hailed as 'saviour' by the populace assembled in the market.

It is a normal reaction to autocratic government in pre-modern societies to express political and economic dissatisfaction in terms of religious enthusiasm. The individual rebel executed hastily by the impatient ruler becomes a saint, whose cult cannot be suppressed even though the 'tyrant' is aware that it is aimed against him. There were, on that basis, numbers of unemployed people only too keen to listen to religious discourses, the implication of which did not so much withdraw them from gainful employment as inspire them with hopes of revolution.[29] The Hebrews formed notionally a theocratic state, and all their economics were based, to all appearances, upon the solidarity of Israel. This was founded upon the revealed will of Yahweh, and what might at first hearing seem to be innocuous spiritual exhortation would fill them with much more solid expectations and portend a commotion. Large crowds gathered in inaccessible places to range themselves behind some religio-political 'shepherd'[30] and this was no more welcome to the Romans than were the Zealots.

26. Jn. 8:33; Est. 13:12. For obstinate opposition to imposed rulers see Jos., *BJ*, i. 243–7, ii. 264–5.
27. Lk. 21:24.
28. Jn. 8:3–6; Test. Gad 4:3, 6. Jos., *BJ*, ii. 234–5, 238.
29. Ac. 4:1–3, 5:17–18.
30. Mk. 6:34; Lk. 23:5; Ac. 5:36–37. Jos., *Ant.* xx. 97, *BJ*, ii. 60ff. (Athrongaeus actually *was* a shepherd and would-be king), 259–60, 261–3 (note how the Mount of Olives is involved).

## §15. PROFIT AND LOSS

However this might be, the Romans like many imperial rulers before them realised that only a healthy and prosperous economy could satisfy their demands. A reasonably stable price-structure, reasonably easy transfer of capital, and a predictable outcome to business transactions, would be essential preconditions for government. Jews' privileges and immunities were preserved in all regions, including of course Palestine itself. Jews transferred their assets from country to country and participated in speculation, often with abundant profits. The multiplication of assets was supposed to be virtuous. A large debt might be the more readily cancelled if the debtor, thus freed, became thereby obliged to his former creditor and thus, out of gratitude, gave more in various services, than the money released was actually worth.[31] The human gain outweighed the monetary loss. A sharp calculation of the margin was usual and went on in large-scale, even the largest-scale transactions, and in petty business and casual loans. This social consideration we have met before in another guise (§13).

Taken to its logical end the system would have made Jewish strife against their rulers unnecessary. The Hebrews could have shared their natural resources and their foreign income, and freedom from Roman rule would have offered less advantage than risk. Indeed, on that basis, the theocracy would have been no less real in transcendental terms for being merely notional in political terms. The Romans, after all, did nothing to hinder the cult as such—at most they wished their own patronage of it to be recognised openly, and their influence over the High Priest, even if it operated corruptly in some aspects, merely prevented the established cult from becoming a focus of rebellion, which was surely an advantage to all concerned. But it was to the Romans' financial advantage to support, not only law and the security of property, but also acquisitiveness and insistence upon rights: charity kept the poor alive, even if fellow-feeling seldom achieved more than that,[32] but if people were less concerned with profit than they were with the solidarity of their own society less would be yielded from taxes. The fact that internal administration was insecure, that private property was often to be enjoyed only as long as Zealots or other brigands did not rob or destroy it, and that individual performance was always unpredict-

31. Lk. 7:41–43.                                    32. 1 Esd. 9:51.

able, all this encouraged the Hebrews to opt for personal safety instead of corporate tranquillity, personal wealth instead of corporate exchange—and this both expected too much from the imposed Roman system and continually prevented it from achieving its own objects. Jews knew that their rulers' notions did not agree, basically, with their own: but they disagreed as to whether traditionally Jewish methods of resolving the problem ought to be used. There were always too many hot-headed nationalists about.

Against this background each one bustled about and attended to his business,[33] exploited his own plot of land or craft.[34] A ripe harvest was to be harvested.[35] Every asset was to be made to show a profit.[36] One withdrew capital from an unproductive enterprise and invested it elsewhere.[37] Modesty in asserting one's claims or pursuing one's interests was deprecated.[38] Nothing must lie idle.[39] No waste could be tolerated.[40] It was against conscience to do so. But rubbish would be burnt or otherwise restored to nature.[41] Subject to recognition of solidarity (as above) recalcitrant debtors were sent to gaol.[42] While false measures were by no means unheard of, the characteristic measure of the market was generous.[43] While counterfeit coins circulated the good man tested each one before passing it on.[44] The means of deception existed; but the nation was in the course of disciplining itself to obviate, and avoid them. Yet, if this fostered individual gains and commercial efficiency it did nothing to forward the ideal Hebrew self-balancing economy, which would break down all too easily. Roman individualism set the Hebrews the worst of examples.

## §16. SOLIDARITY AND COMPETITION

We cannot emphasise too strongly the strength and value of the Jewish belief in national solidarity. Utterly opposed to the individualistic ways of the West, the Hebrews placed, at every turn, an

33. Mt. 7:13; Lk. 14:28 (realism the ideal).
34. Mt. 7:24–27.                                                    35. Mt. 9:35.
36. Mt. 3:8–10, 7:16–20, 12:33, 21:33–41, 43; Mk. 4:20; Lk. 13:6–9, 17:7–10; Jn. 15:2, 4.
37. Mt. 13:12; Mk. 4:25; Lk. 12:48b.
38. Si. 4:21.                                                        39. Mt. 25:14–30.
40. Mt. 5:5, 7:6, 9:16, 26:8–9; Lk. 12:33 (people would even let their purses wear out).
41. Mt. 3:12, 5:13, 7:19.                                          42. Mt. 5:25–26.
43. Mt. 7:1; Mk. 4:24; Lk. 6:38.                           44. Mt. 12:35; Lk. 6:45.

obstacle in the way of the individual's pursuit of gain and accumulation. Gain at another's loss was in any case detestable.[45] There was a kind of partnership of all Israelites, based on kinship, in the produce of the soil.[45a] Odd as it may seem, this notion may have a part to play in explaining the extraordinary ambivalence of the role of the peasant (cultivator one day and brigand the next) who, at any rate in Galilee, was already developing his reputation as a terror to his fellow-countrymen, Jews as well as gentiles.[45b]

The gleanings and the corner of the field were reserved for the poor.[46] Even one's own property was subject to this tacit charge in their favour. Neighbours, whether poor or not, continually borrowed utensils and transport.[47] The Jewish law was strict in making every borrower insure the thing or creature borrowed, to the extent that he must compensate the owner for damage in *any* event, whatever the cause of the loss, unless the owner were actually associated in the work for which the loan took place.[47a] This seems harsh, but it tended directly to encourage gratuitous loans of articles for use and facilitated, as it evidenced, the continual sharing of assets. Fussiness over the terms of the transaction, perfectionism in ascertaining what precisely was the intention, and pedantry in distinguishing the different types of relationship between the ordinary peasant borrower and lender (a pedantry for which our more affluent society has no use) went hand in hand with an ethos which required the Hebrew not to turn aside from one who needed the use of his asset. Competitively equipped in method, the society was not competitively orientated in outlook. Reciprocity was the very life of society.[48]

The law of overreaching, as it is called,[49] shows this clearly. The law took it for granted that the buyer and seller would agree upon a price, and that the agreement, once the property was transferred,

45. Mt. 25:24–26; Lk. 19:21. But one might gain from one's associate's efforts: Jn. 4:37–38.

45a. Jos., *Ant.* iv. 236.    45b. Jos., *BJ*, ii. 581 (habitual malpractices).

46. Mishnah, Peah (throughout). A succinct account of the provisions referred to above may be found conveniently in Maimonides's Positive (Affirmative) Commandments nos. 120, 121, 122, 123, 124 (the forgotten sheaf), and 130 (the triennial tithe for the Levite and the poor), which can be studied in C. B. Chavel, *The Commandments* (London, Soncino Press, 1967). Jos., *Ant.* iv. 231–2.

47. Mt. 5:42; Lk. 6:34–35 (reciprocity taken as commonly presumed).

47a. *Nov. Test.* vol. 13 (1971), 241–258.    48. Mt. 5:46.

49. Literally 'constructive fraud' (*ona'ah*). Mishnah, B.M. IV. 2–4.

actually or fictionally, was the basis of the deal. But, like some other ancient societies, the Hebrews could not accept the proposition, taken for granted amongst us, that the price agreed is the final price irrespective of the parties' respective profit and loss. Altogether apart from fraud or misrepresentation, the seller could retract if the price was excessively low, and the buyer could retract if it turned out to be too high. A small profit from circumstances was allowed—but a considerable one was regarded as hostile to the solidarity of Israel and could not be tolerated unless the loser waived his right to annul the transaction.

Further, there seems no reason in strict law why a skilled man should not set up shop near his former master or in competition with other men in his craft. In many Asian towns all the smiths of a particular guild are found in the same street or quarter. Yet the traditional Jewish law forbids competition between tradesmen if a new arrival settling too nearby must diminish the livelihood of another already pursuing the same trade.[50] The rule is like the rule amongst scholars that a legal opinion is not to be given by a pupil, even long after he has, as it were, graduated, if his teacher resides within a certain distance of him, and thus could easily have been resorted to by the inquirer. And to preserve respect for the teacher this is invariably observed even though the pupil, to his preceptor's delight, had surpassed him as much in wisdom as in learning.

## §17. THE POLITICAL AUTHORITY AND ITS ORGANS

We have now, in a broad outline, most of the chief characteristics of the Hebrews, other than those relating to the unseen world of which they, like other Asians, were keenly conscious. But we have not understood as yet how far these were subserved by the State. We gathered earlier that the aims of the Roman administration, taken as a whole, operated adversely to the realization of the Hebrew ethos. This was not the conscious intention of the Romans; it was a by-product of the supremacy over an Asian nation of a Western organization. Asians are not 'organised' nor do they organise themselves—rather, they aggregate, cohere, or coagulate. If one imposes an organisation of any kind upon them, it is bound to be foreign to

50. It is true that the developed Talmudic law admitted restrictions on freedom of trade gradually (see G. Horowitz, *Spirit of Jewish Law*, New York, 1953, pp. 328–30), but the principle of not removing the neighbour's landmark was available for all such rules from far earlier than the Mishnah.

them and they will react unfavourably to it, distort it, caricature it, and eventually one or the other must be fragmented in an explosion. There can be no doubt but that the ruthless, single-minded Romans were, in our terms, a 'Western' nation. True, the West, as we know it, was not yet formed or identified, but in the clashes between Asians, such as the Persians or the Parthians, on the one hand, and the Greeks, the Macedonians, and the Romans on the other there never was any doubt but that different cultures or civilisations, as well as different racial groups, were at war. The antipathy the Hebrews felt towards Greek religion and society and the fascination the cult of Yahweh had for certain Greeks and even Romans certifies quite as well as the ancient phenomenon of anti-semitism that the gulf was not merely one of language. Let Hebrews speak Greek, they still spoke it with an Asian accent (pp. 49–50).

To grasp what happened some effort of imagination is needed on our part, even though we see Asians constantly, and anthropologists' programmes adorn our television. That there is some broad conti-nuity between the Romans and ourselves is proved by the ease with which Roman law and the Roman political outlook, which was accepted readily enough in Greece for so long, was adopted and admired in all Western countries, including the 'fringe' Westerners, the Slavs and East European peoples and the mixed descendants of the Iberian races in Central and South America. Even the Anglo-Saxon races and Scandinavians were not unmoved by Rome, and admiration not seldom passed over into emulation. Thus to compare the Romans in Syria and Arabia with the British in undivided India, Ceylon, and Burma on the one hand and the Portuguese in China, India, and Africa on the other would not be wildly inappropriate. And the correspondences are illuminating. We may occasionally borrow terms from the experience of the latter to explain the predicament of the former, of course without implying any identity between the two.

From the Roman point of view what was required from the inhabitants was that they should live at peace with each other, with the Senate and People of Rome, and with Rome's allies. They should afford means of self-realisation for the Roman genius, a market for the merchants of Rome and her allies and tributary peoples, and pay (naturally) by way of tribute for the privileges Rome provided. In order to facilitate these objects Rome enlisted and stationed in Syria legions, many of them drawn from Asian populations and even including some Hebrews, which could be used to keep the peace as well as to defend the province from invasion or subversion. Had the Romans prior to Augustus been models of loyalty and co-operative zeal the Hebrews would have been fully justified in their admiration for them. As it was, provided one forgot that Romans too could fall into factions,[51] it was evident that the rulers of the eastern Mediterranean had an utterly different attitude to law, government, and society from their own. They might be viewed from two aspects: Romans had an excellent team sense, subordinating their personal desire for prestige to the commonly agreed policies of the State in whose policy-making they took part in various ways;[52] while on the other hand the policies were not only discussed, but also implemented, because of the uniform and elaborate devolution of command whereby those properly authorised and required to perform an operation either performed it or suffered the highly disagreeable consequences.[53] Hebrews regarded themselves as essentially egalitarian, not subject to overlordship by individuals apart from the latter's prestige; they regarded with contempt the Hellenistic rulers' delight at being called Benefactor,[54] when it was far from clear who benefited from their rule; and it is small wonder that in all their calculations even the most Hellenistically educated potentates took the resentment of the Hebrew vulgar into account.[55] The Hebrews may have envied the Romans' individualism and single-minded drive: but they knew its limitations, and on the whole greatly preferred their own cohesive ways, their instinct for reciprocation and solidarity.[55a]

Asian societies, like enormously inflated African tribes, had, and in some measure still have, no such idea of government as the Romans had. Naturally they could learn it as a technique, parrot-fashion. Decisions are made by a gradual process, as opinion

51. Jos., *BJ*, i. 218.    52. 1 M. 8:14–16.
53. Mt. 8:5–9; Lk. 7:8. Jos., *Ant.* xviii. 265, *BJ*, ii. 195 (the verbal resemblance between this passage and Mt. 8:9 is remarkable) and esp. ii. 577–80.
54. Lk. 22:25. 'Protector' was a title that could be conferred by a vanquished people on its conqueror (Jos., *BJ*, i. 385); 'Saviour' could be adopted by a successful captor of a city he had besieged (!) (Jos., *BJ*, i. 295). On 'euergetes' see A. D. Nock, *Essays in Religion and the Ancient World* (Oxford, 1972) II, 725 ff. A more normal case: Plut., *Titus Flam.* ix. 16.
55. Mt. 21:46, 26:5; Mk. 11:18, 14:1; Ac. 5:26. Josephus often refers to the Achilles heel of the Hebrew nation, *to pléthos*, 'the mob'.
55a. Mishnah, Avot II. 3.

ferments. Consensus, not majority nor election, determines policy. The Hebrews actually learnt decision by majority under Roman rule—they had been ignorant of it previously. In Asia, when decisions are finally arrived at they are translated into action only if and when the prestige-holding individuals who have the opportunity for the time being to implement them feel free to do so and are not impeded by personal considerations.[56] The curious and characteristically Asian quality of insouciance (periodical abdication of responsibility and decision) could hamper prompt action even when the chief, who is expected to take it, is really free to do so. Asian societies function by the coincidence of a myriad of forces, basically of a personal and even sentimental nature, which no computer could analyse or predict.

The Romans were aware of this, knew that a new and dangerous purpose and motive could be heralded by signs which purported to be religious, not secular, and accordingly took as much care as possible not to offend the Hebrew religion, so as to leave the secular arena free from unpredictable and irrational forces which would subvert the tranquillity of the State and therefore its economy. Festivals were the periods when sedition was most apt to break out.[57] The Hebrews, like Hindus and Muslims of today (not to speak of the inhabitants of Northern Ireland, or of the island of Cyprus), were habitually alert to detect any insult to their religion, real or imaginary and to make a commotion, under the cover of which pecuniary or political advantages might be obtained.[58] The Roman governor, like a schoolmaster, was known to attempt to teach them that it was not worth their while—which they naturally resented and attributed to the Roman's brutality. But it would be quite wrong to read into Hebrew behaviour the forethought, planning, and organisation which have existed in those areas I have mentioned, particularly the last two. And where organisation is wanting, people fail to learn from experience, and the whole are at the mercy of undisciplined and fanatical elements which can impose upon the credulous.[59]

I have called the set-up a Romano-Hebraic condominium: a mouthful, and not a convenient expression, but it indicates the unpleasantly vague and sinister system, if system it can be called, providing what the sociologists would (inappropriately) call the 'framework' within which Jesus and his audience lived. Though

56. Mt. 9:31.                              57. Jos., *BJ*, i. 88, ii. 10–13, 42, 224.
58. See p. 79 n. 28 above.                59. Jos., *BJ*, i. 347, vi. 286–7.

Rome was the ultimate mistress she allowed partial self-government to the Hebrews in an interestingly subtle way, which must carry the blame for the terrific explosions which developed into the disasters of A.D. 70 and 132. Then the Hebrew homeland was progressively desolated and its surviving inhabitants, in large measure, scattered. The germs of these suicidal movements were already grown in Jesus's lifetime, and his audience were, unknown to themselves, preparing for the catastrophe. A penetrating eye might have foreseen this. Sceptics have not failed to stigmatise as fake prophecies (pious forgeries) all the gospel passages in which Jesus refers to coming disaster. They seem to fit aptly the *combined* results of the *two* greater Roman Wars and so it was suggested that they must have been foisted upon Jesus by Christians who had knowledge of those events, up to a century or so after the crucifixion! Josephus, who actually lived through the first Roman War, does not give the impression that the Hebrews were adequately warned by their native leaders of the probable effects of their intransigence until the time of the procurator Florus (A.D. 64–66), when such warnings were given with vehemence. All the gospels attained their present form (apart from trifling points still in debate) *after* A.D. 66; though of course their raw materials, including the greater part of the raw materials used by St. John, were in existence before then. All the gospels were in circulation before the reign of the emperor Hadrian, which began in A.D. 117. To delay, musing upon the significance of this, would not be to our present purpose.

Briefly, the condominium operated in this way:[60] the territorial divisions called 'tetrarchies' were delegated to descendants of the Idumaean Herod the Great (d. 4 B.C.) as 'kings'. They were responsible for levying taxes[61] and keeping law and order. After Herod Archelaus was deposed (A.D. 4) his tetrarchy was placed under the direct rule of the Roman procurator. Each ruler was removable by the emperor in Rome, and the inhabitants had the right of sending to Rome and complaining about the ruler's performance of his duties. Procurators were changed frequently, and they too were subject to this kind of harassment. The native rulers, though puppets,[62] could imagine themselves to be more or less independent despots while the procurator wielded the powers of the emperor as

60. Mk. 13:9.  61. Lk. 2:1.
62. Lk. 13:32. The fates of Herod Antipas and Archelaus show the position clearly.

his deputy. Naturally a single man, even with a corps of ministers and agents, could not control what was a teeming population, nor attend to their intrigues, factions, quarrels, and multitudinous unpredictabilities. Thus the day-to-day running of society was left in the hands of functionaries belonging to the previous system, which was inherited like the current coinage by Herod the Great from his Hasmonaean predecessors, and by them from the Seleucid and Ptolemaic imperial systems from which the Maccabean family had only temporarily rescued the Hebrews.

That system was itself an uneasy dual system. In order to carry out the instructions of the governor for the time being, judge-magistrates,[63] with mixed judicial and administrative powers, were appointed to the districts. These operated on the same basis as the Hellenistic magistracy to be traced from Egypt to the Black Sea. They were a bureaucracy, a cadre of police-and-revenue authorities, but each linked, *via* his patron, with the ruler, rather than associated together as a corps. Most of those appointed to territories occupied by Hebrews were bound to have been Hebrews by race and religion, many of them bilingual in Greek and Aramaic. The local tetrarch acted as a court of appeal (or revision) from their decisions.[64] As we shall see, their duties conflicted, automatically, with the requirements of the sacred scriptures of the Hebrews' notional theocracy. But then it *was* only notional, was it not? The real rulers were the Senate and People of Rome.

Alongside this bureaucracy of single administrative 'judges' there were the native authorities whose powers and constitution were traditional and customary and went back far earlier than Alexander the Great, let alone Herod the Great. Their appointment (if such a taking of office can be called appointment), their powers, and their rules, were acquiesced in, but not authorised by the governor.[65] Custom was law, and custom, as usual, was the creature of the silent and unobserved forces of social change, however slow that change might be. Hebrew courts, convened *ad hoc* or on a more or less regular basis, took note of matters of private law, like divorces, the sale of estates of insolvents or deceased intestates, the guardianship of widows and minors, and similar matters. Disputes between work-

63. Lk. 18:1–8.
64. Josephus praises the methods of Philip (d. A.D. 34): *Ant*. xviii. 106–7.
65. Josephus himself attempted to give such a system constitutional backing: *BJ*, ii. 569–71 (after A.D. 66).

men and their employers would be heard by these 'justices', and similarly disputes about boundaries and buried treasure, for these men would be authorised to tender the oath, the traditional ordeal by which the Hebrews quietly solved so many of their disputes.[65a]

I doubt very much whether the administrative judge was authorised, or would be allowed by public opinion, to tender an oath to anyone; the only oaths he would be familiar with would be the invocations of the life or genius of the emperor, with which a process in his court might be initiated. That was, after all, pagan procedure and his court was virtually a pagan court. Crimes under Hebrew law were a very sensitive subject. The jurisdictions clashed.

While the 'judge' did not apply scriptural or traditional customary law (unless, in the interest of good government, he used his discretion so to do), the customary tribunals could not apply Hellenistic laws or the proclamations from the palace. These they could not interpret and perhaps did not understand. It was a crime to refuse the use of any means of transport to a Roman soldier: Jews could neither recognise nor hinder this right of impressment.[66] True enough rabbis had similar rights by custom, which doubtless they would never have to enforce, but this provided no analogy for the ruling power. If a crime at customary law could be punished by a flogging[67] or sentencing to restitution at an enhanced rate the customary court could enforce this without formality. If the defendant attempted to escape the penalty or defied the court it would turn informally to the magistrate for his help, alleging a threat to order and good government.[68] Not that we are speaking here of abstract justice. The lay justices were inclined to take irrelevant matters into account, and bribery was no less to be feared amongst them than in the magistrate's court.[69] For this reason a single, pious arbitrator, some rabbi, would often be preferred, and the parties were regarded as bound to follow his decision.[70]

Where extreme measures were needed, and the Hebrews' customary, 'internal' system was not sufficient, they turned, as in subsequent centuries we often find them doing, to the magistrate for his help,[71] asking him to enforce a similar, or sufficient sentence, in

65a. Heb. 6:16.    66. Mt. 21:1-3, 27:32; Mk. 11:3, 14:14, 15:21.
67. Mt. 10:17-18; Ac. 5:40; 2 Co. 11:23-24.
68. See last note. The terms chosen in Mt. 10:17-18 are precise.
69. This is envisaged at Mt. 21:33-41; Si. 32:17, 40:12; Test. Reub. 3:6.
70. Lk. 12:13-15.                    71. Mt. 20:19; Mk. 10:33, 15:1.

order that deficiencies in the application of Jewish law should nevertheless be made up somehow. Un-Hebrew measures ought, they hoped, to be enforced *mutatis mutandis* in a Hebrew manner.[72] Crimes carrying the death penalty at Jewish law could not be punished by the customary methods. Naturally the power of life and death was reserved for the governor, for otherwise his control of the State would have been nominal. Consequently the more zealous of the Hebrews would try to stone the offender quickly by a kind of lynch-law,[73] hoping that the governor would not get to hear of what they had done. Caesarea, his headquarters, was far from many places in that extended territory which was the Hebrews' homeland.

Now the coexistence of two legal systems, overlapping to a considerable extent *de facto*, was a grave embarrassment and undermined public morale.[74] Under the Hebrew system as in force ideally, under a traditional Hebrew monarch, the Jewish law was in the breasts of the elders, from village to village (the kind of administration conjured up by the biblical word 'gate'),[75] and was studied academically in cultural centres, of which Jerusalem itself would naturally be the chief, and tricky points of law whether ritual or secular were decided by a large assembly of the learned, whose decision had all the force of moral and religious as well as political authority. Judges would both recognise and enforce this law. As it was, however, the village elders and trustees of the synagogue could only *excommunicate* a Jewish offender who refused to obey their decrees (e.g. to divorce his wife to whom he was showing cruelty),[76] or tried, for example, to exact usury on the basis of a document to which the magistrate's court would not hesitate to give effect.[77] And if their sanctions were limited their procedure also restricted them. A Jewish court would be scrupulous about testimony:[78] two eye-witnesses must exactly agree—the Hellenistic magistrate would not require any such strict proof, and might even proceed on suspicion alone. Nor would he use adjuration, available to Hebrew tribunals and indeed in general.[79] Moreover the foreign system did not apply

72. Jos., *BJ*, i. 209, 214.
73. Lk. 4:29–30; Jn. 8:3, 59; 10:31–33; Ac. 7:58–59. Lynching is connived at by the authorities at Jos., *BJ*, i. 550.
74. Read Mt. 5:21–22, 25–26 in the light of what follows.
75. Mt. 16:18.
76. Mt. 18:15–18, 23:34; Jn. 9:22, 34, 12:42, 16:2; 1 Esd. 9:4; 3 M. 2:33.
77. Lk. 16:4–9. *LNT*, 56ff.                           78. Mt. 26:60.
79. Mt. 26:63; Lk. 24:48. Mishnah, Shev. IV. 1, 3.

the healthful Hebrew rule that the witnesses must themselves be executioners,[80] subject to the proviso that if their testimony could be called in question, and they were proved to have plotted to destroy the victim, they would suffer the like fate. A Hebrew who had renounced Judaism in order to collaborate with the rulers would simply sneer at the decree of excommunication, and threaten the elders with punishment from the administrative magistrate for hampering him in his functions. Self-help, much used in those days, might be employed with impunity in cases where the Jewish law would never have sanctioned it.[81] On the other hand the Jewish law adopted a standard of restitution which no Hellenistic court would order or enforce.[82] I need hardly add that the Roman procurator could validly act, in his capacity as judge, only within the Roman law; his jurisdiction as political governor was, of course, as wide as anyone could wish, but the Jewish law was not officially known to him (whatever he may have learnt privately from collaborators).

Non-Hebrews living and working in Hebrew districts, and Samaritans, could, of course, not be made amenable to any customary discipline except in front of the traditional tribunal of their domiciles of origin,[83] or the administrative magistrate of their residence. Hence there was every temptation for the ordinary Jew to do what the rabbis abhorred, namely to escape from the customary law, to appeal over the heads of the customary court, the court of the elders, to the magistrate, to allege some political or revenue aspect to give him jurisdiction, and to demand that the elders be prohibited from proceeding with the case, or, if the case was concluded, to reverse their decision.[84] The magistrate might act fast, unless he himself were under pressure.[85] A decision might be given, on behalf of a defendant in a cause pending before a customary tribunal, against the plaintiff, who had barely got his day fixed for the elders to hear his case! Thus the Law held to be sacred by the natives was virtually set aside. The tranquillity of the State and the efficiency of the revenue system required that the synagogue should be at this disadvantage. The brotherhood of all the children of Israel could not stand up for long to this subversion. They must

80. Ac. 7:58.            81. Mt. 5:38–41; Si. 33:29.
82. Lk. 19:8.            83. Lk. 23:7.
84. Lk. 12:58 (Satan drags the plaintiff before God!).
85. Si. 7:6.

explode against their rulers, or die.[86] They exploded, and were within a fraction of dying.

Such being the menace of the dual judicial system, even the division of political power between the Romans and their puppets on the one hand and the traditional aristocracy on the other was fraught with danger, quite apart from the delicate personal relations involved.[87] The natural leaders were the priestly hierarchy, the scholars (rabbis), and the rich and powerful Jews who had acquired prestige sometimes after generations of meritorious service and the accumulations that went with it. Some of them realized that the Romans were efficient and would secure them a much-needed peace. But there were intrigues between the leading families, not to speak of manoeuvrings to bring into prominence or power one or other of the main religious sects (§26). There was a triangle of forces between the peasants and urban masses and their heroes, the hierarchy and natural leaders, and the foreign rulers. Each could combine with another against the third.[88] The Temple, the focal point of this most religious nation, was no sanctuary, and was itself repeatedly a pawn in a political game.[89] The Romans used the policy of divide and rule.

They took away the supreme political power from the Hebrews as a whole: neither the surviving officialdom, nor the hierarchy, nor the rabbis could make final political decisions; but within the limits permitted by the Roman constitutional and fiscal settlement, the priests and notables retained their responsibility for the welfare of the nation,[90] the maintenance of the Temple cult,[91] and its finances (subject to Pilate's interference) and gave final justice as between Hebrews provided no death sentence was to be imposed. The society and culture of the nation appeared to survive intact: a deceptive appearance, as I have shown. Within the shadow of power the

---

86. This was the attitude of the leaders and the majority of the public: Jos., *Ant.* xviii. 266, 271, *BJ*, ii. 174. Martyrdom for the faith was almost a luxury in the eyes of self-consciously normative Jews: *BJ*, i. 650, 653.
87. Lk. 23:12
88. Mk. 3:5, 6:20, 14:10–11; Lk. 23:2.
89. Mk. 14:49. Josephus's experience, taking sanctuary in the Temple, was quite exceptional. Many had failed in such an attempt.
90. On 'chief priests and notables' see above p. 56, n. 171. Mk. 14:53; Jn. 1:19, 22; Ac. 4:6–7. Their agents: Ac. 8:3.
91. Ac. 21:31; cf. Ep. Jer. 6:28. Jos., *Ant.* xviii. 30 (text, but not meaning, doubtful).

various elements of the native prestige-holding classes combined and recombined and waited for the day when, they supposed, full autonomy would return to them. Vain hope! Their own incapacity to consolidate a workable political system capable of warding off all foreign aggression made it certain that autonomy would not be theirs. A compromised Hebrew leadership, pretending to independent power and eager not to be detected as operating under Pilate's sufferance, sought to gain the support of rabbis, and thus restore their fallen esteem in the eyes of the populace. On the other hand those elements that were better suited with things as they were would think twice before rousing the enthusiasm of a city mob which could easily call down indiscriminate repression from a nervous procurator. The followers of a religious leader whose aims were purely spiritual, in the sense that he aimed at no political revolution but only a return to righteous living, would be alarmed at any attempt to foist upon him, and upon them, a programme of a nationalist character.[92] The two could be so easily confused.

But we must be absolutely clear on one point which might otherwise escape us. Since 'righteousness' did not exist except as a quality of obedience to Jewish Law, the Torah, which contained both secular rules and spiritual injunctions, side by side and intertwined, a religious teacher, characteristically telling his hearers what to do, could not possibly keep aloof from political questions. His teaching must have its secular consequences and implications, or it was not Jewish teaching at all. Somewhere, and sometime in the not-too-distant future, there would be a Jewish community that would put his teaching into practice, and money and power would flow along the channels which, invisibly, his teachings were digging out. And the very fact that pagan courts and pagan laws hindered, directly or indirectly, the application of his teachings was itself an offence to his programme, a rebuke to his efforts, a challenge to his pupils, and a threat to his own survival.

### §18. THE HEBREWS' NOTION OF THE STATE

It has been necessary to enlarge on the political background to this extent because the popular memories of, and obvious fondness for, monarchy tend indirectly towards obscuring, for us, the secular implications of all the religious revivalism in the Hebrew homeland of the first century A.D. We are aware that the 'power of the sword'

92. Mk. 10:48.

lay with the surviving tetrarchs and with the governor-procurator
Pontius Pilate, whose position on top of the volcano created by the
clash of Roman and Asian ideas of government is correctly noted
in the story of Jesus's Passion and in the creeds of the church. The
gospel stories show his coping, admirably it would seem, with the
crafty Hebrew elders. Their civilization, in their own eyes, impera-
tively demanded their revealing (I do not say flaunting) how, in
reality, the ruled manipulated the ruler, as in Asian contexts, under
colonial or imperial powers, they always have. It is not in their best
interests to show this, but, in a crisis, they must and will. Obsequious
demeanour normally lulls the incautious foreigner into the illusion
that he is where he is because of the will-power, discipline, drive,
and interests of his own government at home. Occasional flashes and
rumbles of the storm warn him that the reality is more complex: it
will cost the imperial power more than the country is worth to keep
control by force, whereas a little leniency here, a little temporising
there, will enable the native subjects to derive from their foreign
'bosses' advantages far outweighing the loss of independence—for
example, internal peace. The Hebrews had not forgotten the blood-
shed and destruction caused by events leading up to the accession
of Herod the Great.

How true this was is shown by the Hebrews' notion of the State.
They inherited it from two sources, the bible, with its mythical
picture of human government endeavouring to live up to the
demands of Yahweh, and folk-memory of actual princes, princelings,
petty monarchs, and tribal chiefs, who had little in common with
the biblical characters, except their strong and interesting personalities. The memories, out of which folk-tales naturally spring, were
revived by the behaviour of the Herods. Since government after the
republican period (or from Aristobulus I, 105–104 B.C.) had been
consistently monarchical in fact if not always in name, the Jews
thought of rule as essentially kingship. This old-fashioned idea of
the State as utterly personalised in one man was to last, after all,
into modern history. Its inappropriateness to describe how the
Hebrews actually lived is not to our purpose, for what we need to
know, the peasant's idea of kingship, is a direct key to his fantasies
and aspirations, and, more important, his capacity to visualise
Yahweh. Just as the father–son relationship (§2) is a pattern of
Yahweh's relationship to Israel and to Israel's ideal representative,
so the king–subject relationship told the Hebrews how they must

'stand before' their Creator. The picture is not an edifying one, and my reader must reassure himself that he is undergoing an educative experience before he reads the next paragraph.[92a]

To the Hebrews the king was the one to whom all who had anything to offer offered gifts by way of homage.[93] He was self-centred, masterful, not subject to question or argument,[94] capricious,[95] unpredictable,[96] capable of savage repression,[97] vindictive,[98] ruthless, petulant,[99] dependent on favourites, partial to his friends,[100] not bound by 'natural justice' nor compelled to observe modern notions of fairness. He would listen to any accuser, and would grant requests channelled through a servant to whom he was obliged.[101] He was capable of changing his mind, and was actuated by a mania for power.

His person and his prestige were paramount but in all his dealings with his subjects their benefit formed a factor in so far as it conduced to his, and not *vice versa*.[102] This unpleasing, and doubtless faithful picture, had a mitigating and realistic side. If the subjects needed their king to keep them in order, to prevent their falling apart in intrigues, faction, and lawlessness, their king certainly needed them.[103] He was the ideal prestige figure, the source of 'rewards' and honours, the host whose hospitality was most sought after.[103] His luxurious, glorious[104] living, wasteful and over-conspicuous consumption, dictatorial ways, and tyrannical methods,[105] placed him at the summit of a prestige-pyramid, amorphous but real to the Hebrew mind. They hoped and pretended that their king was also their father. If a father could be imperious and capricious, so a king could be indulgent, forgiving, and as interested in preserving his subjects as a father was in the eventual prosperity and respectability

92a. Greeks were quite prepared to believe Asians thought God an absolute monarch: A. D. Nock, *Essays* (1972) I, 47.
93. Mt. 2:11; cf. Mk. 11:8; Si. 20:27–28, 35:4(6).
94. 1 Esd. 4:3; Ws. 12:12 (but cf. Si. 4:27).    95. Mk. 6:27.
96. Mt. 14:7; 3 M. 5:30, 38–42.    97. Jos., *BJ*, i. 71, 270.
98. Lk. 19:27, Tb. 12:7.    99. 2 Esd. 1:24.
100. Mt. 25:35; 1 M. 10:61–64, 11:25–27; 2 M. 4:47.
101. Mt. 10:32, 12:41, 18:19–20, 25:35; Lk. 11:29–32; Ws. 18:22; 3 Bar. 11:2–7; Test. Dan 6:2; Bab. Tal., Hag. 12b. The concept of the mediator was so well established that conscience can be called or treated as a mediator before God without apology for the metaphor at Philo, *Spec. Leg.* i. 234–7 (ed. Colson, vol. 7, 236–8), where notice the word *paracleton*.
102. Mt. 18:23–35. *LNT*, 42.    103. Mt. 10:31, 20:1–16; Ba. 2:17.
104. Mt. 4:8.    105. Mt. 6:11, 7:21.

of his sons, however wayward. The reciprocity between king and subject and between father and son, curious as it was, amounted to a peculiar solidarity. The Hebrew ideal king was not the mere exploiter of the exploited: there was a valid exchange between the two parties to the relationship.

One who knows his bible will at once ask, what of the shepherd? The father–son image, and the king–subject image both depicted Yahweh to the Hebrew mind. And Yahweh also shepherds his people, as the kings and emperors of the ancient Near East were shepherds of their sheep-like subjects. Traditional Hebrew imagery saw the shepherd as inherently fit to govern men. The notional king of Israel, David and David's successor for the time being,[106] was a shepherd, or like a shepherd. And it is fair to ask, were shepherds not exploiters of the sheep? The answer is simply that the shepherd was viewed as the man who, with his staff and sling, guided the sheep, protected them from wild beasts and birds of prey, led them to pasture, and accounted for them, every one, to the sheep's owner, whose servant he was.[107] The fact that the sheep's owner used the wool and (when it was quite old) the meat of the sheep and goats, was an aspect which, if not quite neglected, did not predominate in the shepherd motif. The kings were shepherds answerable in theory to the god whose creatures their subjects were and who could, at any time, call upon them to explain the conduct of their charge. And it was, after all, no more objectionable to think of Yahweh shearing his sheep than to think of him as a farmer harvesting his crop.[108]

In the ebb and flow of kingdoms[109] (for kingdoms had frontiers), the expansion of empires, the putting down of revolts, and expelling of invaders, messengers had to be sent to each village to announce the 'good news' of the ruler's incorporation of territory, so that everyone knew to whom taxes must be paid, and who would protect them, or at least pretend to do so. Border villages were at especial risk.[110] Similarly horsemen would go round and proclaim a new sovereign on the death of the previous, and the accession of the new. Kingdoms required their messengers or they could not be regarded

106. Mt. 20:30; Mk. 10:47, 11:10 (note 'father').
107. Mt. 25:35; Mk. 10:32.      108. Mt. 9:35, 13:30, 38, 41; Mk. 4:26–29.
109. Mt. 12:43 (gardening metaphor: a liberated territory is fit for occupation by foreigners), 24:6; Lk. 14:31–32 (speculative wars), 19:13, 22:29; Si. 10:14–15, 25.
110. Jos., BJ, i. 334, ii. 235.

as real.[111] It might be a matter of urgency to get as many villages entered in the ledger as possible.[112] The better the king's servants' reputations the more his kingdom would be welcomed.[113] If they looted the new acquisitions the inhabitants might engineer a revolution. On the other hand a good recruiting officer could recruit men willing to leave their families and go to war for the kingdom.[114] Residents of one State who had worked for the accession of the territory to another (and thus were acting in subversion of their existing sovereign) might suffer for their loyalty to the stranger, but when their favourite came to power they would naturally profit outstandingly by the change and be honoured for their previous sufferings.[115]

### §19. WHERE RELIGION AND THE STATE OVERLAPPED

As we have begun to realise, the Hebrews did not distinguish between religion and law: nor between religious and secular life. In this they resembled Asian nations with the limited exception of China. An example of the outlook would be the rule that there is no repentance in religious terms unless there has been restitution (where practicable) in secular terms.[116] Scripture (§21) which, along with oral traditions in the case of the Pharisees, was the reference-material in all disputed matters of conduct, did not separate the requirements of the unseen world from that of common sense or practical utility. What was rational often had a religious backing, and no superstition was regarded as irrational. By the time the Romans began to outdo the exploits of Alexander the Great they had already left their own religious and ritual law to the care of priests, and their constitutional, civil, and criminal law had been developed on an almost entirely rational and pragmatic basis in which reference to traditional wisdom-texts played no part. Utility entered constantly into their debates. Whereas the learned elders of the Hebrews could only declare law after a comprehensive study of the scriptures and their traditional glosses, the legislative organs of

---

111. Mt. 3:2, 4:17, 10:7, 21, 34; Lk. 12:32. A. D. Nock, *Essays* (1972), I. 79–81, has interesting remarks on *evangelion*, but his scepticism at *J.T.S.* 11 (1960), 65 is speculative (it was not a question of formal expression of homage only).
112. Mt. 11:12. Especially if the acquired territory was to be leased to a third ruler: Jos., *Ant.* xviii. 114.
113. Mt. 5:16.          114. Mt. 10:37.          115. Mt. 5:3–12; 2 Esd. 1:35.
116. Mt. 27:3. See Philo cited at p. 95, n. 101 above.

Rome, as in the modern world, reserved entire freedom to alter and enact laws to suit convenience and the requirement of inevitable change.[117] Amendments were no doubt tardy, cautious, and partial. The idea of codification lay many centuries ahead. But there was no theoretical obstacle to change. Religion did not hamper it. On the contrary the Roman religion tended to subserve changes of policy, and when the imperial saviour from chaos and confusion wished or asked to be honoured as a god the god-minded Asians and Hellenes found no difficulty whatever in complying with these wishes—that is to say, except the Hebrews, the vast majority of whom regarded all gods except Yahweh as illusions and regarded Yahweh himself as too jealous to tolerate their genuine attachment to any man as a deity, even as a matter of etiquette or a form of speech.

The demands of their religion were also legal so far as the rabbis were concerned. What their sacred law did not command was indifferent and would not, it might be suggested, bind them in conscience at all. We have seen how the Jewish law authorised and required judicial penalties which the Roman denied in practice, substituting an alternative at their own option. The Romans, for example, would not order a woman to be stoned for adultery.[118] The Jewish law was defective in that it did not provide for the punishment of certain crimes and misdeeds, and when it attempted to make up the gaps in the scriptural law of crime and punishment its only sanctions were flogging and, ultimately excommunication. As long as the civilisation was self-sufficient and independent, the internal penalties awarded by customary chiefs had been effective. The boycott was a good deterrent. But when the Hebrews were interpenetrated by foreigners and foreign ideas and the ranks of 'sinners' swelled, the traditional ways were not enough. Robbers therefore were attended to by the Romans, as they had been by the previous administrations, as a police undertaking or military concern. Action against robbers was typically a necessity falling outside Jewish law and *de facto* supplementing it.[119] The Jewish law went so far as to

117. When the Hebrews wanted a word for 'law' in the sense of enacted legislation, to which one refers as a norm of conduct or instruction for administration, they could not find one in their own vocabulary; they therefore naturalised the Greek word *nomos*, which appears in rabbinical writings in the guise of *niymos*.
118. *LNT*, 168, n. 1.
119. Mk. 14:48. Jos., *BJ*, i. 204, 304–16, ii. 253 (crucifixion of brigands), 271.

recognise that decapitation with the sword was a penalty which could be inflicted by any civil power while maintaining good government. Crucifixion was another penalty long since known to Levantine rulers[120] as a deterrent for offenders who could not be made amenable to Jewish customary courts, or whose wrongdoing was not an offence at native customary law, or, if an offence, was not punished by death under that law.[121] Attempts were made to harmonise foreign jurisdiction with Jewish custom.[122] The crucified were taken down rapidly so as not to be seen on the Sabbath and the penalty was assimilated so far as might be to a scriptural penalty known as 'hanging up' the body of a malefactor who had been stoned according to the customary system (Dt. 21:22–23). Jews seem to have accepted readily enough a penalty for political crimes which has no biblical authority, namely amputation of the hands.[122a]

But these adjustments did not touch the heart of the problem. Was the Hebrew nation in its homeland ruled by Yahweh, through his agents, or not? The civil law and 'righteousness' were often at variance, as 'sinners' noted with satisfaction.[123] Religion taught consistently that the Hebrews had been conveyed, 'sold', to the 'nations' for their (the Hebrews') sins. One day their 'father' would forgive them and reinstate them in his favour, on the basis that they had been chastised enough. Therefore the *de facto* rulers were to be obeyed. But only so far as the religion allowed! Secular administration and perhaps taxation, the mechanics of political life under the Gentiles, were the scourges sent by Yahweh.[124] But the requirements of the Law must be observed. Circumcision, the Sabbath, the laws of marriage and divorce, the dietary laws, the laws of sacrifice and tithe—all these and much more could not be touched by Roman or any other legislators. Yahweh had spoken, through Moses and the prophets, and one could only interpret his words, neither add to them nor subtract from them. Obey, said teachers, the ruling power so far only as religion permits![125]

This was a proposition which the Roman governor could understand. He could discreetly keep quiet on such high constitutional

120. Mk. 8:34. See last n. Plutarch, *Titus Flam.* ix. 4 (ed. 1968, 11/2, 38) (Macedonia, 197 B.C.); Pauly-Wissowa, *Real-Encycl.* viii (1901), 1729. 14 (Punic!).
121. Lk. 23:41 (accepted as normal).     122. See p. 90, n. 72 above.
122a. Jos., *Life*, 171–7; *BJ*, ii. 642–4.     123. Mt. 5:32.
124. Mt. 5:38–41; 2 Bar. 5:3. Rulers rule by God's will: Jos., *BJ*, ii. 140; *Ant.* xv. 374.     125. Mt. 22:15–22. *LNT*, ch. 14.

matters. But he knew well enough that Caesar would have, in any event, the things of Caesar.[126] Yahweh was apparently a projection of the Hebrew mind and experience, and Caesar, as yet, could not care for the rights of Yahweh. The problem was not resolved—nor the State's impatience with the religious conscience terminated—until the emperor became (nominally) Christian, nor perhaps even then until the problem raised by the heresy of Arianism had been, as it were, cleared up by the beginning of the fifth century.

126. For non-Romans (and perhaps for many Romans?) the very word 'Caesar' caused a chill of apprehension: Epictetus, IV. i. 41–50, 60.

# THIRD LECTURE

# *The Mental and Intellectual Scene*

## §20. 'AS IF'

When reading the Old Testament or the New there is a temptation
to think in condescending terms of 'myth'. Myth has been described
as man's understanding of reality, expressed by him in terms
appropriate to the majesty or awe of the theme, and the intricacy
of its relation to himself. It is beyond my present concern to speak
of the presence or absence of mythical elements in the New Testament. It is sufficient if it is clear to the reader that Jesus's contemporaries were quite used to what I can compendiously refer to as
'as if' talk. Since we are habituated to 'as if' ourselves, the discovery
that someone spoke in those days of a thing as existing, whereas he
meant only that it was 'as if' it existed is not a startling discovery. As
we shall soon see, 'as if' is an expression which identifies many
types of metaphors and dramatic or poetic diction. I shall try to
illustrate this style of speaking, but not to analyse, still less catalogue
all its manifestations. But it is essential to grasp that each as-if
statement was 'triggered off', initiated, by an objective or subjective event, the scientific description of which had been ignored
or overlooked.

We have legal fictions, and social fictions. The expression 'not at
home' is often a fiction: it is not a lie, it means that the person sought
is, for all practical purposes 'as if' he were not at home. Some
fictions are so well rooted that it would be bad taste to expose the
realities. There is the mental fiction that decisions are made on
rational grounds; the truth is that reasons are alleged afterwards to
support a course determined upon on quite other grounds. There
are so many legal fictions (which fit very well in the category of
working 'as ifs') that one does not know where to start. There are
conclusive presumptions (e.g. as to the source of title to property)

which one may not challenge. The legitimacy of a child is a fiction, which experience never verifies. Irrespective of actual paternity he is 'as if' he were the husband's child. It is a social fiction that marriage can be ended by divorce, and by divorce only. It is a social fiction that appearances indicate reality, that, for example, the wealthy are more worthy than the poor, the elderly wiser than the young, that females are more charming than males: all these are contrary to fact but we habitually behave 'as if' they were true. A professional fiction is that consultants know more than general practitioners, and professors are more learned than lecturers. Some fictions are built into dramas: putting on a surplice makes one more holy; gestures do duty for thoughts. At the Trooping of the Colour, which is a huge drama on totally fictional lines, one might well exclaim 'Stop! That object you are venerating is not a Roman legion's standard, and you are not Romans, for it is a piece of embroidered rag and you are Britons entertaining each other with a ceremony. That lady on the horse is not the Commander in Chief and if any one should take the salute at the parade it should be the yachtsman who figures as prime minister.' The exclamation would simply demonstrate that one was at the wrong show, not in that drama at all. Sentiment cherishes fictions, and people would think the exclamation 'unseemly'.

Educationally, fictions are necessary. Even our spelling is fictional: 'would' is read as 'wood'. The sun 'rises' and 'sets'. Electricity 'flows'. Humpty Dumpty unquestionably fell, and no one can be heard to say that Miss Muffet did not run away. Fictions, formulas, untested hypotheses which express something of value—there are so many of them, and life would not get on without them. A lecture asserting that Humpty Dumpty did not fall would be pointless. And yet the psychological function of Humpty Dumpty is trivial. Some fictions belong to the psychosomatic world and it is hazardous to tamper with them, as Freud did. But if we are to understand Jesus's world we must know a little about the 'as if' upon which they worked, the fictions around which life functioned; without committing ourself, of course, to accepting them; provided we know that we too cannot get on without an array of fictions as numerous and perhaps as awesome as theirs. Where should we be, for example, were it not accepted that examiners and administrators are incorruptible? It is not quite true, but even to suggest that the lid be lifted, and the truth revealed causes distress, emotional excitement. It is *as if* they were incorruptible, and that 'as if' earns its bread:

that is the drama in which we indubitably are. Satan, and Hell, are no longer in *our* drama, but I think Heaven still is. Incorruptibility was not in *their* drama, and with them it was *as if* all widows were poor and oppressed, though powerful and oppressive widows must have existed to everyone's knowledge. To them the word 'orphan' suggested the idea of helplessness and being exploited. It is worth noting that we are having to move out of one 'as if' into another, when we refer to 'the working classes'. That makes me think of a very notorious 'as if', namely the promise on our banknotes. It is an absolute fiction, but that does not prevent me from picking one up and tendering it.

If a fiction to which we are completely used suddenly comes alive we are very much impressed.[1] It can be disturbing. I get the impression that the apostles preached that a vast number of fictional biblical characters and stories and ideas had been collectively verified and exemplified in the life of their hero, Jesus. It was *as if* the drama had been played out. Even if the facts did not correspond exactly it was *as if* they had. A man who tells one some items of one's past can be described as one who 'has told me everything I did'. Jesus himself is depicted in the gospels using 'as if' in several ways. 'Behold thy son; behold thy mother': a fiction created by mere will.[2] John the Baptist is 'as if' Elijah—provided one has the mental adjustment to see him so.[3] The law relating to marriage has an internal logic which must be taught and will be grasped by those who see it correctly: whatever the facts of life marriage is *as if* indissoluble.[4] For those that take spiritual nourishment bodily hunger is *as if* satisfied.[5] *Enduring* is 'as if' one gained one's life, even if one lost it in the process.[6] Whether Sodom and Gomorrah really perished is unimportant, it is *as if* they did, for the purposes of the

1. As at Mt. 21:4–5, 12.        2. Jn. 19:26–27.
3. Mt. 11:14. Cf. Lk. 16:16.
4. *LNT*, 368–9, 383. For those that accept a bold teaching it is true: Mt. 19:11.
5. Mk. 6:37–44, 8:1–10, 16–21 (a teacher must 'feed' his hearers or he is no teacher).
6. Lk. 21:16, 18–19. For the martyrs who endure to the end (Mk. 13:13) are saved (*ibid.*). This, in St. Luke's view, is the same as acquiring 'life' (i.e. the 'life to come') expressed 'as if' one escaped alive (in fact, better). A paradox expressed elliptically, without the simile being stated. No one can say that the 'life to come' is life as we know it (on the contrary: cf. Jn. 10:10).

teaching, which a true student will not question (or he leaves the teacher–pupil relationship).[7] One may demean oneself to Yahweh in a manner not really representing the facts, since it is *as if* it were necessary (for the benefit of bystanders).[8] Jesus certainly rode on the donkey (we need not doubt it) but it was *as if* to enact, mime, the words of Zechariah. In teaching action ekes out words, and is often far more potent. Teaching requires that facts be taken up and expounded *as if* they meant what they evidently did not. John the Baptist was *as if* he testified to Jesus's identity as the Messiah: in fact his testimony was irrelevant and unnecessary. But since the disciples and the public generally believed that Elijah would come first, and that the redemption process involved the two characters, Elijah and the (or a) Messiah, the testimony of John was 'as if' valid and useful: Jesus says this in so many words, or at least St. John wishes us to understand that it is *as if* he did so.[9] This is independent of the possibility that *St. Mark*, drawing attention to the Baptist, wishes to signalise the beginning of human testimony to the Messiah's having come.

It is not difficult to understand now how it was possible to see an inward and fundamental truth in a myriad of discrete, unrelated events, which an instructed eye could organise into an intellectual whole, into a truly educational mosaic of narrative.[10] The withering of the fig-tree was *as if* it were due to Jesus's curse—there was no examination to see whether a worm was at work with the speed mentioned in so many words at Jon. 4:7, 10. It happened *as if* it were a re-creation of the Garden of Eden in which Adam, before the Fall, had, as the only tenant-gardener, a special relation to the fruit-trees. The scientific explanation of the fig-tree's fate is neither here nor there. Not that the tree did not wither (Mk. 11:21)! No one challenged the fact effectively. The instructed eye understood, and taught, *why* it did so. If one accepted that 'as if', one related the unseen and the seen worlds, which is what all this story is about.

I find the phrase 'as if' handy; but there is an alternative. We may find in John Marsh's *Saint John*, which appeared in the Pelican Gospel Commentaries in 1968, a striking contrast between statements which merely relate *what took place* and statements which relate *what was going on*. Many a statement which appears to say what took place is really, without deserting narrative, telling us *what*

7. Mt. 10:15, 11:23–24.          8. Jn. 11:42.
9. Jn. 5:34.          10. Mt. 1:22–23, 2:6, 15:17, 23; 4:15, 8:17.

*was going on*. The example he chooses to make his point is that of the Baptist who was clothed with camels' hair and had a leather girdle around his waist: irrespective of his clothing, which had no *intrinsic* interest, the Baptist *was*, for the purpose of the narrative, Elijah (cf. Mk. 1:6 with 2 K. 1:7–8). I should say the Baptist, choosing his form of self-advertisement, was 'as if' Elijah; but it would be equally possible to ignore the Baptist's awareness of what he was doing, and simply say that the coincidence of facts symbolised a coincidence of role, the role being imputed to him by the Evangelist or, most probably, the latter's source. Now Elijah was, by the first century A.D. already an 'as if' figure himself. True, he was a historical character; but he had already acquired the quality of a symbol of the unfinished programme of redemption—and we all know that to say that a thing is unfinished is as good as imputing to it the desirability of completion.

Let us take some illustrations of 'as if', or 'what was going on' from completely secular quarters, and we shall find it works out well. There can be no doubt but that the busts of the emperor, or even his statue, could have done no harm whatever to Jerusalem or its people. A few bits of metal, a polished piece of marble, some completely harmless artefacts which deserved no more attention than the craftsman's skill could command! Killings of men, women, and children in Jerusalem, apart from the gruesomeness of the acts, the moral damage done to those who committed them, and the suffering, apart from pain, inflicted on those who lost relations or means of support, or even peace of mind as a result of such barbarities, were, at most, brutal, uncivilised acts, unworthy of a so-called civilised people. That would be the sum of it, and no reader will differ with me on the point. But, turn to contemporary accounts of these things. They reveal a totally different approach. The Hebrews regarded the 'idols' as if they were a foul miasma, physically and mentally intolerable, worse than the bubonic plague would be to us. To lose their lives rather than permit their entry into the Holy City would be an honour, a privilege; there was no hesitation whatever in putting the alternative to the brutal foreigner directly: 'Take them in, if you must, for you are no doubt under orders; but so are we, and you must kill the lot of us first.' This is historical fact which not even the most hardened sceptic has ever dreamed of doubting. The Hebrews were that sort of people. Then what of the killings inside Jerusalem? We should say that, suffering apart, they amounted to nothing that horses, hooks and chains, some buckets of water, and a few good brooms could not deal with. I am never tired of repeating that Flavius Josephus lived through the events and participated in many a crisis himself. His book on the Jewish War (apart from other writings of his) maintains the thesis that the crimes committed against Yahweh inside the City where he had chosen to pitch his dwelling, establishing his Presence amidst his people, mounted up from the times of the earliest Herodians onwards to such an accumulation that no means of purification would suffice; and Yahweh would level with the ground the abode in which his Presence could dwell no more. 'Impiety' was like a stink, but not got rid of so easily.

From what is fact I can move at once to speculation. The reader knows what is called the Transfiguration (Mt. 17:2). It is described in St. Matthew and St. Mark as if such a process of change of appearance were not unique, were not beyond description in one bald, unexplained word 'transfigured'. A thing, and a person, can have normal shape, which is what it is; in moments of revelation the thing which has its normal shape is suddenly discovered in its real significance, it is 'as if' it had another shape: and the shock is not less violent because that 'true' shape has been there all the time, obvious enough to an observer who had the intuition, or experience, to recognise it. Now we do not know what happened on that mountain-top when Jesus was 'transfigured' but what the Evangelist was trying to tell us was conveyed in an 'as if' form. Or, to employ John Marsh's phrase, what was 'going on' was that the disciples realised for the first time who it was they had to cope with, the man whose words and acts had prepared them for the shock, but had not imparted it.[10a]

### §21. SCRIPTURE

An outstanding fiction of the Hebrews was their scripture, the canonical and other inspired writings. No one knows whether Adam existed, but who would dispute it? It is *as if* he did. Moses himself

10a. 'Naturalistic' explanations of apparently supernatural events testified to in the gospels and Acts were popular about 150 years ago and are now eschewed by theologians: but if the Transfiguration were to be scrutinised as an account of an instance of 'dissociation' (during which conversations with dead 'saints' may well occur and the subject changes his appearance alarmingly) interesting results might accrue (see p. 127 below).

may not have been fictional in historical terms, but the Deutero-nomic Lawgiver was probably fictional, and Abraham bears all the marks of being a fictional ancestor. But in their view the holy spirit had caused countless generations of Hebrews to speak of their history (including their present) in terms of stories which lived because they were educationally effective. Society hallowed the scriptures and scripture provided the constant intellectual and poetic skeleton round which the flesh of its mental life was formed. If anything was to be known for certain (whether spiritual or secular) it was from the scriptures.[11] These had an absolute value and close interpretation of them made a man into a scholar.[12] A preacher sewed texts together in his head and a pastiche of scriptural phrases made many a telling (if cryptic) lesson: in that way Mt. 11:25 (= Lk. 10:21) is made up from Is. 28:9 and 29:14—without the references the reader could be in the dark. Since scripture performed this function, entirely excluding all foreign and imported cultural material, it was a living corpus, much more than would appear from the visible text, the letters written on parchment.

Since the Dead Sea finds we know their script exactly, and any student who, for fun, wanted to pretend to forge a piece of a scroll could copy a part of the Torah of Moses, or a portion of one of the greater prophets, say, Isaiah, and though he cannot be certain that his spelling would agree with any complete scroll actually existing in Jesus's time he can be quite sure that his forgery could have been opened and sung out, in the elaborate cantillation used in the synagogues, by Jesus himself or by any of his literate contempor-aries.[13] Just as one can handle coins that might have been in Judas's purse,[14] so one can write, and read, a text which Jesus could easily have declaimed and then expounded. Then, it would have been holy. It is worth remembering that when a Roman soldier burnt part of a scroll he caused pain, not less physical than mental, and for the uproar he thus stimulated he paid with his life.[15]

But no written text would give *us* all the information the letters conveyed *then*. The letters were unpointed (they had no vowel signs except the 'jot' for 'y' and the *vav*, for 'o' or 'oo') and they

---

11. Mt. 2:4; Mk. 12:26–27; Jn. 5:39.          12. Mt. 5:17–18, 19.
13. Lk. 4:17–20. The scroll of Isaiah, published by M. Burrows as the *Scroll of St. Mark's Monastery* (I, New Haven, 1950), could very well have been handled by Jesus himself; not that there is any reason to think that it was.
14. Jn. 13:29.          15. Jos., *BJ*, ii. 229–31.

permitted many alternative readings, all of which were viable con-
currently. If a scribe, as the experts in the text were called, adopted
one reading he did not thereby deny or denigrate another reading
or interpretation. All were possible, though not all always equally
relevant. Then in between the lines of text, as it were, were woven
explanations and enlargements, completing what the text left
obscure or implicit. This is *midrash*, 'interpretation', in essence a
gloss upon a particular text. It often figured as an exposition of the
text with obviously fictional and invented additions. *Midrash* was
the result of the work of generations of scholars, thinkers, mystics,
and poets, and it had accumulated. One example will serve. Yahweh
is talking to Adam—I put the biblical text in Roman type and the
*midrash* in italics.[16]

> Gen. 3:17: And unto Adam he said, Because thou hast hearkened
> unto the voice of thy wife, and hast eaten of the tree, of which I
> commanded thee, saying, Thou shalt not eat of it: cursed is the
> ground for thy sake; in toil (*or* sorrow) shalt thou eat of it all the
> days of thy life; 18. Thorns also and thistles shall it bring forth
> to thee; and thou shalt eat the herb of the field; *and Adam sorrowed,*
> *and his face sweated, and he prayed the Lord that he might not be*
> *counted like cattle, nor be tied to the manger along with his ass, but*
> *might be able to stand upright*[17] *and labour with the labour of his*
> *hands, to make a distinction between the children of men and the*
> *offspring of cattle, and the Lord said—*
> 19. In the sweat of thy face shalt thou eat bread, till thou
> return unto the ground; for out of it wast thou taken: for dust
> thou art, and unto dust shalt thou return.

Another form of *midrash*, equally admissible and equally common,
was to associate passages of scripture, thus linking as many as three
forms of sacred or inspired writings (see, for examples, p. 150 below).
Thus the provisions of the Torah were illuminated from the stories
in the historical books, stories which every Hebrew child knew, or
from the oracles of the prophets, which, being cryptically phrased,
were available for many an ingenious and far-fetched application, or,
finally, from that curious development amongst the Hebrews, the
spiritualised maxim. The ancient East was fond of apophthegmatic
'wisdom'. Short sayings, paradoxes, worldly-wise propositions (like

16. *Theology*, vol. 74 (Dec. 1971), pp. 566–71.          17. See Lk. 13:15.

'Do not winnow in every wind!') were taught as if they were principles of good practice, good manners, shrewd reflections on life. But in the form of wise counsel, under the cover of worldly maxims, information about the unseen world was given: the result was immensely popular.[17a] Thus a first-class *midrash* provided, as an interpretation or application of a verse in the Law, material from elsewhere in the Law, from the prophets and from the wisdom literature.[18]

The latter was growing in the time of Jesus and numerous documents now treated as apocryphal, for example, the Psalms of Solomon and Ben Sirach (Ecclesiasticus) were then regarded not merely as edifying, but even as inspired. In the sense that they included perennial truths they were capable of being connected with ancient scripture as if they formed one piece. And although long years of oral tradition, the gradual obsolescence of the Hebrew language (in favour of various forms of Aramaic), and the dispersion of schools of study had conspired to make many places in the written texts uncertain or undependable (even nonsensical in places) this did not diminish the educational and spiritual value of the material. The system of Sabbath instruction and bible study kept a constant demand for texts and for homilies about them. Difficulties with textual accuracy and integrity only enlarged the scope for the imaginative gifts of the authors of sermons and lectures, namely the rabbis. If scripture lives, as it did amongst the Hebrews, it must move, not merely in its interpretation, but also in its text. Only the elaborate fossilisation of a text by methods adopted in India by the Brahmins for Vedic recitation could have prevented this, and Vedic methods were not applied, even in India, to preserve the text of law books (e.g. Manu) from corruption, and even enlargement, at the hands of those who relied upon it as a tool for the settling of day-to-day problems.

A still further midrashic method was to explain everyday events and tendencies as bearing out prophetic oracles.[19] Thus a group

17a. *E.g.* Qo. 5:7–8 (= 8–9) has a double meaning: (i) corruption has a natural limit as the fields must be tilled (and the agriculturist must be able to live, however many parasites batten on him: cf. Lk. 18:5); (ii) God punishes rulers and shows his verdict on them by way of the harvest (Mishnah, R.H. I.2).

18. Some such quaint *midrashic* linking may explain the apparent error at Mt. 23:35.

19. Mt. 15:7; Mk. 9:12–13, 11:7–10, 32; Lk. 24:27; Jn. 12:41; Ac. 1:16, 20, 2:25, 30, 18:28.

whose situation was unique politically or on a religio-political basis could claim that scripture foretold their dilemma and illustrated their motives and those of their 'enemies'. Scripture lived in various guises in everyday life. Naturally the enemies, not living in *their* drama, ridiculed their use of scripture and claimed, tit for tat, that scripture showed that *their* behaviour was reprehensible. All Hebrews, however, would agree that the Romans and their allies 'were' Esau, that it was 'as if' they were the Edomites—and that scriptural and midrashic references to Esau and his career, character, and future, foretold the discomforts the Hebrews suffered, and their eventual, long-hoped-for vindication.

The canon of scripture was not settled.[20] A penumbra of pious writings, conceived in archaic style and biblical idiom, put forward popular and traditional opinions in the form of revelations by the patriarchs, the sons of Jacob in their so-called 'Testaments', for example, or Enoch. These would not be read in the synagogue service, which confined its regular readings, so far as we know, to the Torah and the Prophets. But they were educational reading for the pious and a sermon-maker could legitimately borrow a phrase or an idea from them.

Scripture was relied upon to provide a justification for ways of life, and the scriptural stories could be cited as precedents *as if* they were historical.[21] In the 'as if' sense scripture was true, irrespective of the place which the citation or quotation would take in the original. By Jesus's time even the psalms of David were counted as if they were Torah.[22] The habit of quoting and alluding to the sacred text without giving a clear reference, or giving only the vaguest reference, cannot have helped accuracy,[23] and it was all too easy for men who knew scripture by heart to confuse similar passages. Granted that no one was going to refer rapidly to the original to check its appropriateness, quaint and far-fetched analogies from scripture could clinch an argument if the result would consist with piety. Scripture spoke with what was called the holy spirit, and therefore could not be convicted of error. And it spoke for contemporaries, however improbable the subject-matter or however symbolically the antiquated (and sometimes unedifying) tale must be

20. Si. 33:16.
21. Mt. 10:15, 24:15,37; Lk. 4:25–27, 17:30. 1 Tm. 2: 13–14.
22. Mt. 22:43; Jn. 10:34, 15:25.
23. Mt. 12:7.

taken if it were to make any sense at all.[24] All teachers must at least appear to go back to scripture, and the sacred word was something to conjure with. One could, and plainly people did, read it without understanding it at all.[25] It provided amulets to protect and sanctify the person[26] and to protect a dwelling: its frequent repetition brought, it was thought, a holy condition to the individual repeating it, and so used were scholars and students to citing scripture on any and every occasion ('as it is written . . .') that the affectation became a habit which was so acceptable in terms of the higher culture that its absurdity could pass unnoticed.[27] Indeed, so hard was this work of poring over the sacred text, if one took it seriously over a long period, that there was a chance it would disturb the mental balance.[28]

## §22. LAW

We have already noticed what was the administration of law, or rather laws, amongst the Hebrews in Jesus's time (§17). The Torah, interpreted according to the notions of schools taught by series of teachers and kept in a certain degree of uniformity by decisions of the supreme rabbinical court (the Sanhedrin) at Jerusalem, was the Law, binding in conscience on all Hebrews and (save for some rules that applied only to the Land of Israel) to Jews overseas. Its contents and techniques have been the subject of a multitude of works of every degree of popularisation or specialisation. Since its content was common knowledge, and the technique of deriving the most elaborate or exquisite rule from scripture was immensely popular and deservedly controversial, sermon-makers and lecturers could count on their audiences' knowing the main rules of commercial, agricultural, criminal, family, and procedural law,[29] and recognising the principal indications whereby one determined a fairly common issue in any one of those fields. Everyone knew, for example, that one witness was sufficient if the wife of a man who was alleged to have died abroad wanted permission to remarry; but that in criminal cases two witnesses were essential.[30] The Law was derived as much from *unwritten* custom as from the scriptural text; that custom has

24. 2 Tm. 3:15–17. Scripture speaks to *us*: Rm. 4:23, 15:4; 1 Co. 9: 9–10, 10:11; 1 Tm. 2:13–14.
25. Ac. 8:30.          26. Mt. 23:5.          27. Paul at Ac. 23:5.
28. Ac. 26:24. The celebrated Ben Zoma (about A.D. 120–140) studied till he had a beatific vision, from which he never recovered.
29. Jn. 8:13.                                        30. 1 Tm. 5:19.

been successively organised and reorganised by Pharisees under the name of 'oral law'. This was supposedly derived from Moses at Mt. Sinai, since the Hebrew people would not have persisted in practising rules that could *not* be traced directly to scripture unless their original lawgiver (Moses) had authorised them! Thus, the Law of Moses in the time of Jesus already included oral law.[31] Scribes sympathetic to the Pharisees' educational and moral ambitions for the nation (§26) assisted in enabling the oral and the written law to be taught and applied as a coherent whole. Legal discussions bored no one then, as they would now. It was an intellectual exercise that suited public taste,[32] and was a means whereby rabbis indirectly advertised their fitness to be judges, arbitrators, or trustees (§7).

In reality the Law certified, documented, witnessed, within limits, the beliefs and customs and usages of the Hebrews. Many characteristic notions found little or no place in scripture (e.g. the blood feud) and many magical practices were discountenanced by scripture and rabbis alike. A downright contradiction of scripture as taught by the scribes would naturally strike the hearer as an attack on the culture, betrayal of the civilisation, a breach of the barrier which separated the Hebrews from the heathen—quite apart from the anger of Yahweh and its possible consequences. Unless the offender could show that his action was supported by a biblical-historical precedent,[33] or arose from an intelligible, rational interpretation of scripture,[34] especially by an allowable analogy,[35] he would be in danger of punishment. The society did not doubt but that its cult, and its Law, must be protected from insult or flagrant defiance on the part of a member.

The Law prescribed observances (§25) and documented many a taboo (§24). Coupled with the Prophets it exhorted to virtue and pronounced doom upon vice. Small wonder that it was spoken of as a 'yoke' or 'burden'.[36] The moral standards of the post-exilic Hebrew people were inculcated by repeated denunciation and tales of woe merited by offenders of the past. The formal and specific rules of private law must therefore be read along with these overriding requirements of the moral aspect of Judaism.[37] One must

31. Jn. 9:28.          32. Mt. 23:16–22.          33. Mt. 12:3, 5; Mk. 2:25.
34. Mt. 12:8; Mk. 2:27; Mt. 12:25–26, 17:25.
35. Mt. 12:11–13; Lk. 13: 15–16, 14:2–6.
36. 2 Bar. 41:3; Mt. 11:28–30, 23:2–3.
37. Mt. 9:13 (about undiscriminating legalism).

not 'place a stumbling block before the feet of the blind': this meant
that the unwary must not be deceived. One must not 'remove his
neighbour's landmark': this meant that any kind of unfair competition, subtraction of reward or infringement of long-established rights
was forbidden. A maxim such as 'great is peace',[38] would govern
many a situation where it would be unfair or inexpedient to enjoin
a Jewish rule where natural equity was more appropriate, especially
in dealings with the everlasting heathen.

Punishment was indeed a part of the Law, but it was a commonplace proposition that what was not confessed, punished, or com-
pensated for in this life would be punished hereafter.[39] And there
were a whole range of rules which, if broken, could not be upheld
in an earthly court, but must be punished by Yahweh, in his own
way and his own time. The 'soul shall be cut off' (though it was
never quite clear what that meant), or the individual would meet
'death at the hands of Heaven', perhaps sudden, and certainly
untimely death.[40]

Many acts of legal consequence were done on earth (i.e. in the
Hebrew courts) which were regarded as binding upon Heaven:[41] the
determination of the New Moon, for example, the intercalation of
the additional month to correct the calendar, and so forth. Which
day was the Sabbath was determined by man, not by Yahweh, who
would punish the Hebrews for breach of its taboos. The priest's
decision on the fitness of a person for entry to the Temple, to present
offerings, and the fitness of the offerings, would be attributed to
Yahweh. This was a convenient overlapping of the two worlds, and
one hesitates to imagine what would have been the result of a
different outlook.

Summaries of the Torah were educationally interesting or
amusing. Commandments (there were so many of them) could be
epitomised or weighed up comparatively.[42] Odd as it seems to us, it
makes good sense in an oriental environment in which some
dilemmas involve breach of at least one commandment, whichever
course is adopted.

Our survey is not complete without mention of legal tricks or
devices.[43] However reprehensible these seem to the Western mind

38. *LNT*, 251.                    39. Bab. Tal., B.B. 88*b*. See below, p. 154.
40. Ac. 5:5 (see Derrett at *Downside Review*, vol. 89, no. 296 (1971), 225–32).
    2 M. 3:27 (cf. Lk. 1:20).
41. Mt. 16:19.              42. Mt. 7:12, 22:36.              43. Mt. 15:5.

they come naturally to peoples governed by a written scriptural law, since rigidity can only be avoided by subtle interpretation, analogy, and devices. The *erub*, by which fictitious residence is acquired in order to extend the Sabbath-limits, seems to have been in use in Jesus's time, though, e.g., Sadducees might have disputed its validity. At that rate one must tread neatly around scriptural prohibitions.[44] If Yahweh had wished devices and restrictions to be unavailable he should have told Moses accordingly! Even though there is no legislative power anywhere, scriptural law can never become obsolete. Therefore the scholar-interpreter must find inherent limitations and conditions such as the words could not originally have contemplated.[45] On the other hand, a moral teacher may well extend or expand a text, by contending that it is not exhaustive (e.g. the 'neighbour's landmark' type), but only illustrative and indicates the tendency that should be followed.[46] He can also refer to fundamental legal provisions which automatically restrict detailed provisions.[47]

## §23. SUPERSTITION

Many taboos were superstitious or were largely so, and many observances were essentially superstitious, but since they form topics to themselves I have thought best to exclude them from this section, which is a rapid survey. By 'superstition' I mean a practice based upon belief not susceptible to rational verification.[48] It is of the essence of our study that we recognise as a fact that the ancient world, and particularly the ancient East, understood unseen forces, powers, influences as in no way less real than seen and empirically verifiable factors. To this day Asians of the highest integrity and highest educational qualifications (including several known to me personally) are convinced that unseen forces rule all life, that their will and tendency can be discovered by more or less occult means, that actions ordinary in themselves have occult significance and

44. Mk. 3:5 (the man himself acts, and the Sabbath prohibition is obviated)·
45. Mt. 19:8.                                              46. Mt. 19:9.
47. Mt. 19:4. *LNT*, 372. Mt. 12:7; see above, p. 113.
48. I do not follow the definition in the *Shorter Oxford English Dictionary*. Many superstitions are indeed founded on fear. All religions are in a sense superstitious, since in so far as they are religious they are not founded on objective (as opposed to subjective) verification—but they are not always based on fear; and if 'ignorance' were cured the religion would not necessarily vanish.

power, and that 'holy' people can do miraculous cures of sickness of all kinds and can 'materialise' solid objects from the air or from nowhere. They cannot be convinced that the 'miracles' at which they have been present personally are charlatanry or conjuring tricks (as they are) and they are deeply hurt at the suggestion, for example, that the hairy rustic who is widely believed to be possessed of miraculous powers of healing is a clever confidence trickster.[49]

A senior judge of the Supreme Court of an Asian country, sometime judge of the Court of Appeal in another Commonwealth territory, a prolific legal author, an LL.D. of London University, a man who has observed fraud and trickery all his long working life, swears that he has seen an amulet materialised in the palm of a fakir's hand (he showed it to me with pride) and 'holy' honey appear on the glass cover of a portrait of the above-mentioned rustic. This does not mean that those miracles happened, they did not—they were artful tricks, done in the interest of increasing faith (as in the case of pre-Reformation tricks by monks, exposed by the royal commissioners and defended by the monks as being *permissu superiorum*). India is, and was, the mother of all magic and confidence tricks. But the sincere conviction which these highly respectable and responsible men and women evince is much more interesting. They earnestly desire and believe that that unseen world and its potency (of which they have no doubt) should be available for them. And their belief projects itself upon the talented 'holy' men who pander to this appetite (and by constant acting eventually persuade themselves that they have occult powers), and these professional entertainers (I cannot in fairness call them parasites) seriously try to live up to the bogus role imposed upon them by universal demand.

However, there is something more to be said. When the 'miracle' is understood by the former sufferer and his relations to be a healing miracle, other factors enter into the picture. When strong emotional stimuli are brought to bear upon the sufferer in an entirely new context (a 'cure', if you like, which has not been 'tried' before) they

49. Jos., *BJ*, ii. 585ff., for a startling Jewish example (there are others in his work). The credulity Asians show towards confidence tricksters masquerading as psychiatrists *and the astonishing cures actually effected by the latter* are illustrated by a case detailed in S. Venugopal Rao (of the Indian Police Service), *Facets of Crime in India*, 2nd ed. (Bombay, London, etc., Allied Publishers, 1967), 121-3.

can certainly produce results which science has not yet explained. These are reported in Asia in our own day amongst individuals who are innocent of religious faith in the Western sense, but who are certainly open to strong emotional stimulus in a naïve and uncritical way. The coming of Mao's China has produced in Chinese medical men and their patients a fixed (and irrational) belief in the impossibility of its *not* producing cures in even the most apparently hopeless cases, and the most sceptical Western observer cannot deny that at the very least the 'gospel' of the 'kingdom' of Mao has actually made the paralytics believe they can walk, and has made innumerable witnesses testify that men now walking and actually working were incurable invalids a matter of a few months before. Ross Terrill, described as an Australian-born expert from Harvard, and apparently innocent of religious partisanship for Chinese communism, reports (*Observer Review*, 9 January 1972, p. 25, cols. 7–8), 'Most had lain in bed for years, and the marks of the bedsores were on them like burns'. Public interest in identifying the miraculous does not diminish the reality of the experience of those who claim to be cured: and it would be a bold man who would deny that a claim to be cured is the same as being cured, or go a little further and deny that a naïve faith in an irrational force was a significant element in the cure, or, if you like, a qualification for being cured. From my own experience I can testify that *behaviour*, and certainly *attitudes* can be changed instantly by the application of the right emotional force (rational or irrational) at the right time and in the right way, and rational argument is powerless in comparison with it.

It was believed that diseases (and presumably many injuries) were due to sin, on the part either of the individual or of his forebears. It followed that if anyone was empowered to release or forgive sin he could mitigate the effects of illness, if not cure it altogether. The concept, whereby illness is traced to sin, is so opposed to the presuppositions of a scientific age, with its system of education based on observed cause and effect, that unless it can be (at worst) tolerated modern man is bound to regard it, and those who acted as if it were true, with scepticism, if not ridicule. Solidarity (as we have seen) was a comprehensively potent principle. Illness, though ostensibly individual, was bound to be seen as a misfortune for the group. A woman's illness interfered with her duties towards her husband's guests. Many illnesses of psychological origin may have been due to subconscious resentment at the group's expectations from the patient. What was the difference, whether a male member was paralyzed, or in gaol?! Illness and punishment were the same in social terms. It was crimes against other groups that were punished (if at all) by death, flogging, enforced restitution, etc. A group was penalised through its member if his illness could be viewed as divine punishment for an unexpiated religious offence within the group. If one could attribute an illness to sins committed by a member *other than* the patient, chances of remarkable cures by sin-diviners would be enhanced. But no one doubted but that Yahweh, the 'just judge', sent scourges to the group through the illnesses of individuals; and to detect and 'treat' the consciousness of unexpiated guilt seems to have made all the difference to a patient's capacity to recover. We know that the will to live, cessation of fear of the complaint, and an expectation of recovery play an enormous part even in our sceptical and materialistic age.

## i. Destiny

Inconsistencies do not trouble the Asian mind. The Hebrews of the time of Jesus believed in fate, in predestination, and in the inevitable tendency of events.[50] At the same time they believed that their own spiritual conditions, i.e. their stock or repute with Yahweh, collectively rather than individually (because of notional solidarity, p. 44), would affect fate. Yahweh, as the book of Jonah showed, could change his mind. Faithful service of Yahweh gave hopes of a long life.[51] The occult forces were subject to the predestined condition that moral goodness could deflect the power of fate, or that though the fated evil would come, some fragment or remnant of the group could escape. The Hebrews' view of fate was essentially pessimistic, qualified by the concept of the survival of a remnant, for whom frustrated joy would transpire. This is a projection of centuries of experience of blind destruction, barbarity, and oppression by warring foreign rulers' armies, or at the hands of their own fratricidal factions. A remnant escaped, but only a remnant. Destiny had a way of declaring or disclosing its secrets through the significance of ordinary acts which were done, and words spoken, in ignorance or inadvertence. Ordinary life was full of omens, symbols for those

50. Mt. 1:3, 5, 6; Mk. 13:10, 11, 14:21; Lk. 1:9, 16:29, 22:36 (cf. 49); Ac. 13:48; Tb. 3:17, 6:17, 10:12. Sadducees affected to care nothing for Fate: Jos. *Ant.*, xiii. 171–3.
51. Jos., *BJ*, i. 462.

with eyes to recognise them.[52] Retribution, Nemesis, was eagerly recognised: fate had its justice, come what might.[53]

## ii. Palmistry

The destiny of an individual could be known from his palm(s) on which all his past and his potential for the future were written.

## iii. Astrology

Scholars and mathematicians knew an elaborate science whereby destiny was declared in amazing detail by reference to the conjunction of planets influencing the place of birth of an individual at the time of birth. It is not known how highly developed it was then: Babylonian, Greek, and Indian astrology reveal that the science was by no means in an early stage by the first century. However irrational the theory or bizarre the methods, the results of astrology are unquestionably valid to a large degree and prove that by haphazard or amateurish means some real factor of life has been broached, though not explained. The emperor Tiberius, Jesus's contemporary, was a great astrologer. The many tales told of his proficiency may be exaggerated, but he would not have devoted so much of his considerable brainpower to this science had its contact with reality not been obvious. While trained men cast horoscopes the village stargazers predicted events by merely scrutinising the heavens. And strange stars were readily accepted as portents.[54]

## iv. Numerology

It was widely believed that numbers were magically significant, that certain numerals had particular power, that numerical coincidence was meaningful.[55] In a culture in which ciphers were letters all numerals must be expressed in what can be read as sounds, often words. Therefore words and names have numerical values and significance can be obtained from that if one is intent on divining

---

52. Mk. 10:50, 14:54 (cf. Jr. 36:22–23 and Mishnah, Yoma I. 8, II. 1); Lk. 2:2 (cf. 1:69: Quirinius = q r n = 'horn'), 13:2–4, 22:36. Jos., *BJ*, i. 331, 377; *Ant*. xviii. 284–8.
53. Jos., *BJ*, i. 72, 82–84, 179. Mishnah, Avot II. 6.
54. Jos., *BJ*, vi. 289 (the star of destruction stood over the place). Astrology and the Jews: Jos. *Ant*., i. 156, 167–8; Bab. Tal., Shab. 156*b*; Tosefta, Kidd. 5. 17.
55. Mt. 1:17. An *as-if* genealogy.

destiny (*gematria* is the name of the Hebrews' fanciful divining by use of the numerical value of words or phrases).

## v. Names

This was especially true of names, the numerical value of which is supposedly significant. Children were named in order to perpetuate some family tradition, but no one was ever unaware of the meaning of a name (all names had literal meanings or allusions). A child's name was often intended to commemorate an event or predict an influence for his destiny. The Hebrew bible is full of play with names, and the tradition that names must throw light on the bearers' natures is so widespread that Philo, in his allegorical interpretation of the Torah, has no shame in making the biblical characters little more than symbols for the qualities their names suggest. 'Name', as in primitive cultures, often stands for the 'power' of the bearer.[56]

## vi. Birth

With the topic of childbirth itself we reach a point at which modern ideas continue those of the ancient world. Increased scientific knowledge has not explained the *why* of conception. The Hebrews viewed childbirth as symbolic of destiny in a most intimate way. No conception took place without the co-operation of the holy spirit.[57] None, that is to say, since the mythical giants were born from women impregnated by the fallen angels. Pregnancy was symbolic of patience, the pains of childbirth the storms of life in the throes of destiny, and the actual delivery symbolised redemption, release, joy, fulfilment. Fertility, conception, and birth were the great taboo areas of life (as was death), wrapped in mystery and awe,[58] a proper focus for old wives' tales and superstitions. The birth of a son was especially valuable (no angel says 'Thou shalt conceive and bear a daughter').[59]

## vii. Angels

Contact with Yahweh was never doubted, and there were many means of communication with him. The Hebrews stood before him in prayer and referred to him in casual 'pious' ejaculations and remarks day in and day out. The words needed to 'glorify Yahweh', when occasion arose, came easily to the tongue. But communication

56. Ac. 3:16, 4:30.        57. Mt. 1:18, 20.
58. Lk. 1:41, 44.        59. Lk. 1:25.

was not a mere reflection of his omnipresence. Rather he was a kind of king with limitless courtiers and his messengers and agents were angels.[60] So well imbedded was this notion that the announcement of coming events, good and bad, the communication of some special fact or idea which could not have been arrived at by simple deduction,[61] were referred to Yahweh's messenger, not to any intuition or exceptional intelligence on the part of the individual. I have no doubt but that the generality of Hebrews had then, as many primitive, illiterate people have still, a skill in the nature of clairvoyance and/or telepathy which survives only in a residual form in educated man. But the arrival of ideas later confirmed by experience was attributed not to a natural power, but to angels. This was the idiom in which such mental processes were referred to. Hyperbolically, one spoke of deep knowledge withheld even from angels.[62] Angels could act as harbingers of punishment,[63] as testers or examiners of men,[64] as helpers,[65] or as simple representatives of the divine presence which could not with propriety be visualised as keeping company with men in terms of daily intimacy.[66]

People knew a few facts about angels, worth noting. They shone.[67] They looked young, but of no identifiable gender (they are masculine linguistically, but that is honorific). They had no organs of excretion or reproduction[68] and when they seemed to eat or sit down this was an illusion.[69] Angels do not eat or drink, nor do they sit down (it is doubtful whether they have more than one leg). They are dressed in brilliant white cloth, wrapped round them (for they do not need to walk or run, they just appear).[70] A statuesque figure wrapped in white would at once be recognised as an angel.[71] The vision would be expected to terrify. Names of angels, and their particular func-

60. Mt. 1:20, 2:13, 19; Tb. 12:12.     61. Test. Reub. 3:15.
62. Mk. 13:32.     63. Mt. 13:41, 44–49; Sus. 55.     64. Lk. 10:20.
65. Mt. 4:11, 18:10 (under the age of puberty—see §24—children are pure [Mt. 19:14–15] and in good communication with Yahweh), 26:53; Mk. 1:13; Ac. 12:15; Ep. Jer. 6:7.
66. Jos., *BJ*, ii. 401. Qo. 5:5 (= 6).     67. Ac. 6:15.
68. Mt. 22:30 (Lk. 20:36b is not so good, because *on earth* bad angels *did* have intercourse with the 'daughters of men', long ago: Gn. 6:2).
69. Tb. 12:19.
70. This prepares the mind to accept the disappearance of apparitions without scepticism: Lk. 24:31.
71. Mt. 17:1, 28:3; Mk. 9:3; Lk. 24:4; Ac. 1:10; 2 Esd. 1:39–40; Test. Levi 8:2.

tions, were esoteric 'information' beloved of the probers into the occult world.[72]

## viii. Dreams

It need hardly be said that dreams were interpreted as indications of destiny.[73] The references to dreams and their interpretation in scripture make it clear that this was beyond doubt. The question was which dreams were to be believed.[74] That people would act, in matters of vital importance to their families, on the basis of omens contained in dreams, seems to have struck no one as in the least remarkable.[75]

## ix. Heavenly voices

A curious characteristic Hebrew notion was that heavenly voices (literally 'daughters of a voice') made occult pronouncements.[76] Sometimes they were heard by the person addressed alone.[77] Sometimes they could be heard by others as well.[78]The rabbis in the next centuries often noted that a knotty problem had been solved by this process. It is difficult to identify the psychological origin or basis of this notion. It is difficult to see what a heavenly voice could do which an angel could not. It seems the phenomenon could be confused with thunder,[79] and this gives a clue. Thunder was regarded as an omen in the pagan world, and it may well have been so in popular Judaism. Omens may have been read into the rather rare occurrence of lightning (and so thunder) in daytime in an apparently cloudless sky. If a debate were in progress, or a critical situation were developing, the noise could be interpreted as supporting the speaker or main actor in a significant way. Since this could be abused it is not surprising that rabbis at one time forbade people to believe in a heavenly voice supporting a false teacher.

## x. Demons and ghosts

The coming and going of human life, its vitality and consciousness, were associated with the coming and going of the spirit. At death the

72. Lk. 1:19, 26; Tb. 3:8; 3 Bar. 11:2–7; Test. Dan 6:2.
73. 2 M. 15:12. Jos., *BJ*, i. 328, ii. 112–14, iii. 352.          74. Si. 34:6.
75. Mt. 2:12, 13, 23.                              76. Mt. 3:17, 17:5; Mk. 1:11.
77. Ac. 22:9; Test. Levi 18:6–7; Jos., *Ant.* xiii, 282 (for the motif of burning incense cf. Lk. 1:9–11). Midrash Rabbah, Song of Songs, VIII. 9, 3.
78. Jn. 12:28; Ac. 9:47.                                        79. Mk. 9:7.

spirit left. The ubiquitous belief that the spirits of the dead jealously torment the living (if they are not appeased) survived amongst the Hebrews. Thus tombs would be the natural abode of someone inhabited by an evil spirit.[80] From the earliest times Hebrews had the charitable and humane notion that psychic or mental distress, physical disorders both pathological or 'functional', were due to the person's being occupied, taken over, as it were, by an evil spirit,[81] since the body is only a dwelling for a spirit[82] and an evil one can as well inhabit it as a good one.[83] Apparitions were visualised as spirits having unsubstantial form,[84] often omens.[85] These could be detected by their abode (ruins or tombs) or their incapacity to eat and drink.[86] From these beliefs it followed that the Lord of Spirits, Yahweh, could control their movement. Similarly the Lord of this World, Satan,[87] had power over evil spirits.[88] A magician conjured with them,[89] and with their names,[90] but at his peril.[91] When an evil spirit was identified or suspected by reason of the physical or mental disorder, the relatives of the afflicted (whether Hebrew or pagan) naturally turned first to a spirit-worker (i.e. what is called in practically every other culture 'witch-doctor', or, for the difference is not always substantial, shaman),[92] next they turned to a sin-diviner (i.e. one who found out by reason of whose sin this 'punishment' had fallen on the house),[93] and then only to a physician in our sense of that word.[94] If the remedies applied by the first two did not kill the patient the third opinion might save him, and physicians were known to be expensive. Indeed the boundary, apart from the size of the fee, between the witch-doctor and the physician was ill defined. One who cured a psychosomatic disorder by utilising the patient's superstition (a vast number of ailments must have been susceptible to such cures) would be credited with power over evil spirits, whatever his own view of the matter, which might or might not coincide with this explanation of his success.[95] In A.D. 69 Josephus saw one Eleazar draw a demon out of a man's nostril and

80. Mk. 5:2.                                                           81. Mk. 1:25.
82. Mt. 12:43 (the desert is too pure for them: §27), 17:16–20 (Mk. 9:25, 29).
83. Mt. 10: 19–20.                                               84. Mk. 6:49; Mt. 14:26.
85. 2 M. 5:1–4, 10, 10:29–30, 11:8.
86. Mk. 5:43; Lk. 24:41–43; Ac. 10:41.
87. Mt. 4:1, 5:25, 10:25; Mk. 8:33.          88. Mt. 9:34.          89. Mt. 12:24.
90. Mk. 5:9; Lk. 8:30.                    91. Ac. 19:14–17.          92. Mt. 12:27.
93. Sickness is an affliction of Yahweh: Si. 30:19–20.          94. Si. 38:9–15.
95. Mt. 8:32, 15:26–28; Mk. 1:34, 7:30.

order him to upset a basin of water as he went, never to return: the method, practised in the presence of the emperor Vespasian (known for his superstition) and his sons (both emperors-to-be) was based on exorcisms said to have been composed by Solomon.[95a] Eleazar was an exorciser of demons and general healer: Josephus says Jews specialised in this method of healing. In this area magic, suggestion, and real medicine would overlap. An opinion which, it seems, many might share is that 'false' doctrines were entertained and propagated under the influence of demons.[96]

The traditional role of Satan, who trapped people into sin,[97] defeated their hope of vindication in the heavenly courts, so depriving them of supersensory benefits and otherworldly delights, was still accepted. Piety, it was thought, must always be alert against this force of evil.[98] This charitable concept placed the source of wickedness, as it were, *outside* the person; it removed or lessened the burden of natural malice or carelessness, but it did not fail to prove that the Hebrews knew the deceitfulness of personal plans, the fallibility of individual judgment.

### xi. The evil eye

Envy, admiration, jealousy, bad and good sentiments known the world over, must have been common then, since they will so often have given rise to irritation and unpredictably hostility, often secret and often taking the form of witchcraft. The tendency was so much feared that, as in parts of modern Asia and Africa, glances of envy or admiration were thought enough to blight prospects, diminish returns or bring disaster:[99] and not everyone had an amulet powerful enough to avert the evil eye.

### xii. Clairvoyance

A recognised means of identifying a person of exceptional powers, assumed to be of supernatural origin, was the ability to read thoughts,[100] to know of happenings at a remote place,[101] to identify a deliberately or accidentally disguised person, and to know the truth of any disputed question (e.g. the identity of a thief of some stolen property). Such powers may not be so extensive as claimed

95a. Jos. *Ant.* viii, 45–9.                          96. 1 Tm. 5:1, 3.
97. Mt. 6:13, 16:23; Mk. 1:13; Bab. Tal., Gitt. 52*a*. 1 Tm. 3:6–7; 2 Tm. 2:26
98. Jn. 13:27.        99. Si. 31:13; Mt. 6:22. Mishnah, Avot II. 9, 11; V. 13.
100. Mt. 9:4; Mk. 2:8; Jn. 4:29–30.                101. Jn. 1:48–49, 4:19.

by those who undoubtedly possess them, but clairvoyance is a real phenomenon, unfortunately exaggerated by the credulous who seem only too ready to attribute limitless ability to people who possess a power, which is not miraculous merely because it is uncommon. Prophetic power, in the sense of an ability to foretell the future, was generally attributed to rabbis of exceptional holiness.[102]

### xiii. Reincarnation

Scriptural Judaism gave little support for the belief in reincarnation. But popular Judaism accepted it in principle,[103] naturally without very clear and precise definition. Since personal and individual resurrection was believed possible (§31), and patriarchs and specially holy people of biblical days were believed to have 'ascended' to heaven whilst still alive (§31), it followed that the reappearance of the spirit of the deceased in another body,[104] retaining the power of the original host of that spirit, was to be reckoned upon as a possibility.[105] It is futile to be too logical in such a field of inquiry. Metempsychosis was widely accepted in the Hellenic orient, as of course in India (whence it may have come), and there was every reason for this Hebraic superstition to become established.[106]

### xiv. Miracles

In the East (p. 115) it is not the believer in miracles who is rare but the sceptic. The unseen world impinges continually on the seen and the progress of scientific thought has no impact on this supposed category of higher truth to which the populations tenaciously adhere. Their world-view cannot stomach the notion that miracles do not occur. How much more true must this have been in the ancient world! The Hebrew concept of miracles was complex. Evils could be miraculous, and they could be a sign, a warning of the trend of destiny, as much as good happenings. The unseen world asserted its reality by *signs*,[107] which authenticated people, or their claims. A miracle which was against the course of nature (e.g. sight given to a man born blind) would certainly qualify as a 'sign', namely a

102. Jos., *Ant.* xv. 373, xvii. 41, 43; *BJ*, i. 78–80, ii. 159. The High Priest is a prophet in this sense (*BJ*, i. 69).
103. Mt. 14:1, 2, 16:14.                     104. Cf. Mt. 10:28.
105. Mt. 17:13, see also p. 122, n. 82 above.        106. Mt. 8:28–32.
107. Targum on Is. 7:11; Si. 36:6.

warning that the unseen world demanded recognition, homage. Miracles demand responses, they do not occur *in vacuo*.[108] Some miracles were associated with the End of the Age (§31). The world would be turned upside down, nature would return to the Golden Age. Miracles could thus be scrutinised to see whether they came within this category. Could it not be possible that miracles adequate in quantity and quality would not merely presage, but even hasten the End?

Since Hebrew attitudes were constantly confirmed by their religion, by study and repetition of scripture and other inspired literature, and by long-inherited superstition, in the view that the unseen world kept company with, and interfered in daily life, it was unthinkable that miracles should *not* occur. Individuals, whose materialism got, as it were, the better of them, or who were conscious of insufficient submission to the divine commandments would hesitate.[109] Were they worthy of a miracle?[110] Had they the faith, which was the essential prerequisite to receive one?[111] Correctly, the Hebrews realised that for psychosomatic experiences the appropriate psychic state was essential,[112] and the sceptic did not lend himself to the miracle-worker's art.[113] A sinner was, in his own mind, unfit for a miracle.

Thus miracles, discharges into the material world from forces believed to lie above it, as it were, were regarded as proof of the performer's *merit*,[114] capable of being deducted from it, as if a treasury of merit would be exhausted if nature stepped aside too often to meet the needs of the doer and those who believed in him and so were his associates.[115] A good miracle would be done only by the extremely holy.[116] An imposter thought he could walk on water.[117] But magical and outrageous feats were commonly done by men claiming holiness, who were only practising upon a credulous public, supplying wonders and utilising faith. Skilfully exploiting the people's credulity and appetite for marvels could bring in a vast income, and there was no reason why a practitioner should not live

108. Mt. 11:21; Jn. 2:11, 23; Ac. 4:16.        109. Mt. 16:4.        110. Lk. 5:8.
111. Lk. 17:19.                    112. Mk. 9:17–25. Even for gentiles: Ac. 14:9.
113. Mt. 13:58, 14:31; Mk. 6:6.
114. Mt. 12:38; Mk. 8:11 (cf. Dt. 6:16; Is. 7:11–14; Mt. 4:7); Mt. 16:1; Mk. 16:17–18; Jn. 2:18.
115. Bab. Tal., Taan. 24*a*.                116. Jn. 5:11, 9:16, 31, 33, 10:21.
117. 2 M. 5:21, 9:8. Derrett, *Zeits. für Rel. und Geistesgeschichte*, vol. 24 (1972), 153–5.

well upon the gratitude of his public. On the other hand, a man who did *not* work miracles, whether gratis or on the basis of voluntary contributions to his mission, would be thought to be a man of small merit, of merely verbal holiness, a windbag. The thaumaturge was not necessarily holy, he might well be a good confidence trickster. But how could a man of established holiness not be a thaumaturge, given the propensities of his public?[118]

One New Testament miracle deserves special mention because its implications can be checked. Everyone knew that solar eclipses can occur only when the moon is new. Eclipses last for five minutes at the most, usually very much less. When, at the time of the paschal full moon, St. Mark speaks of darkness from the sixth to the ninth hour he refers to a state of affairs not coinciding with an eclipse. The statement of St. Matthew (27:45) adds nothing. But St. Luke (23:45) adds that the sun was eclipsed (if we follow Nestlé's text, which is the most widely used). The alternative text printed in the Textus Receptus, 'and the sun was darkened' could be a correction of Luke (to avoid an obvious falsity), or it could be the original, but clumsy text, at the point where Luke adds Yahweh's mourning, as it were, to the Marcan tradition of an apocalyptic cataclysm. In any case what is being depicted is not a clue to the date of the Crucifixion (!) but a response, as it were, in nature to the bereavement, as it were, of Yahweh and the End of the Age (then visualised as beginning to appear). What is described is not some natural phenomenon, but the state of the participants in the drama, expressed in terms of the world which was assumed, as a matter of course, to be in sympathy with them. So far as they were concerned it was *as if* the sun's light went out (which could not be expressed in Hebrew idiom without a threefold occurrence, therefore the three hours). It has nothing to do with a solar eclipse as a natural phenomenon, nor was the sun eclipsed: but for those who participated it was *as if* a solar eclipse had lasted as long as three hours. This is not my rationalisation of my text, it is my understanding of what St. Mark's text told St. Luke, how St. Luke reacted to this, and how he passed on the information to his own hearers. But neither evangelist stopped to explain the irony: darkness covered the earth so that the Messiah's light might shine upon Jew and gentile alike! So says Isaiah (60:1–3) as interpreted in *Pesiqta Rabbati*, 36.

118. Mk. 6:2.

This is the point at which to raise the sensitive but unavoidable subject of spirit-possession, called by many anthropologists and psychiatrists 'dissociation'. The Anglo-Saxon mind rejects the notion with such violence that we can be sure that subconsciously even the Anglo-Saxon is aware that it is a part of truth (mercifully hidden from him, for if he began to practice it he would wonder if someone would pick his pocket or he would reveal secrets no one was intended to learn!). The Hebrews (like Indians of today) were perfectly familiar with it as a phenomenon, but it was a rarity. Plutarch in his *Life of Marius* tells us of a certain Martha who made a good deal of money out of Westerners' curiosity about this Asian 'gift': like Simon Magus, she could turn the Western appetite for quasi-religious charlatanry to good account! Africans have institutionalised it, and it has penetrated into organised religion, where the anthropologist has long been studying it at leisure. By a process akin to acute and prolonged day-dreaming the 'dissociated' person ceases to be conscious of surrounding reality and begins to utter sounds, which are usually babbling ('speaking with tongues', in New Testament language—and see Ac. 2:13), but in adepts it can take the form of intelligible utterance, and even answers to spoken or unspoken questions. Since what is said often could not be said by the speaker when in a normal state (because too tactless, presumptuous, or knowledgeable) the 'voice' is attributed to a deity. During spirit-possession the 'dissociated' person acquires supernormal strength, endurance, and insensibility to pain (he can run, for example, vast distances); he can also show evidence of memory and intelligence, also apprehension of the future and the inwardness of events, impossible when in a normal condition. Some facts need to be noted: 'possession' can be induced by 'trigger' sensations, e.g. sights, smells, sounds (e.g. rhythms); the 'possessed' person always utters (if he can speak intelligibly) conservative, orthodox views; and while the ability to be 'possessed' is associated with the wild anxieties and tensions of primitive and 'under-developed' societies (and seems to be a necessary release from them), its supernatural by-products (e.g. prophecy) never transgress the needs of observed reality. The 'possessed' prophet or priest in fact subserves the real world and its ultimate advantage. Everywhere the New Testament uses the phrase 'in the spirit' one must enquire whether spirit-possession is not alluded to.[118a]

118a. M. J. Field, *Angels and Ministers of Grace* (London, Longman, 1971). Philo, *Vita Mosis* i. 283; Eusebius, *Hist. Eccl.* v. 16 (tr. Williamson, 218).

## xv. 'Baraka'

I use this Arabic word to express an idea which certainly existed in popular Judaism and exists now throughout the Islamic world from Morocco to Malaysia. A holy person (usually a man) is believed to have the means of conferring blessing, i.e. some of his immanent power, by touch (as by placing the hand on the visitor's head),[119] by his garments (whether he is wearing them or not),[120] and by his shadow.[121] When he is dead pilgrimage to his tomb conveys this 'blessing' and by offering to him a prayer one can obtain his spiritual assistance, from the unseen world, in one's aspirations, whether spiritual or (as is by far the most usual) secular. One confers a favour on him by visiting his tomb, and he, in the 'other' world, does what he can for his visitor. This is yet another transference to the unseen world of an idea well established in daily life. I do something to please you, and whether you like it or not you are in honour bound to do me a good turn in due course.

## §24. TABOO

This section is difficult and delicate to write, yet it cannot be avoided. The New Testament is replete with references to it, often indirect and sometimes silent. Ancient societies were afflicted with taboos, the debris of millennia of fears, superstititions, observances, and habits. Some of them were quite absurd. Rational explanations for some are forthcoming, which impress the uneducated. Taboos have a stranglehold on the person, more than rational exhortation can have, and the teacher who can hook his moral teaching on to a taboo is skilled indeed. For breach of a taboo causes a sense of guilt, whereas moral misdeeds are usually justified fairly easily in the miscreant's own mind. He can always find a justification for doing what he wants to do.

A prime taboo was the avoidance, fear, and hated of the ritually unclean. Much uncleanness, as we have already noticed, is relative. One purified oneself for a particular purpose, and a lower degree of purity was adequate for a lower purpose. Pharisees purified their eating vessels, themselves, and their clothing in case they had

119. Mt. 19:14–15; Mk. 10:13; 1 Tm. 4:14, 5:22.
120. Mt. 9:20–21, 14:36; Mk. 6:56; Ac. 19:12.                    121. Ac. 5:15.

accidentally contacted impurity in a public place.[122] They believed
that bread was a taboo object, and hands had to be rinsed before
eating it.[123] In their view one must avoid impurity and one must not
enter the houses of people who did not observe impurity-taboos,
nor allow them to enter one's own home.[124] Houses were made
unclean if strangers entered them and poked about, strangers who
were suspect of not observing impurity-taboos. The concept, from
its origin, had no moral aspect, and, since I have no doubt but that
the behaviour of Pharisees resembled Brahmins in this particular, I
am sure no visitor was offended when he observed his host and his
family turning out the house and washing all the vessels susceptible
to 'uncleanness', or sending some to be immersed in an immersion-
pool, the moment the guest's back was turned and before he had
reached the corner of the street. Nothing personal, you understand!

Anything to do with Yahweh was 'holy', and intensely tabooed.
For someone to walk into the Holy of Holies was an idea which
would thrill the Hebrew with horror (his hair would erect). The
presence of Yahweh, even to the mind's eye, required the removal
of sandals or slippers, which cannot be worn in the presence of one
whom the wearer honours. The 'holy' and the 'unclean' were tabooed
in strikingly similar ways. Contact with either defiled one. The
procedure of purification, rinsing, immersion, and so forth was
prescribed both for those who became unclean and for those who
contacted the extremely holy. 'Holy' did, after all, mean 'separate'.
After touching a scroll of the canonical scripture one's hands must
be rinsed before touching any 'common' thing. The holy and the
common must not be confused or evil would result.[125] The non-
purified was 'common'. The people who did not have the time, or
who doubted the validity of these customs, were naturally a source
of ritual danger to the meticulous, who called them 'common',
'accursed', 'people of the country'.[126] If the observance of ritual
purity was bound up with the destiny of the nation, those persons
(the majority) were traitors! This was an attitude to be found
amongst Pharisees.

122. Mt. 23:25; Mk. 7:4; Jn. 18:28; Ass. Mos. 7:10; Mishnah, Hag. II. 7;
     Bab. Tal., A.Z. 52b. It will be recollected that all 'purifications' (as of
     vessels) were valid only to the extent of the purpose for which they were
     purified: 2 Tm. 2:21.
123. Mk. 7:2.                          124. Mishnah, Demai II. 3.
125. Jdt. 16:18.                                126. Mk. 7:2.

The left hand, used for lavatory purposes, was inauspicious even after it had been washed, and must never be used for 'noble' acts. The left side was the ignoble side.[127] The head was the noblest part of the body, the feet the humblest: to attend to the needs of the feet an act of the utmost humility.[127a]

A corpse defiled one who touched it (for seven days, provided the 'decontamination' process—with the water of the ashes of the Red Heifer—was observed), or anything on which a corpse was placed.[128] Anyone who walked over a corpse or a part of one, if it were in a shallow grave, was automatically defiled.[129] Only virgin rock failed to give a passage to corpse-defilement.[130] Very rapid burial was usual, and tombs had to be visited for three days to ascertain that the corpse had not revived. If one wanted to engage in any holy activity elaborate decontamination from death-pollution was necessary. Secretions from the body[131] were, as it were, dead (though this reason seems not to have operated on their minds) and they defiled automatically, with different effects in each case. Semen, menstrual blood,[132] urine, faeces,[133] spittle[134] (including drops emitted in, e.g., shouting), defiled. The touch of a menstruant defiled.[135] Sexual intercourse defiled,[136] and in theory the partners must immerse themselves immediately thereafter. Lepers were unclean and defiled one who touched them, likewise certain 'creeping things'.[137]

Idols, too, pollute,[138] even (so some said) when no longer objects of worship by anyone. Anything pertaining or possibly pertaining to the worship of heathen deities certainly polluted.[139] Hellenic ways, including the wearing of the characteristic Greek hat, were abhorrent.[140] The notion of suicide rather than being polluted by the heathen was culturally acceptable.[141] The dietary laws were

127. Mt. 6:3; Mishnah, Zeb. II. 1; Lk. 1:11; 1 Esd. 4:31; Ac. 3:7. Bab. Tal., Ber. 61a, 62a.
127a. 'Be dusty with the dust of the feet of the wise': Mishnah, Avot I. 4.
128. Mt. 23:27–28; Lk. 7:14; Tb. 2:5, 9; Si. 34:25 (30). Jos., Ant. xviii. 380.
129. Mt. 21:39; Mk. 5:2; Lk. 11:44.          130. Mk. 15:46.
131. Mt. 15:11; Mk. 7:15.                    132. Mk. 11:2; Ps. Sol. 8:13.
133. Mishna, Yoma III. 2. Jos., BJ, ii. 149 (Essenes).
134. Si. 26:22; Bab. Tal., Hag. 20a, 23a. Cf. Mishnah, Sheq. VIII. 1.
135. Mk. 5:33.          136. 2 M. 6:3–4.          137. Mk. 1:41.
138. 1 M. 4:45, 15:47.          139. 2 Co. 7:1; Ac. 15:20, 29, 21:25.
140. 2 M. 4:13.
141. 4 M. 17:1. Even rogues could be obstinate to the point of suicide: BJ, i. 312–13.

partly derived from age-old superstition and partly from a determination not to eat with, or to be suspected of eating with, idolaters. The anti-gentile tendency of the whole system was overt and obvious.[142] The Sabbath was a taboo day. Work on the Sabbath,[143] even walking more than the prescribed distance;[144] and cultivating, or recovering debts, during the Seventh Year were taboo.[145] I have said that breach of taboo is more excitement-creating than breach of a moral rule, and the Sabbath provides a perfect example. The unexpected prominence of this topic in the gospels reflects contemporary facts. The adjustment of the civil law to these taboos would form a topic of absorbing interest. We find that the Pharisees had a schedule of prohibited objects, e.g. a piece of cloth in which threads of two or more materials had been woven, or meat seethed in the animal's dam's milk, from which no enjoyment or profit whatever could be obtained. Another example would be leaven at Passover.[146] But there were other less tainted objects, e.g. the hire of a harlot. This could be sold, the taint did not pass to the money thereby obtained, and the latter, or things bought with it, could be enjoyed safely.[147] Unrighteous mammon could, at least in one view, be given in charity: money does not stink.[148] I have already explained the psychological difference between taking in charity (as a beggar) and taking in reciprocity, which involves solidarity and sharing of taint (if any). A guest would not eat the profits of extortion, unless he were himself a 'sinner'; but the same man reduced to poverty could safely accept the food as charity! I think this is an appropriate point at which to insist that there could be no possible objection to this fussiness and scrupulosity, which perfectly fits the ancient oriental mind: any objections would be to the rules arrived at and their practical application and effects; an improved version might be infinitely more fussy and scrupulous.

A notable taboo, which must be taken seriously, found also in other Asian societies (notably in India) is the false concept that the reproductive urge is evil. Sexual pleasure is regarded as inherently

142. Ac. 10:13–14; Est. 14:17; Jdt. 11:12; 1 M. 1:63; 2 M. 6:18–19; 4 M. 5:25–27, 7:6.
143. Lk. 13:14; Jn. 9:16.                    144. Mt. 24:20; Ac. 1:12.
145. 1 M. 6:50, 53.
146. Mt. 26:17; 1 Co. 5:7. Mishnah, Pes. I. 1, II. 1–2.
147. Mt. 19:21, 26:8–9.                    148. Lk. 16:9.

bad. The instinct is as much subject to rational control as any other, but the ancient civilisations (*except* the Western) concluded that because the sexual drive makes men hanker after other men's women, and intrigue to get them, and since those women fell an easy prey to a determined admirer, the drive must be the work of Satan. The 'evil inclination' and Satan were virtually synonymous. Etiquette and society itself were largely aligned to the avoidance of sexual stimulation (to keep Satan's scope down) and a heavy taboo on all sexual activity saving that directed to procreation[149] gave a particular character to the culture. It distinguished it profoundly and conclusively from the Greek. The Greeks must have thought the Jews collectively neurotic. Jesus's comment on Peeping Toms[149a] would strike Greeks as crazy.

Metaphorical use of the ritual law was already known by Jesus's time. Baruch speaks of 'defilement with the dead' as a metaphor for misery.[150] The deliberately defiled was said to be worthy of death.[151] Handwashing could signify a clear conscience.[152] The notion that moral delinquency adheres to the delinquent as does ritual impurity, so that one is, as it were, soiled by sin, was a metaphor finding ready acceptance.[153] It is very ancient in India, where the vocabulary equates 'sin' with 'stain'. Since abhorrence attached to defilement it was a notable moral advance to see wrongdoing as equally in need of washing off.[154] The idea emerged that immersion in 'baptism' (the same word used for removal of ritual impurity) cleansed an individual from guilt.[155] A new life could be started. No one in his senses would now imagine that a bath would wash off sin, or would make for a new life. But it would be quite another matter if we habitually thought that sin adhered like a defilement, that ritual purification removed taint (irrespective of any concept of hygiene): and the notion would be most attractive if reconciliation with Yahweh could not be obtained by way of offerings and penance because, in the circumstances (of extortioners and so on), restitution to those wronged was impossible, or offerings would not be accepted

149. Tb. 4:12; Ac. 15:20, 29, 21:25.
149a. Mt. 5:29 is an application of the general principle stated at Mt. 18:9. Mt. 5:30 refers to a Don Juan's oaths that there is nothing he will not do for a lady teetering on the brink! *Divorce* is the next topic. See p. 204.
150. Ba. 3:11.                 151. 3 M. 7:14–15.                 152. Mt. 27:24.
153. Jos., *BJ*, i. 506. Ws. 2:16. Philo, *Spec. Leg.* ii 27.
154. Mt. 15:20, 23:25; Mk. 7:19, 21–23; Si. 40:29–30. 1QS V. 19–20.
155. Josephus has a brief but significant discussion at *Ant.* xviii. 117.

by the Temple authorities (e.g. in the case of ex-harlots). Since abhorrence in an Asian society is a social phenomenon ('Do not sit near me, you are defiled!'), and since an exactly similar abhorrence arises whether one is unpurified or has committed a moral breach of society's laws, a confusion between ritual taint and moral taint would be all too natural. In fact it would not be going too far to say that *sin* was regarded as a personal condition rather like a sprain, which could be amenable to the appropriate treatment. One could, in the same breath, speak of the wicked, the ritually unclean, and the man who neglects to perform sacrifices, as if the same quality and amount of attention or forethought would keep an individual from all three accusations.[155a]

A testimony to the age of this development is the notion of blood-money—not blood-money as compensation for the loss of a relative, but money tainted by having been acquired in breach of a scriptural commandment not to betray the innocent.[156] Then we have several instances from Jesus's world of sarcasm against those who were fastidious about ritual impurity (they made a fetish of it, as we should say), and gained prestige thereby, whilst being none too scrupulous about their social obligations; clean without, but dirty within: a delightful notion.[157]

We have already encountered the taboo on the Name of Yahweh,[158] the superstitious veneration for the Temple,[159] and the accepted euphemisms which avoided reference to tabooed events (e.g. 'sleep' was used as a euphemism for death).[160] By rending one's garments one sought to avert the evil omen of the tabooed expression.[161]

## §25. OBSERVANCES

The Law contained a vast number of negative commandments, things not to do (e.g. coupling different kinds of animals to the plough), and a smaller number of positive commands (e.g. to tithe one's produce). The true Israelite observed all these, commencing

155a. Qo. 9:2.  156. Mt. 27:6; Test. Zeb. 3:1.
157. Philo, *Quod Deus*, 7–8 (ed. Colson, vol. 3, 14); the same *De fug. et inv.* 153 (ed. Colson, vol. 5, 92).
158. Mt. 5:34. Bab. Tal., Kidd. 71*a*.
159. Mt. 12:6, 26:66; Mk. 11:16. White clothing is needed to enter the Temple: Jos., *BJ*, ii. 1.
160. Mt. 9:24 (irony).
161. Mt. 26:65; Mk. 14:63; Ac. 14:14. See above, p. 70, n. 256.

with circumcision.[162] He did not await compulsion from above; it was a matter of cultural integrity, group habit.[163] The rules were a nuisance, a burden. The Hebrews made a virtue out of them as if they were superior to the heathen, who did not observe so many regulations. Observances were a part of 'righteousness'.[164] 'Righteousness' was popular and the more observant a man was the more righteous he was thought to be.[165] Blessings before meals were an outward sign of piety which seems to have had a taboo origin.[166] Opposition to observances as insufficiently spiritual (cf. Zc. 7:5) was at least thinkable;[167] but all reforms would tend to reinforce the significance of approved observances—a life without observances would be characteristically heathen. The laws concerning diet were not observed *in their entirety* by all the population, but the substantial number of the 'righteous' obeyed the laws so scrupulously that authorities making a corner in 'pure' oil in wartime could make a huge profit;[167a] and travellers to the West under Roman escort had to subsist on a diet of nuts and figs.[167b]

Apart from compulsory acts, like tithes, redemption of the first-born, purification after childbirth,[168] attendance at festivals like Passover, the celebration of feasts and fasts, the Jew enjoyed a great many rituals which enabled him to present himself before Yahweh in various guises. Offerings and vows,[169] and in particular sin offerings were one-sided transactions in which the Temple and ultimately the priests benefited[170] and the individual obtained a sense of satisfaction. The Temple was *par excellence* the location of Yahweh's 'presence'.[171]

Gifts in charity formed a large part of the observant Jew's life. Prayer and blessings associated with many activities punctuated life with consciousness of the activity of Yahweh in all things.

Attention to multifarious abstentions and enjoined actions could well produce a perfectionist and complacent attitude which conflicted with recognition of unenjoined but basic duties; and teachers might well be sarcastic about individuals who were pleased that they had performed all the commandments, but had nevertheless fallen

162. Lk. 2:21; Ac. 16:3.                          163. Mk. 1:44.
164. Mt. 3:17. Even when the motives were ambiguous: Jos., *Life*, 290–1.
165. Mt. 5:47, 48; Mt. 23:5; Lk. 16:4.        166. Mk. 8:6, 6:40. Jdt. 11:12.
167. Jn. 4:23; cf. Mt. 23:4.          167a. Jos., *Life*, 74–6; *BJ*, ii. 591–3.
167b. Jos., *Life*, 14.                      168. Lk. 2:22 (mother and child).
169. Lk. 21:5; 1 Esd. 2:7, 9, 4:44–45, 5:53.
170. Mt. 8:4.                                    171. Lk. 24:53.

short of moral perfection. The picture of Hebrew life as a joyless and burdensome one is probably untrue. It is pleasant to think one has done many duties and obtained public approval, and status thereby. But the burden aspect is present, and it might well distract those who are proud of it from other aspirations, e.g. building a coherent society free from faction, which would have been far more useful. But I have explained, have I not, that in Asian societies utility is of secondary importance?

The theory that Yahweh required all those observances could hardly be countered, when scripture contained so many testimonies that he had done so, and the rabbis wove round these a veritable net of virtually additional requirements. It was hard to be an observant Hebrew, but harder still, in view of Judaism's being coterminous with Hebrew society, to abandon the observances. If Nigeria may afford us a parallel, how does the Ibo become a Yoruba? In India the problem of how one moves out of caste mores and prejudices is virtually insoluble. But if one becomes educated, takes a higher degree, and is called 'Mister' or better still 'Doctor' one can refuse to answer questions as to one's caste and pretend to be a super-caste person. This automatically gives one a religious and social freedom (e.g. matrimonially) to which one would otherwise aspire in vain. But Greek-speaking Jews were still Jews, and amenable to synagogue discipline. For non-Hebrews wanting, strangely, to become Jews the problem was not so great. Males could (after instruction) be circumcised (admittedly quite a sacrifice),[172] and females could simply undergo the proselytes' immersion.

A theory that one could still be a Jew, practising much fewer observances (with a minimum of taboos) and still claim to have Yahweh's authority for so doing might well strike many as *prima facie* a brilliant and progressive suggestion. But most holy men and purveyors of holiness asked for additional observances: more vows (provided, of course, one could be sure of fulfilling them), more immersions, more abstentions, and more restraints.

## §26. SCHOOLS OF THOUGHT

Contemporaries, Josephus and Philo, have given a great deal of information about the Sadducees, Pharisees, and Essenes, supple-

172. Jos., *BJ*, ii. 454.

menting, and to a certain extent improving our view of the religious sects existing in Jesus's time as indicated in the gospels and Acts.[173] It would be out of place to attempt even to summarise what is known about them, especially since our knowledge of the Essenes has been greatly increased by the Dead Sea finds, if, as is generally believed, the Dead Sea people were Essenes. All these sects were 'students of Moses'.[174] The Sadducees, because of their opposition to Pharisaic developments of oral law, and their lack of belief in the world to come (they did not accept apocalyptic manifestations as justified by scripture) were able to involve themselves in political and economic life more thoroughly, and they were associated with the aristocracy. Amongst the Pharisees there were two schools, those of Hillel and Shammai—it is not impossible that there were more of which we have as yet no knowledge. Their respective followers appear to have been content to differ on numerous points of detail.[175] Divergencies in ritual law need not matter greatly; in family law they did—yet these two schools of Pharisees could differ on both.

Josephus tells us of the Essenes, separatists devoted to exceptional holiness and enjoying what looks like a community of property—a feature evidently taking to its logical conclusion the solidarity of which I have spoken so often. The Dead Sea sect certainly did oblige those who passed the various stages of initiation to hand over their assets to the community. Neither the Essenes nor the Sadducees survived, for practical purposes, the last Roman War, and it seems the Dead Sea sect was gravely crippled in the first. Phariseeism remained to produce, in due course, normative Judaism. The former's long hostility to Christianity (now happily much abated) derives from Christian refusal to acknowledge sympathetically the validity of Judaism after the church became predominantly Gentile. The early church, indeed, had earlier identified the Pharisees as that section of the Hebrew society which was most consciously concerned to eliminate the peculiar cult which ultimately became Christianity. And Christians' behaviour compromised Jews in the eyes of the

173. The basic material on the major schools is collected conveniently in the articles under those names in Hastings's *Encyclopedia of Religion and Ethics*. G. F. Moore's *Judaism* is a valuable treatment of the subject historically. Apologetic works on the Pharisees, though useful in other connections, are not relevant to our present approach.

174. Jn. 9:28.                                    175. Mishna, Hag. II. 2.

Romans, while Jews' refusal to accept Christians as part of themselves deprived the former of an immunity the Romans had conceded
to the Jewish religion and its customs.

There is no doubt but that, since religion, politics, and law were
closely intertwined, the teaching of life included superstitious as
well as empirical elements. About superstitions full consensus was
bound to be a vain hope. Argument about superstitious matters had
no anchorage except habit. Schools in which such studies went on
were scarcely hard-and-fast affairs. Students could conceivably pass
from one to the other and from one teacher to another within the
same school. All schools had a great reverence for scripture, all
appealed to it, but there was no agreement on how it should be
interpreted. The bread differed, not because the wheat was different,
it was the teachers' leaven that differed.[176] Teachers had no shame
in crying up their wares, as it were, or in advocating their particular
theories, which they obviously took very seriously.[177]

Manners in dealings between the schools were bad,[178] and feeling
sometimes ran as high as enmity.[179] They ridiculed one another[180]
on the basis that they taught *fruitless* teachings,[181] or caused other
people's students to *stumble*.[182] 'True' teaching (and teachers were
naïve enough to suppose that their version was 'true') bore fruit (in
the students' deeds, and merits); and put people on a straight path.
Schools were prepared to defy each other's rulings in action. The
(almost) unpardonable step could be taken of pointing out that an
opponent's teachings were good as teachings, but they did not find
any reflection in his life.[183] He was a bogus teacher, for he did not
practise what he preached. In Asia teachers must live their teachings;
those that do not are soon exposed. The generic name for such a
poseur was *hypocrites*, 'hypocrite'. Action by a teacher was itself a
precedent and supported his rulings, and so a contrary life automatically undermined his activity. Since popularity meant money,[184]
to undermine a teacher's prestige was a damaging thing to do. And
if a teacher were really popular (as by preaching lax or easy doc-

176. Mt. 16:5, 12. 1 Co. 5:7.                    177. Mt. 11:28–30.
178. Mt. 12:34, 23:15, 33; Mk. 3:29.             179. Mt. 12:14, 26:3–4.
180. Mt. 15:3–9, 17:10; also 23:15; Mk. 7:6–13.
181. Mt. 12:36.                                  182. Mt. 13:21, 18:6; Jn. 7:12.
183. Mt. 23:2–3. A public rebuke for living a lie: Ga. 2:11–14.
184. Proved by the story at Ac. 8:9–13, 18 (true in kind if not *ad hominem*);
     also Ac. 19:19. The principle: Ga. 6:6.

trines)[185] others were wildly jealous.[186] The very fact that some scholars are seen approving of other teachers' ideas only confirms how critical the attitude was.[187] But etiquette required that one should not criticise a man who had initiated one;[188] for one belonged to a school by initiation in it—different schools could criticise each other's founders, there was little mutual criticism within the school.

Since teachers were highly respected and money was dedicated for their support and their students' there was competition for public favour and for students. Academic poaching occurred,[189] which could be referred to as 'thieves coming into the fold' (the students are, characteristically, sheep), or the work of wolves dressed in sheep's clothing![190]

Abuse and sarcasm as between the schools was evidently common.[191] Teachers of one school queried the behaviour[192] of students of another and tactful inquiries might mask insidious intentions.[193] But it was the convention that all teachers should be open to question on any matter, no matter how abstruse, and it was normal to suspect questions to be a trap, whether they were or not.[194] Bystanders would be delighted at smart answers, provided these relied upon unquestioned biblical sources, however far-fetched the invocation might be. Thus anyone might put a question, however ridiculous the set of facts propounded, at the risk that he too would have to answer some conundrum or be the butt for his intended victim's irony.[195] A series of smart answers[196] would diminish the questioners' ardour and the teacher under questioning would hold the field temporarily. Perhaps it is fair to add that a failure to answer a conundrum was not necessarily a disaster.[197] Legal conundrums, we have already seen, were exceptionally popular.[198]

Behind all this discussion, some of it being pure advertisement, lay an uncomfortable thought. A Sanhedrin would not condemn an opinion easily: it could not be packed with any one sect. To condemn any opinion worked to the disgrace of individuals (as the early General Councils of the Christian church discovered). Thus in

185. Mt. 11:28–30 (cf. 23:4).
186. Mk. 11:18 (obviously he 'bewitched' his audience!). Ga. 3:1.
187. Mk. 12:32, 34 (mutual approval = mutual humiliation); Lk. 20:39.
188. Lk. 7:30.     189. Ac. 13:43–45, 50, 14:2.     190. Jn. 10:5, 8; Ac. 20:29.
191. Mt. 12:34, 23:13; Mk. 12:12, 12:38.     192. Mt. 12:1–2, 15:1; Mk. 7:2.
193. Mt. 17:24.               194. Mt. 12:10, 19:1, 22:34–35; Jn. 8:5.
195. Mk. 12:18–23.          196. Mt. 22:15–22, 23–33, 46; Ac. 18:28.
197. Mt. 21:27.                          198. 2 Esd. 4:13–18.

theory any opinion might be *true* which utilised accepted *midrash* technique, even if the individual *midrash* were novel. All approaches to religion and life were potentially valid. The violence of the language of the schools could not hide this. The opponents were 'sinners',[199] 'sons of the Pit', and all possible unrighteousness was attributed to them; but it was not possible, at that period, for them to be proved wrong. Signs from Heaven seldom resolved these quarrels.[200] On the other hand a small court of Sadducees might well condemn to a thrashing a Pharisee whose behaviour threatened their idea of public order,[201] and it was possible for an accused man to embroil a mixed court of Sadducees and Pharisees by making out that the charge against him really contained an element on which the schools were sharply divided.[202]

Rival witch-doctor-scholars easily formed into camps, no doubt to protect their own 'practices'.[203]

I hope I have said enough, though it barely scratches the surface of what is known of sectarian views, to show that the concept of 'the Jews' was an artificial one, invented by Christians as part of an apologetic for the first church. They were bound to explain their want of success, and to attribute it to a national failure, as part of Yahweh's wrath. To the heathen, no doubt, 'the Jews' was a viable concept; and this Christians rather readily inherited, though in the process they lost contact with the world the gospels portray. Widely differing opinions and practices occurred: there were 'common' and 'observant' Hebrews even within the same family (much to the embarrassment of the latter).[204] What linked all of them was the ideal concept that the children of Abraham were a unit, bound by a fundamental solidarity, the more appealing to the sentiments for its not being realised often enough in experience.

## §27. THE ASCETIC AND ASCETIC PRACTICES

We cannot accept the Hebrew traditional taboo on sexual activity: but it is not impossible to understand how it arose, or to accept that it had tremendous force. Fornication created a guilt-complex of a near-neurotic character. Offenders felt they were prejudicing their status as Hebrews, which was absurd: but that is how the culture was. We shall have no more sympathy, I am afraid, with the pen-

199. 1 En. 104:10.    200. Mk. 8:11.    201. See Mt. 23:34.
202. Ac. 23:6.    203. Mk. 9:38.    204. Bab. Tal., Hag. 25*b*.

chant for asceticism, which likewise rested upon false foundations,[205] and was likewise part and parcel of the ancient Asian world, where it is still to be found (notably in India).

Asceticism is foreshadowed in Jer. 35 in connection with the Rechabites and in the book of Judges in connection with Samson. It is contrary to the doctrine that Yahweh promised the children of Israel a land flowing with milk and honey. Naturally that promise was subject to the proviso that they should not get 'puffed up' and forget him. Presumptuous forgetfulness he would punish. Asceticism took several forms, but throughout it assumed that enjoyment of Yahweh's gifts was a possibility from which one could opt out, as it were. Pharisees' puritanical outlook was somehow connected with their view of Sodom (and its fate): unnecessary consumption somehow suggested being 'puffed up',[206] and it was thought that asceticism would protect against this. The basic idea was that if you refuse benefits and forgo delights you gain spiritual merit, by making Yahweh into a kind of creditor. By refusing food (fasting)[207] one makes oneself thin and miserable and Yahweh is moved to compassion. Abnegation is in this way profitable.[208] Just as a guest who refuses food puts pressure upon his host whom he embarrasses thereby, simply by forgoing enjoyment[208] the Hebrew obtained from Yahweh some consideration which mere prayer would not have obtained. Thus vows to be uncomfortable, such as the Nazarite vow[209] or vows which meant keeping the hair of the head uncut[210] (apart from the Nazarite vow, which had this and abstention from wine as its more obvious signs), were popularly supposed to be meritorious. It is a fact that self-discipline has a bracing effect, and

205. Early Christians expected to be believed when they said that those who preached asceticism did so under the influence of demons: 1 Tm. 4:3.
206. Lk. 16:19.
207. Mt. 4:2, 6:17, 9:14; Si. 34:26 (31); Test. Reub. 1:10; Ps. Sol. 3:9 (8).
208. Mk. 9:43, 10:23.
209. Mt. 26:29; Ac. 21:23–24; 1 M. 3:49–50. A reader of Mishnah, tractate Nazir, who did not know the background, but knew the cultural history of India, would think that the material had somehow come from India. The whole concept of Nazarites (Nazirites) has a most primitive and further-eastern character. Hebrew women used to take vows which involved the shaving of the head and a (would-be) 'sanctified' condition: Jos., *BJ*, ii. 313–14. Apparently if the head was shaved she did not need (theoretically) to cover it when in prayer (the angels would not be perturbed by woman's sexual glory, her long hair): 1 Co. 11:5–10.
210. Ac. 18:18. Apart from a vow an effeminate practice: 1 Co. 11:14.

deliberate abstention from pleasure gives confidence to those who are, or imagine themselves to be, weak-willed. The lack of blood-sugar in those who fast induces visions and abnormal psychological states,[211] and these factors combined gave people under vows, or otherwise practising asceticism a claim on public approval. This remarkable claim to prestige was hugely admired in the East, and still is. The abstainers imagine they have supernatural powers and are able to make it seem as if they have, if the credulity of their admirers matches their ambition. Popular superstition, that 'holy men' could work miracles more or less to order, certainly flourished in Jesus's time.[212] It is for this reason that the natural assumption in the West, that conduct or admissions against one's interest are tokens of sincerity, cannot apply here, since an ascetic was a privileged person and gained more in prestige than he lost in comfort. Asians and Africans, as a whole, live stoical lives, inured to hardship, suffering, and pain, bearing the violent ups and downs of life impassively: for them to give up wine,[213] haircuts, going near the dead, and even intercourse with their wives (whose opinion might not be consulted) would cost them so little that what is remarkable is that they were so highly admired.[214]

Ordinary people fasted,[215] some regularly, e.g. widows. This was thought, for reasons stated above, to give them an advantage over others, who followed nature's injunctions and kept themselves in good physical shape. Fasting no doubt kept sexual urges at a minimum, and, as we have seen (§24) the sexual urge was believed to be a bad thing. Vows of celibacy by men and avoidance of all contact with females were also thought meritorious,[216] but it does not follow that the commandment to increase and multiply would be set at nought by this: experience of an arranged marriage until the birth of a child might set a naïve individual on the road to a vow of celibacy.

211. 2 Esd. 5:20, 6:35.   212. Lk. 23:8; Jn. 4:11–12.
213. Lk. 1:15.   214. Mt. 3:4–5, 10:8–10; Mk. 1:6.
215. Mk. 2:18; Lk. 18:12.
216. Mk. 14:13; 2 Esd. 6:32. There is a story in the Babylonian Talmud of a female bedmaker who testified (!) that her employer's sheets had never shown signs of a nocturnal emission. This was evidence of very superior holiness on his part, seeing that he was a total abstainer from sexual intercourse. That story breathes the atmosphere from which the New Testament comes, but we must not be afraid of recognising nonsense as nonsense.

It was believed that leaven adulterated bread.[217] Urban life, based upon cultivation (the fate of Adam) was fancifully believed to be inferior. True purity was to be found in the desert,[218] whence the nomadic patriarchs had come. To live among the hills on natural foods, self-grown, was thought to equal enjoyment of an atmosphere of purity and truth. The primitive notion that the person, the self, was affected by foods going into the body had this corollary that life apart from civilisation, sustaining oneself on automatically growing substances was somehow more holy and more worthy.[219]

An ascetic, having a position superior to all 'worldly' people could afford to be scathing about them and to speak even of and to rulers with a unique freedom[220]—until one of that kidney caught him and silenced him, a fate from which, it seems, angels would be no protection. We know that the Baptist felt it his duty to rebuke Herod Antipas for questionable proceedings within the borders of the family law,[221] and the self-appointed jurist paid for his temerity. He would not have been imprisoned had he not expressed his views on the marriage law too loudly or too persistently, and Herodias would not have had his head if he had not been in prison. It was a mark of the ascetic, or 'holy man', a sign of his prestige, that he did not handle money.[222] Other people did his shopping for him.

## §28. THE TEACHER AND THE ROLE OF THE STUDENT

Apart from the synagogue (to attend which one did not have to be literate, still less literate in Hebrew as opposed to Aramaic) there was no organised education in Palestine. Fashionable people sent their sons to Hebrew equivalents of the Greeks' sophists, and an attempt was made to project the Jewish ethic in terms of contemporary 'wisdom'. Technical education, namely in trades and crafts, naturally flourished (for livelihoods were made by it) but this was a matter of apprenticeship; new techniques were rarely acquired, and imitation far outweighed initiative or individuality. Education (as world history confirms) has been in the interests of the family, the religious sect, and the state in that order. Education in the child's interest, as a means of maximising the personality, is

217. Mk. 8:15. 1 Co. 5:7.
218. Mk. 1:35; Lk. 1:80. Jos., *BJ*, ii. 259–60, 261–3; *Ant.*, xx. 97.
219. Mk. 1:2–3; 2 M. 5:27, 6:1–11; Mart. Is. 2:11; Jos., *Life*, 11.
220. Mt. 3:7, cf. 11:15, 12:13–14; Lk. 13:32
221. Mt. 14:4; Mk. 6:19.
222. Ac. 3:6.

an entirely modern idea. When could spiritual education safely conflict with the interests of the family, the religious cult, or the State? An uneducated, but spiritually alert, and controversially excitable populace provided an audience which had serious limitations, but great potential. Impatient of abstracts, insistent upon practical relevance, eager to be entertained as well as instructed, it virtually forced its teachers to rely on concrete illustrations, particularly shrewd and comical ones, and to teach through pictures and maxims rather than continuous and reasoned argument. Problems of what one did in everyday dilemmas interested everyone, and solutions to practical difficulties had an allure for minds avid for generalisations but unable to arrive at them independently. Small wonder that amongst the Hebrews Law was the unquestionably superior medium of instruction, Law as the articulated presentation of Life, not law as it is understood in modern Europe and America.

The teacher was a theologian *and* a lawyer. He based his teachings on scripture and saw himself as enacting scriptural roles, for the teacher was in a sense the heir, though usually a far inferior one, to the extinct line of prophets. He expected the public to be interested in him as well as in what he taught. His life was public and no one became a teacher unless his life passed as a worthy one by popular standards. Students could apply to him,[223] but he reserved the right to choose the most likely youths or men to be his disciples and there were no conventions in this regard. A skilled teacher could see potential in unexpected quarters.[224]

The teacher spoke in the way beloved of Asians, in crisp, memorable phrases, making use (especially in debate) of maxims, proverbs, analogies, and similes, forms of speech still highly favoured in the East. An apposite choice of maxims and metaphors was the sign of the accomplished public speaker and 'wise man'.[225] Of childish puns, which Semitic languages greatly favour, they were inordinately fond.[226] Sometimes the ancient method of miming prophecy was used.[227] At the same time esoteric teaching would be given to his students, the inner circle at least, the élite.[228] This would be worth a lot to them if they eventually became teachers in their turn.[229]

---

223. Jn. 1:39.                              224. Mt. 5:19, 9:9; Jn. 15:16.
225. Si. 6:35, 18:29, 20:20, 28:33, 39:2.
226. Lk. 9:31 contains what the Evangelist's advisers regarded as a permissible pun: *exodos* = (1) death, (2) (second) Exodus; Mt. 23:29 (*boney/baney*).
227. Ac. 21:11.          228. Mt. 13:3, 18, 35, 15:10.          229. Mt. 10:27.

Cryptic words, conveying subtle versions of simple thoughts, were highly admired.[230] One could take home a cryptic teaching and decode it, and enjoy retailing it and its explanation to one's relations and neighbours. Stereotyped allusive diction was also in vogue: light, water, cup, bread, wine, salt, and other common but valued objects could convey the Law, the holy spirit, wisdom, and so on.[231]

A special class of teacher was the healer, the thaumaturge who specialised in curing ailments. The connection between the two activities is not obvious, but I trust I have explained how it came about (§23, x, xiv). One who knew scripture by heart and interpreted the secrets of Yahweh had obviously been favoured by Yahweh and had merited favours from him. Thus to conquer evil spirits and effect cures by psychological means,[232] operating on people as if they were physical organisms entirely obedient to the healer who cleansed them (as if weeding them) of their evil lodgers, was not only to prove one's holiness and fitness to be a teacher, but a natural activity on the part of one who could use scripture authoritatively and apply timeless wisdom to individual problems. A successful healer would link his cures with the prevalence of sin, and physical cure could underline the moral issue raised by the household in question. In spite of the sombre touch to a happy occasion the healer-teacher would be immensely popular,[233] since every young person cured was money in his relatives' purse. At this point religious students, whom agriculturalists everywhere view ambivalently as parasites, came into their own and earnt their corn. Healers who could operate at a distance and so save relatives the cost and trouble of transporting the sick would be doubly popular.[234] Jesus himself is portrayed in the gospels as attributing his own success to the in-breaking of the Messianic Age (§31).[235] Since teaching and healing often went together it was natural to presume that heathen who were not admitted to the first could not benefit from the second.[236] Yet we find Jesus convinced by argument (backed

230. Jn. 3:3. Learning formulae was part of the student's task: 1 Tm. 3:16, 4:9–10; 2 Tm. 2:11.
231. Mt. 5:15, 6:23, 26:39, 42; Mk. 8:16–21; 1 En. 48:1, 49:1.
232. Mt. 8:1–2, 3, 17.
233. Mt. 4:24; Mk. 1:28, 45.
234. Mt. 8:13; Mk. 6:55.
235. Mt. 11:2–6 (cf. Is. 29:18–19, 35:5–6 and Targum thereon, crudely understood).
236. Mt. 15:22–23.

by faith) that this was erroneous,[237] a fact which must have increased the apostles' expectations enormously.

Such a teacher would have, as a characteristic, complete independence.[238] In that role he was often an ascetic. He must be uncompromised, free. A man who approached with a request might be sent off with a stinging rebuke, a flea in his ear.[239] Gifts in charity might be made to his 'family', which its purse-bearer,[240] not he, would handle, and those whom he cured would naturally be attracted to his programme, if we may so call his brand of teaching, and to his person and suite,[241] especially if alternative employment were not immediately available. It would be characteristic of such a teacher not to be a burden on one area, and to move about constantly. He would not be married, burdened with wife and children and a daily occupation. He would have more 'power' if he was celibate. This would not mean that he had never been married. Since divorce was free at the husband's option he could divorce his wife, provided she could be looked after (and even otherwise), and so devote himself entirely to his students.

Their concept of student differed utterly from today's. It is not surprising that we distinguish 'student' from 'disciple', though they were once one and the same. Even in Asian countries the Western concept of the university student has almost obliterated the native and traditional role, which can be summed up by saying that the student is a secondary son for his teacher (cf. the instance of Kim).[242] Females might listen to a teacher's lecture, but female students as such were unknown. It was unseemly for women, unless really old, to roam about. A student must be prepared to accompany his teacher anywhere.[243] Some teachers were necessarily itinerant. Students could be of any age, even older than the teacher. The method of teaching was to rehearse the student in biblical passages, to explain their meaning, and to rehearse them in the explanation of the meaning. A great teacher exhausted his text so that no more meaning could be squeezed out of it, and interpretation reached perfection in this way.[244] General religious instruction was given,

---

237. Mt. 15:26–28. Cf. 1 K. 17:4–6, to be read with Ps. 147:6, Jb. 38:41.
238. Mt. 21:23 (usurpation? cf. Lk. 21:38); Mk. 12:13–14.
239. Lk. 12:13–15; Jn. 8:11 (Olympian tone).        240. Jn. 4:8.
241. Mt. 19:21; Mk. 5:18.                            242. 1 Tm. 1:18.
243. Mt. 8:19 (not always into vagrancy); Mk. 1:16–18 (into an insecure job).
244. Mt. 13:17.

making use of all relevant scriptural material (§21). Stories were taught, since these formed staple material for sermons which instructed people were authorised or invited to deliver in synagogues: there must have been a constant demand for speakers, and there were no ordained clergy. Amongst the techniques required for successful story building *irony* will certainly have figured, for it pervades our gospels like an aroma.[245]

The process of rehearsing students in scripture, so that they could be word perfect in the Law and the Prophets was prolonged. Many passages would have been learnt in childhood, and the average man knew, I feel sure, most of the psalms by heart by the time he was 14; but even gifted students must have started young,[246] and if they acquired a word-perfect memory of the Law by 14-15 (as Josephus said he had)[247] they might well be consulted by their less gifted elders and would complete this exacting memory-training by a course of spiritual training. No doubt the agricultural majority sought for likely youths and, as usual, certain hereditary aptitudes were to be found amongst the leisured, land-owning classes. But provided the man 'knew his stuff' the fact that he came from an artisan background[248] would not throw doubt on the learning he displayed. Intrigue, however, or imposture were not enough as (unhappily) they can be in our day, nor was favouritism or nepotism, as could have figured in Jesus's time, sufficient to make a man a teacher, even if he could claim the honorific title 'rabbi'. His students, his sharpest (if usually tactful) critics,[249] moved about with him as if they were his family.[250]

Not that criticism could often be voiced openly.[251] Etiquette kept students in a permanently inferior position relative to their teacher.[252] They were his 'children', 'little ones', 'sheep'. He led and they followed.[253] Obedience was expected from them.[254] A teacher was

---

245. Lk. 24:21; Jn. 7:42, 52, 8:33, 52; so Tb. 5:16, 21, 8:9; Jdt. 12:4, 17-18. A magnificent example in Acts: 2:13 (cf. Mt. 26:29).

246. Mk. 6:2-3.

247. Jos., *Life*, 9-10. No one, I guess, of the aristocracy would have consulted him had he not been of the priestly class himself, memory or no memory! See last note.

248. Ac. 4:13. Si. 38:24.                                    249. Mt. 16:22.

250. Mt. 11:2-3; Targum on Is. 7:3 (cf. Hebrew text). Mt. 12:48-49, 23:15, 26:50 (special circumstances); Mk. 3:33-35; Jn. 13:33, 14:15.

251. Mk. 8:32.                      252. Mt. 10:24, 23:10 (cf. 8); Jn. 15:15.

253. Mk. 9:42; Mt. 28:7.                                    254. Mt. 14:28, 24:9.

responsible for his students' welfare,[255] and every hearer, however numerous these might be, was entitled to the teacher's consideration, exactly like a flock.[256] Inferior in prestige, the student group nevertheless formed a solid fraternity which was in turn responsible for the prestige and welfare of the whole, including of course their teacher. Their rabbi must be saved from disaster and they must try to look after him in a practical way, if he was too other-wordly,[257] just as he looked after them spiritually. And they would bury him if he had no sons to do that duty.[258] The idea of a student carrying his master's slippers and washing his feet was quite acceptable,[259] but not the other way round.[260] Amongst the students the senior in age and progress would want, and have, prestige over the others and would like to inherit his master's mantle.[261] For most of the students would return home and have the chance to become pillars of their little societies. A few would found schools of their own and carry on the tradition.

A student initiated by a teacher would remain always recognisable as that teacher's pupil; though differences between the students respectively of two students of the same teacher (i.e. their academic grandfather) could be rather ridiculous.[262] If the teacher demanded too much of the pupil they could fall out and the relationship broke.[263] But otherwise an utter adherence could be expected, creating a relationship which would last a lifetime. I can give an example from nineteenth-century Bengal which is relevant as it shows the mentality of the ancient East: the teacher, who taught absolute submission to the principle of love (it was a Vaishnava sect) required his students to swallow his sputum, and they did. In the Hebrew homeland, and in the dispersion, a similar attitude *mutatis mutandis* persisted, and has not utterly evaporated. If a student cared too much for his home and family he obviously did not 'belong', and would make indifferent progress.[264] The gifted pupil temporarily forsook all else to pick up what his teacher had to give.[265]

Preachers had no shame about trying their hearers' patience. Oriental audiences are late in assembling, but are prepared to listen

255. Lk. 19:39.  256. Mt. 14:19, 15:35.
257. Mt. 9:11, 26:35; Mk. 6:35–36.  258. Mt. 14:12, 27:59; Mk. 6:29.
259. Jn. 13:5–6, 8, 13; 1 Tm. 5:10.  260. See last note.
261. Mt. 23:8.  262. 1 Co. 3:4.  263. Jn. 6:61, 66.
264. Mt. 10:37; Mk. 10:29–30; Lk. 9:61.  265. Lk. 14:33

indefinitely. The rustic evangelist goes on and on until people drop off to sleep,[266] or until stenographers are worn right out.[267]

The situation is more easily understood if we realise that teaching was engrafting the pupils on to the master.[268] A metaphor used was of the vine; now we should use organ-transplant—appropriately, because something which is the least bit foreign will surely be rejected in the end. The teacher sometimes gave a new name to the pupil to signify his new condition, and to indicate his future life.[269] Those were not 'liberties'; the teacher was authorised to treat them like sons. They imitated him and reproduced his ideas and sayings word-perfect. There was no question of bringing out original thought or individuality on the student's part, no induction.[270] Teaching must bear fruit, but it was *sown*; one *plants* in the pupil, one does not develop the taught.[271] False scholars were 'weeds'.[272] Education was simply a matter of ensuring that traditional ideas, accumulated 'wisdom' were faithfully reproduced without addition or diminution.[273]

The test of successful teaching, no doubt, was perfection in practice, the student's carrying out to the letter what he had been taught.[274] But no student should aim to be better than his master, and not to outshine him was no disgrace.[275] Occasionally a pupil did outshine his teacher. The effect of this would be that teachings would be traced back eventually to the pupil, and his master's name would be forgotten. But at least he would owe almost every-thing to that master who guided his early steps and gave him the groundwork. Normally scholars quoted and cited their teachers and their teacher's teachers. To base one's teaching directly upon scripture was always possible but it sounded odd, impressive perhaps, but idiosyncratic.[276] One who gave a new tradition as well as an old one, was like a man who paid in coins of various reigns: all were

266. Ac. 20:9.          267. 2 Esd. 14:40–42.          268. Jn. 15:2, 4.
269. Mk. 3:17. In history overlords gave their vassals new names: 2 K. 23:34, 24:17; cf. 2 S. 12:24–25. Whence Is. 65:15?
270. Mt. 10:24. See n. 230, p. 144 above.
271. Mt. 13:2, 18; Jn. 15:8. Greeks shared the idea: Antiphon, the *Corpus Hermeticum* (I. 29), etc., cited by A. D. Nock, *Essays* (1972), I, 125 n. 311.
272. Mt. 15:13; or hard soil (Mk. 6:52).
273. Mk. 13:31; Jn. 9:27; Ga. 1:6–7; 2 Tm. 2:2. Rv. 22:18–19.
274. Mt. 19:11, 21.                                              275. Lk. 6:40.
276. Mk. 1:22; Mt. 7:28–29. On the whole subject see Birger Gerhardsson, *Memory and Manuscript* (Copenhagen, Lund, 1961). Jn. 7:18–19.

current.[277] A teacher who claimed only supernatural instruction as his 'authority' must have sounded odd indeed.[277a]

There was nothing to prevent a new school being formed by branching out from an older one,[278] provided the doctrines cohered reasonably well.[279] It was sad when a teacher was lured by government employment, whereupon both he and his students would be lost to independent scholarship in the pursuit of gain.[280]

A well-taught student who really believed what his master told him could go away and do, in his master's name, anything the master authorised him to do—if he failed it would simply mean that his education was not yet complete.[281]

It must have been very disagreeable for students who had learnt the nation's culture at great pains and expense, living rough perhaps, exposing themselves to public curiosity, and enduring their master's irony and sarcasm during their studies, to discover at a late stage that their master's name might be so badly besmirched that they themselves could become neither teachers, nor preachers,[282] nor judges (p. 57), nor healers, nor even synagogue-trustees, but they must go back and pick up, if they could, the threads of their family occupation (if their relatives would let them) and be productive once again. When the teacher was in bad odour followers might be ashamed to be seen coming to him in daylight.[283]

It would be helpful to have some notion of what their teachings were like. I give below two specimens of sermons in condensed form. They illustrated taste and technique as admired about a century after the Crucifixion and there is no reason whatever for doubting that they illustrate the general drift and method of accomplished Pharisaic teachers of the time of Jesus. They are taken from the Mishnah, tractate Avot, otherwise *Ethics of the Fathers*, which is available in several translations. They illustrate the threading together of scriptural texts, the far-fetched use of the latter, and the ultimate moral purpose.[283a]

277. Mt. 13:51–52. See below, p. 176.                    277a. Ga. 1:12.
278. Mt. 9:16–17; Ac. 9:25. Too noticeable a divergence could lead to a ban (a curse) on the deviant teacher: Ga. 1:8–9.
279. Mk. 2:21.                    280. Bab. Tal., Hag. 16*b* (*baraita*).
281. Mt. 17:16–20; Mk. 6:7, 30.        282. Mt. 4:23.        283. Jn. 3:2, 19:38.
283a. *Pirqe Avot* is to be found in Danby's *Mishnah* and Blackman's *Mishnayot* as well as the Soncino *Babylonian Talmud*, but the reader may well prefer C. Taylor, *Sayings of the Jewish Fathers* (2 vols.) which was reprinted in 1970.

III. 3. R. Simeon said, If three men have eaten at one table and have not spoken words of the Law there, it is as if they had eaten sacrifices of the dead (Ps. 106:28), for it is said (Is. 28:8), *For all tables are full of vomit and filthiness; God is not there.* But if three have eaten at one table and have spoken over it matters concerning the Law, it is as though they had eaten from the table of God, for it is said (Ezk. 41:22), *And he said to me, 'This is the table (as it were, the altar) that is before the Lord.'*

III. 15. R. Aqiba used to say, Beloved is *man* for he was created in the image (of God). Greater still was the love in that it was made known to him that he was created in that image, for it is said (Gn. 9:6), *For in the image of God made He man.* Beloved are Israel, for they were called children of God; but by a special love was it made known to them that they were called children of God, as it is said (Dt. 14:1), *You are children of the Lord your God.* Beloved are Israel, for to them was given the precious instrument; still greater was the love since it was made known to them that to them was given the precious instrument, for it is said (Prov. 4:2), *For I give you good doctrine; forsake not my Law.*

## §29. BELIEF AND ACTION

It seems hard to believe that a life filled with taboos and observances could be called imitative, childlike, unreflecting. Yet it must have been as much so for the generality as it was full of intriguing technical problems for the learned. The 'wise' thought too much, and sinned knowingly.[284] The 'simple' sinned, if at all, inadvertently (§30). Insight was not a personal achievement or attribute of the one who had it, but a gift from Yahweh.[285] I do not think there existed the notion taken for granted now, that action does not reveal the state of mind; action betrayed belief and what was not acted was thought not to be believed. Hence action tended to do duty for belief and the cry 'hypocrite!' (§26) was all too easy. With a sense of surprise a near contemporary writes how people cheat and commit adultery and also give in charity and fast. The result, he says, is 'evil'.[286] But a society believing in observances could hardly avoid

284. Mt. 11:25, 18:2–4, 12, 14. 1 Co. 1:26–29.
285. Mt. 16:17, Ga. 1:12, 16. One must heed Yahweh's warnings: Jos., *BJ*, vi. 288.
286. Test. Ash. 2:6–8.

that syndrome. To show that he was still a faithful Jew St. Paul paid out cash to enable some Nazarites to complete their vows in the Temple, and this payment struck intelligent people as conclusive proof of his loyalty to the religion.[287] Private religious belief was obviously as rare as privacy itself. Life was a collective experience, and behaviour, laboriously learnt, was a collective thing, in which there was little room for tolerance. If a man is converted so, automatically, is 'all his house' (§4). The possibility of dissent is ignored. All actions could be tested to see whether they were in keeping with the group beliefs. If they were not the individual was liable to be penalised as a matter of good order (p. 112). The result was that breakaway groups, sects, or communities attempted to establish standards for themselves. But this was not liberty: individualism gained nothing from it. The first church adhered to the Jewish view, and acts that would have been lawful for pagans could result in excommunication and eventual ostracism, with all the wretchedness that penalty entailed in a society that has no use for individuality, and had not discovered 'fundamental freedoms' (which would have been regarded as antisocial nonsense).

Granted that a man's actions *were* in keeping with the group beliefs, the overt justification for them would, in the jargon of the rabbis, ultimately be the *halakah*, 'the right way', the Law. One walks in the paths trodden by predecessors, like sheep. But if a teacher were asked whether an individual should take one of two possible courses he would reply, 'Let all your works be for the sake of Heaven', i.e. all acts are to be tested in terms of the actor's personal rectitude, *not* from the point of view of the effects, political and otherwise, upon the other parties to the action as such. This is typically Asian and the New Testament is instinct with this fundamental notion. This is not quite the same as 'individual morality' as we understand those words. It was a question of the individual's *duty* being *performed*, which duty, duly performed, gives him a satisfaction to which supernatural and superstitious explanations are attached. The reason for action was not that the act was reasonable and profitable, but that the act will be morally healthy (meritorious in terms of the unseen world) if he does it, and he loses if he does not.[288] One must not cause others to stumble, not so much because one feels for them, but because causing others to stumble is a sin for him who causes this; causing or allowing others to break a

287. Ac. 21:23–26, 24:18.            288. Mt. 18:8–9.

commandment is itself a breach of a commandment.[289] The restriction is not applied in their interests, but one's own! One is kind to pagans not because they need it, but so that they may glorify Yahweh.[290] One gives what one can afford in charity not in order that the poor may eat (though the festival of Purim provides an occasion where the opposite view dominates) but in order to build up a bank balance of unfulfilled reciprocity on the part of Yahweh, the poor's protector (§4), an unstealable treasury of merit.[291] It is for this reason that the curses of the poor are to be feared.[292] One stones a blasphemer, a false prophet, or 'seducer of the people', a presumptuous despiser of the sentence of the priests, not because one hates him or is bloodthirsty or has any particular opinion of his opinions or programme (if any), but in order to fulfil the commandment to put away the evil from among Israel (Dt. 13:5, 10, 17:5-7, 21:21).

If a man found himself without a belief, or trust (which would ordinarily occur only when the person in question did not belong to his group), he diagnosed his own condition as a weakness or illness: he did not ask to be convinced, but to be cured.[293] Faith based on conviction was much less acceptable culturally than faith based on external influence and emotional attachment.[294] Naturally: solidarity would otherwise be jeopardised. A faith based on conviction can be argued away. A faith based on a relationship between the seen and unseen worlds gives exceptional fortitude, unusual strength and endurance, which is much appreciated by a community needing 'faithful' champions.

By performing commands one obtained 'eternal life',[295] i.e. one earnt one's share in the world to come, if one accepted the doctrine of which Pharisees made much, namely that the promises of Yahweh were not to be exhausted in earthly individual life. A belief in an existence after the termination of individual life was found amongst Asian nations other than the Hebrews, and, needless to say, in Egypt. There can be little doubt that vague beliefs of this character were part of popular Judaism which Pharisees adopted and

289. Mt. 17:27; Test. Gad 6:4. Bab. Tal., Shev. 31*a*, 47*b*. Pal. Targ., Ex. 20. *LNT*, 255-7, 380.
290. 1 Tm. 6:1; 1 P. 2:12.
291. Mt. 6:19-20, 26:11; 2 Esd. 7:77, 8:33; Tb. 4:8-9, 11; Si. 29:11-12, 34:20 (24); Sec. En. 44:5, 50:5, 51:2. 2 Bar. 14:12.
292. Si. 4:6; Sec. En. 46:1.          293. Mk. 9:24.          294. 2 Esd. 1:37.
295. Mk. 8:35, 10:17; Ps. Sol. 9:9. Jos., *BJ*, i. 650, 653.

utilised, and that it was the Sadducees who were the sceptics here and the deviants. Yahweh requites, the rest thought, and repays all a just man's sacrifice, and sacrifices.[296]

Many meritorious acts redounded to the financial advantage of the doer (e.g. giving 'full measure' brings extra customers), because piety and honesty (which are not the same thing, but are often associated in Asian business circles) made for good business in a country where law was unpredictable and judges possibly corrupt. But this, significant as it surely is, is not a sufficient explanation for the Hebrew attitude.[297] For the Jew's abstaining from intercourse when his wife thinks she has begun to menstruate cannot be said to bring him the slightest secular advantage, nor his refusal to do secular work by the light of the Hanukah lamp.[298] It is clear that subservience to the will of Yahweh, i.e. to standards projected out of the inherited social experience of the Hebrews, was the conscious motive which they attempted to keep uppermost; and their eagerness to hear teachers who taught what was Yahweh's will is clear evidence for this. Therefore no teacher would proclaim or enjoin any particular programme as being expedient, socially desirable, or profitable. If he foretold disaster it would be Yahweh's wrath, not the logical outcome of unreasonable politics. If he urged his followers to fight it would be because Yahweh was to be with them. He would teach only the will of Yahweh and let Yahweh by all means see to it that his teachings were profitable. If they were not, one could only cry with the psalmist that there are no praises for Yahweh from the grave (Ps. 6:5, 88:9-12)!

## §30. SINS AND ATONEMENT

The ancient, especially oriental, civilizations regarded misdeeds as affecting the individual like a disability, which could be cured by treatment. To find the treatment one went to an expert who 'prescribed' the penance. The point of doing this was that unexpiated sins affected one's (and consequently one's group's) success in this life. The rains failed or one's cattle cast their young untimely. Alternatively one, or one's group (in spite of Ezekiel's propositions on the subject), would pay before the last Judge for all misdeeds for which one had not made adequate reparation in this life, or for which divine punishment had not befallen one in this life. Occult ill brought occult punishment, and secret sins were especially likely

296. Si. 35:11 (13). See last note.    297. *LNT*, xliv.    298. *LNT*, 198-9.

to find one out. Sins committed in ignorance were venial, but sins none the less.[299] Sins committed in inadvertence were in a different category from sins committed deliberately.[300] All had to be expiated.[301] Fortunately it was usually agreed that a civil penalty of an extreme character operated also as a penance (it could hardly be otherwise). But where the civil penalty for a crime was a flogging the criminal might have to make restitution to the injured party *and* bring a sin-offering to reconcile himself with Yahweh.

Sins against Yahweh (like marrying a woman and her mother, where the relationship between the two was unknown, say, even to them, as could happen in that troubled world) could only be expiated by an offering to him. Thus if a Sanhedrin arrived, in good faith, at a judgment which turned out, on further consideration, to be wrong, they must collectively expiate this by a collective offering in the Temple.[302] The Law went into considerable detail to distinguish between sins against a positive commandment and sins against a negative commandment, but all that concerns us now is the fussiness and scrupulosity with which the whole was developed. The Hebrews were highly conscious of sin. Well they might be, with an intensely duty-orientated culture, heavily patriarchal socially and with a view of Yahweh which assimilated him to an ideal father or king.[303] Unrepented misdeeds[304] would be 'visited', sooner or later, and no one supposed sins would not find him out. Repeated sin would mean a relapse, not psychologically, as I think I have explained, but in terms of Yahweh's dissatisfaction with the sinner.

This would normally be expected to lead to frequent cases of neurosis. Irrational superstitious opinions trickle over into paranoia and it is certain that Asian cultures tolerate, i.e. fail to diagnose, or even recognise, paranoid symptoms far more widely than we do. It is clear that neurotic and paranoid cases existed extensively in the Palestine of Jesus's time. What is curious is that we know for certain that Asian, developing, and illiterate, and, still more, primitive cultures have an agreeable feature in contrast with our own, namely the warmth of affection between relatives and friends, the deep and irremovable sense of belonging and sharing, which ties Asians

299. Jn. 9:41; 15:22, 24. Mercy was to be expected: 1 Tm. 1:13.
300. 1 QS VIII. 30–IX. 6.
301. Ac. 3:17, 19. Philo, *Spec. Leg.* i. 238 (ed. Colson, vol. 7, 238).
302. Mishnah, tractate Horayot. Cf. Mt. 27:4.
303. Mt. 12:31–32.                                                304. Mk. 6:12.

firmly together no matter what their changes of fortune and domicile. This does a great deal to protect them from anxiety conditions, and secures them against the evil effects of their insouciance (§17) which, until recently, would certainly spell ruin for members of our (passing) achievement-orientated culture with its competitive and individualistic ethos. The ancient, developing, cultures have a very good record of mental health, and minimal suicide rates. Thus the high incidence of acute mental ill-health in Jesus's time is much less likely to have been due to family-tension, or acute poverty, than unbridled religiosity and sin-fantasies. This links up with the widespread belief that the conditions evidenced the presence of evil spirits, and that the latter could be evicted by a sufficiently strong spirit-worker. There is no doubt but that psychic cures were effected, and this might have been assisted greatly if the original cause of the trouble had been in the department of religion, as it were.

Yet, whether or not this is justified, the Hebrew religion as generally understood made adequate provision to avoid neurotic developments. Our modern theologians, who tend to dwell sometimes on the sin-concept (because it no longer exists in our culture), do not always appreciate how the safety-valves worked, and it is clear they did work well. The voluntary sin-offering system enabled a man who could afford it (or had any associate to do it for him) to put himself straight with Yahweh. Granted that the Temple hierarchy may have charged inflated rates for animals and birds guaranteed free from ritual defect, the cost was not exorbitant. The system was a working one.[305] But it meant that sin had a tariff. Alternatively, ridding oneself of property (I do not mean by throwing it into the Dead Sea) for the benefit of the poor, etc., was thought to 'wash away' sin.[306] This fits the notion that sin can be viewed as a debt to Yahweh.[307] Yahweh is creditor and requires payment to himself or to his dependants. The pecuniary loss in favour of Yahweh or the poor proved the sincerity of the repentance, of remorse for the breach of *halakah*: but this is a modern rationalisation of the concept, and I am not sure whether it was explained in those terms in Jesus's time. For example, if it *were* the explanation (and I have voiced my doubt) one wonders how they came to take

305. Mt. 5:23–24. Sec. En. 59:1–2. The priests were Yahweh's agents: Mk. 2:10.
306. Tb. 12:9; Si. 3:30.     307. Mt. 6:12, 18:23–35; Lk. 11:4, 13:4.

it for granted that a friend's payment for an offering would do just as well, and the unseen consequences of sin would be lifted (as where a friend pays a man's fine and gets him out of gaol in our own day)?[308] No doubt payment is payment—and solidarity is solidarity, and that is that.

An unsatisfactory aspect of the sacrificial system was that sacrifices as atonement for sins and sacrifices in performance of vows tended to get confused in the public mind and the Temple, instead of being a source of spiritual instruction and inspiration, could become a place where one 'kept oneself on the right side' of Yahweh, without bothering to know the moral quality of one's actions—a state of affairs asking for jibes.[308a]

Then there was the Day of Atonement. True, on the Eve of that day the Hebrews went through a complete catalogue of sins and expressed their abhorrence of all of them and remorse for having committed them, collectively, in the previous year. The forgiveness of fellow Jews is asked for, and reparation tendered. Assuming that all is square in that quarter Yahweh forgives Israel through the actions of atonement done by the High Priest, who atones for himself and all Israel on that Day,[309] and also through the ceremony of the scapegoat. Every year saw each Jew capable of starting with a clean sheet, even when he had neglected to bring his sin-offering(s). The fact that Yahweh had not yet redeemed Israel from the foreign yoke was proof that the Atonement procedure had not been fully effective: but in such occult matters who could say for certain what the position was?

The concept of vicarious suffering existed in the whole idea of animal sacrifices, and, of course, in the scapegoat. We have already made the acquaintance of individual penance in connection with the ascetic and asceticism (§27).[310] The blood of the animals slaughtered as sin-offerings could be advantageous to the penitent: it was *as if* he offered himself. The revolting aspects of this ancient nonsense should not blind us to the universal belief in those days that life was owed to Yahweh, the Creator, and that it was the highest recognition of him to offer it. The fact that the animal was blameless made its blood more valuable. Through the animals' blood super-sensory situations were created. In a similar way people could take

308. 2 M. 3:36.                                    308a. Qo. 4:17 (= 5:1).
309. 1 Esd. 4:40. Mishnah, tractate Yoma.
310. Test. Reub. 1:10; Ps. Sol. 3:9 (8).

on the blood of an innocent person unlawfully slaughtered: 'his blood be on me'.[311]

The idea that the High Priest atones for Israel was paralleled by a similar notion, that wretchedness atones. Wretchedness, poverty, suffering (however induced) diminish the evil balance of sin, by, as it were, draining off Yahweh's wrath, drawing attention to the partial failure of his promises to give life and plenty to the sufferer.[312] All the blind, halt, and lame are, as it were, Yahweh's creditors and all will be made up to them in the next life.[313] Hence it is an atonement to suffer, especially to die before one's time, still more to be put to death unjustly, no matter by whom.[314] Vicarious suffering[315] could be utilised if one deliberately offered one's unmerited sufferings to release one's comrades from supernatural retribution.[316] This far-fetched belief, based on tribal loyalty and hoary superstition, was part of the mental furniture of the Hebrews. As if it were true, services could conceivably be rendered to the nation, of which it could take advantage. Would they not thereby pass under an obligation to their redeemer? If acceptance followed upon knowledge of the sacrifice of course the result was subjectively real.[317]

Baptism for the remission of sins was an interesting invention.[318] Without actually paying for a sin-offering, one showed one's contrition by a humiliating public ceremony and arose immediately from the water a proselyte, as it were, to a new life,[319] as if those sins had been a ritual pollution from which one were ridding oneself. Naturally one was bound in loyalty to the master who initiated one in this form.

## §31. THE MESSIANIC HOPE

The pessimism produced by centuries of oppression and unpredictable suffering confirmed the Hebrews in the view that the world would end,[320] and the Gentiles be punished, in a cataclysm, which would contain some elements common to many varied and partly inconsistent theories. A representative of Israel, representative also

---

311. Mt. 27:25. *LNT*, 430.   312. Mt. 5:3–12, 19:27; Sec. En. 66:6.
313. Midrash Rabbah, Genesis, XX. 5.   314. Ws. 3:3.
315. 1 QS VIII. 1–19.   316. Mt. 27:23; Jn. 11:50; 4 M. 5:29, 17:21–22.
317. *LNT*, 450.   318. Mt. 3:6; Mk. 1:4–5; Lk. 3:16.
319. Mk. 1:10. See Josephus cited at p. 132, n. 155 above. D. Daube, *Sudden in the Scriptures* (Leiden, 1964), 46–61.
320. Mt. 5:18. Time would be fulfilled (as in a full-term pregnancy): Mk. 1:15; 2 Esd. 7:30.

of Yahweh, whose pre-existence of the world itself[321] vouched for his certainty and eternity, would come,[322] at the End of the Age. Atonement for sins would be at an end, the account books in Heaven would be closed.[323] The chastisement of all sinners, pagan and Hebrew, would follow, and for that purpose a general resurrection would take place.[324] Resurrection was not unthinkable prior to that imagined date,[325] but the general bodily reappearance of the dead, the good to go to eternal bliss,[326] and the bad to eternal punishment[327] along with Satan and his demons,[328] was reserved as a sign of the End.[329] The coming of the End was to be portended by great omens, in which nature would begin to behave as never since the fall of Adam.[330] Even eunuchs would have 'posterity' (Is. 56:3-5).[331] Cataclysmic atmospheric and terrestrial changes[332] would follow upon a period of unexampled lawlessness and wickedness. False prophets would take advantage of this.[333] The sorrows at their height, the Messiah, or possibly two Messiahs, 'anointed' ones, would appear, to reign for ever.[334] Before his or their coming there would be a period of chaos,[335] a war[336] against the powers of darkness by the powers of good,[337] in which the latter would be victorious, while Elijah would appear again and put all to rights.[338]

At the Messianic banquet to celebrate the conclusion of the Holy

321. Jn. 8:59, 10:31–33.
322. 2 Esd. 7:28, 2 Bar. 30:1. The Mount of Olives was somehow associated with this coming: Mt. 26:30. See p. 79, n. 30 above.
323. Mt. 12:32, 25:1–13.
324. Lk. 20:35; Jn. 5:29; Ac. 24:15; 2 Esd. 1:16, 23, 31. A rebirth, or recreation: Mt. 19:28–29.
325. Mt. 27:52, 62, 66; Mk. 6:14–17, 9:26–27; Jn. 12:11 (did not preclude second natural death). Si. 48:4–5, 13–14.
326. Lk. 23:43; 2 Esd. 1:18–19, 8:52.
327. Mt. 5:22, 13:42, 18:8–9, 23–35; Lk. 16:26.
328. Mt. 8:29, 25:41, 46.                    329. See p. 340, n. 159 below.
330. Mt. 21:19–22; Mk. 4:38–39, 11:13, 21–23, 16:17–18; 1 En. 10:19; cf. Is. 32:15, Am. 9:13ff.
331. Jos., Ant. xvii. 45.
332. Mt. 24:16–18 (Ezk. 7:15), 37, 28:2; Mk. 13:2.
333. Mt. 24:11, 24; Mk. 13:5–6, 20–23.
334. Mt. 16:28; Lk. 21:36; Ac. 3:20. The Dead Sea sect believed there would be two Messiahs.
335. Mk. 13:8; Lk. 17:30.
336. Mt. 16:18–26; Ps. Sol. 17:23–27, 32; Si. 29:13. The War Scroll of the Dead Sea scriptures is devoted to this topic.
337. Tb. 8:3.                    338. Mt. 27:47; Mk. 6:14–17, 15:35; Lk. 1:17.

War all the righteous would feast, along with the patriarchs and others of the righteous of history who went to Heaven alive,[339] and and participate in the unseen process of Yahweh's ruling of the world. At the coming of the Messiah all the sins committed since Cain killed Abel would be avenged, a universal judgment would take place,[340] and the bliss of the remnant, or chosen,[341] who achieve a place at the banquet would be endless.

Perhaps even this is too specific. So many notions existed. It was a topic on which scholars and astrologers could hardly be precise, and they were chided for wasting their time on such speculations.[342] The time of Jesus was one in which considerable controversy went on regarding the Law and its meaning together with great interest in what would emerge at the End of Days.[343] Nationalistic fervour gave fuel both to political extremism and quietist piety—both being equally 'authentic' interpretations of Yahweh's will on the subject. The Messiah, son of Joseph, and son of David,[344] was hardly an identifiable person, but an abstraction,[345] a dream and a hope, an *as-if* figure if ever there was one. Their certainty that he (or they) would come was equalled by an incredulity that he would come *now*.

To propose to a Hebrew that the Messianic Age had started, the Messiah was already here, retelling the Law of Moses and healing all the ills of Israel, was to draw upon the faith of the hearer not perhaps more than he could wish, but almost certainly more than he could bear. Anticipation has its own function and to bring it abruptly to a close is to risk an unfavourable reception, if not blank denial: let what is to come remain in the future!

339. Enoch: Si. 44:16, 49:14; Sec. En. 67:1–2; Jos., *Ant.* i. 85; Philo, *Q.Gen.* i. 86; Heb. 11:5; 2 Esd. 6:26, 8:19 (Ezra). Not David: Ac. 2:29, 34.
340. Mt. 10:15, 11:22, 24; 2 Esd. 7:34ff.; Ws. 3:8; Si. 35:12 (15); 1 En. 53:5, 54:2, 63:1, 12; 2 Bar. 40:1, 72:1–6.
341. Mt. 24:22, 31; Mk. 13:24–27; Lk. 17:30, 23:35 (solidarity!); Mt. 13:13.
342. This is what is meant, I suppose, at 1 Tm. 1:4, 4:7; 2 Tm. 2:23.
343. Mk. 12:35–37.          344. Mt. 12:23; Ps. Sol. 17:46 (41).
345. Mt. 22:42; Mk. 12:35; Jn. 7:27.

# Conclusion

I have in mind my youthful reader (p. 16 above) and there are the growing number of more or less serious students of theology. Any of these when they reach this point will be likely to ask, 'Well, what do you expect us to make of this? What are you asking us to do? Granted that we now know more about Jesus's and his audience's background, and, with the aid of your bibliographical note, can put ourselves in the position to know a great deal more, so (if we may be blunt) what?'

Teachers and students of theology, and past students of theology will already have had differing degrees of confidence that they knew about Jesus's world. History, after all, formed part of their syllabus, and New Testament Histories exist in reasonable numbers, though they fell greatly out of favour when the form-critics got to work. The sociology and anthropology of the Hebrews was always *just round the corner*; it was something one almost did, but not quite. The apostles were (when they were not on spoons) figures in stained-glass windows, and not altogether unlike the prestige-figures of our undergraduate world.[1] Teachers and students of theology will have been puzzled by my references. I have explained that they are an almost random selection: this is not only because my lectures were not referenced, and I wanted a short, inexpensive publication, but because, instead of using my work as a comment on the New

---

1. R. Morton Smith puts the point well at *East and West* (Rome), N.S., vol. 20, no. 3 (Sept. 1970), p. 363: 'When one begins teaching in North America one soon realizes (what is becoming true in Europe) that however alienated the average student is from the European tradition, he cannot easily conceive that any people could have a mentality different from his own, even if he easily admits the academic possibility and believes in the relativity of (other people's) values. Many scholars are no less guilty, and interpret the past in terms of the conscious emancipated cynicism of modern materialism . . .'

Testament and Apocrypha, I have used those books as illustrative comments on my reconstruction of Jesus's world. The text comments on the book, not the book on it. And, if my readers have looked up those references, they will have found that in the process I have indicated how those passages are to be taken, often in unexpected ways. But the reader must be assured that I do not deny, or impugn, any other ways of taking those passages: this is not the place to do that, and even if it were it has already been pointed out that the New Testament world regarded all inspired literature, as it were, like a row of onions, to be peeled indefinitely as long as you could see to do the job. You never got to the core.

Granted that my little reconstruction is best illustrated from our New Testament and Apocrypha, my learned friends will ask why I have made such sketchy and fitful use of the Old Testament. 'On your own showing', they will say, 'the Old Testament figured intimately in New Testament times, if sometimes rather crudely and childishly, as the skeleton of all research, and of moral, social, and legal thinking. Why do you not make more of it here? Anthropologists are indeed "this minute" men, and eschew cultural continuity, but surely the sociologist is vitally concerned with what the people think of their society in time; their sense of continuity, and their reliance upon tradition are an essential feature, and particularly (on your own showing) in the case of this culture.' True, but this is where I say the new student of the New Testament must make a conscious distinction. Old Testament stories and the *midrashic* handling of the Law (one should read the Palestinian Targum rather than the Hebrew original) are, indeed, essential 'background' for the student of the parables. But I am concerned with the mental furniture of the audience of Jesus and the apostles. I can no more document that from the Old Testament than a man can describe the civilization of Victorian England with the aid of citations from Shakespeare and the Authorised Version of the bible, on the ground that these were definitely in the centre of the cultural *pabulum* of all literate people during the greater part of Victoria's reign.

My second class of reader joins, at this point, my first. The latter, as I imagine him, has feared that the Jesus-story was ill-told in the Sunday school, in the primary school, and in 'living religions' classes in the secondary school. He has all along had a sneaking sensation of not being up to hearing what Jesus had to say, and he has felt that the noisy 'humanists', and wordy apologists for Christianity have both lost their way, far from the shores of the Sea of Galilee. Holy credulity does not inspire him, and antipathy to Christianity is, he senses, due far more often to a sense of guilt and inadequacy, a fear of facing 'that man pinned up on the gibbet', than to bad teaching, unimaginative handling, out-of-date translations, churchy snobbery, and other unattractive aspects of the quest for the real Jesus.

If I have done my job well he will not waste time asking further questions but will get out his New English Bible, or Jerusalem Bible, or any other modern version handy to him, and go (not too rapidly, I hope) through the gospels, which should be much more real as a result of my 'introduction'. But then he will put them down, and say 'What now?' I do *not* want him to set out on a one-man heresy; nor do I ask him to go around churches to see whether any preacher teaches something which fits in with a historical approach. I am a teacher and I want him to be exposed to Jesus's teaching, to use good reference books to dispel quandaries, or place difficult passages in the proper perspective (remembering that there are some which many have tried to solve in vain), and let the texts speak themselves. I have applied, as it were, a syringe to my reader's ears; perhaps more treatment is needed; let him use my bibliographical note and other bibliographies libraries can supply, and his hearing can be sharpened, so that there is no difference in hearing-ability between him and the rag-taggle crowd that sat and listened to Jesus in the court of the Temple and elsewhere. It is up to Jesus's words to have what effect they may. That is his affair.

The pious are a problem. Religion is a kind of emotional lavage, a personal indulgence, which they keep free from intellectual invasion. I have a professional associate who is a Fellow of the British Academy and is regarded (and paid) as one of our great scholars. I was trying to explain to him my discoveries relative to the parable of the Wicked Vinedressers.[2] He listened fairly patiently and then said, 'I *do* wish you had not told me that. I would *much* rather not know. If you don't mind, I shall go on believing as I always did.' Now subjectively, his views, his beliefs, have supported him through personal danger, and are real, of more value to him than any amount of money. But error is a source of weakness for him and for any whom he himself teaches. Now I am not saying

2. *LNT*, ch. 13.

that what I was telling him was the final truth. There is no signed commentary on the parable, authenticating any interpretation of it, 'I, Jesus of Nazareth, meant so and so'. I may well be wrong. But so may he. An open mind is essential, and even a Fellow of the British Academy has something to learn from tackling the 'as if' concept. His own beliefs are *as if* true for him; but that does not mean that the factual information on which they are based cannot be greatly improved. The *as if* is not destroyed thereby. It is strengthened. The heart does so much better if the head agrees.

No, I want neither the intellectual nor the man in the street to become first-century Jews. One must sympathise with them while one finds their ideas repugnant. One must be adaptable, like the good German-speaker who puts his heels together and bows when he shakes an older person by the hand, though he would never even dream of doing so when he is introduced to a fellow Englishman. The Englishman has actually to learn to take a lady's hand and kiss it, in some continental environments; and the continental lady, even in her own home, has to learn not to offer her hand palm downwards to an Englishman who is not a real 'linguist', in the sense in which I use that word. These trifling examples show what I mean.

How is my reader getting on with his cultural education? I suppose he knows now that when Jesus is depicted as feeding Judas like a child he is to be visualised as doing so with the right hand? When you imagine yourself eating out of the same pot with the Twelve, it is your right hand you put in. If you put the left hand in, the pot would at once be taken out and thrown on the dung-heap. They would know you were quite mad, and your future would be a matter of long and anxious discussion. When you want to part from them (we will forget about any absurd indiscretion) you do not say cheerfully, 'Well, I'll be off now!' You touch their feet in the order of seniority and stand quietly waiting for the senior member of the group to permit you to leave.

Jesus referred to sacrifices and altars: what did he mean by that? He spoke of alms and of love: did he mean by them what we mean? He spoke of 'Caesar': was 'Caesar' another word for the State, and if so what kind of State? 'Love thy neighbour': what did his audience understand by 'neighbour'? 'The Son of Man came not to be ministered unto but to minister, and to give his life as a ransom for many.' What does that mean in terms of doing something for someone? Listen to his words with the ears his Hebrew hearers

had, and the effect can safely be left to the speaker. A brain trained
to receive them will hardly fail to respond.

But in this respect we and they are not different. The heart and
the head (poor team-mates) are still there, the average weight of the
brain is the same, and the heart often holds the brain back. The
arrow may reach the centre of the bull . . . and yet fall out. There
are factors which defy the process of communication, just as there
are bodies that will not respond to certain medical treatments which,
on purely chemical grounds, were calculated to work without fail.
It is just as well that I am no preacher, and not personally concerned
about the success of the gospel. . . .

. . . As it is written in the book of the prophet Isaiah (6:9–10;
Mk. 4:12): 'Hear ye indeed, but understand not; and see ye
indeed, but perceive not. Make the hearts of this people fat, and
make their ears heavy, and shut their eyes; lest they see with
their eyes, and hear with their ears, *and* understand with their
hearts, and turn again, and be healed.'

# Cultural Ignorance: St. Paul's Boast of Disinterestedness

When I sweated and suffered in the East as a young man I never thought that my experiences would be of use to anyone. It never occurred to me that the intimate knowledge I obtained of life and manners there could provide an essential clue to many a biblical episode, nor that by imbibing Asian notions of prestige, so opposed to ours, I could see into the mind of St. Paul in a way hidden from Western readers of the apostle. But to an Asian, with his preconceptions of destiny (p. 117), this would not seem strange: odd only that when I sat cross-legged wagging my head sideways in (real or pretended) agreement with some wiseacre 'telling me what' I did not realise that it was not all in vain.

One lesson I learnt which I still believe, though it is inconsistent with Western ways of thought: prestige is upheld by giving much and taking little, and he who takes least is the most prestige-worthy. If many come to my house and none invite me to theirs (or invite me only as a matter of form) I am superior to them, and the greater their status, and the more frequently they come, the more gratification I receive from the fact. The European who is never invited, and to whom no offers of hospitality or the like are made, feels despised, and shrinks under this contemptuous treatment. The Asian is proud of not receiving anything. One holy man I consulted once took this to such lengths that the only thing that could be offered to him was camphor, which was not put into his hands, or at his feet, but burnt in a lampstand in the centre of the little hut he lived in. He was, by the way, a clairvoyant, and made some very remarkable 'pronouncements', some of which have come true in an astonishing way—but that is taken quite for granted in the East.

St. Paul's words in self-commendation at 1 Co. 9:16–18 have not been understood, and are incorrectly rendered in all our translations.[1] The passage is seldom discussed, and the most recent critical treatment to come to my notice is not based on Asian experience.[2] There is no point in my reprinting any old translation, since it will simply mislead readers. They may consult the bibles lying to their hands and compare the text with a much more nearly correct attempt I offer below.

At this point an acquaintance of mine, who is a believing Christian, made the following comment: 'Does it really matter whether you improve, marginally, our understanding of 1 Co. 9:16–18? Your point, I gather, is that there is a great deal which the specialists have still to learn, and you are favouring them with specimens. That's as may be. But, while I admit there is much we do not know, I am not at all sure that I care about the "pedantry" with which you are supplying us. We do not know when the Lord Jesus will come again in glory. We do not know what are the delights of Heaven or who will share them. We do not know what are the pains of Hell and who will endure them, or how. But what we do know, namely that we are saved by faith in the Redeemer, is enough for me, at any rate. The bible is full of incomprehensible things, and always has been. We struggle along, and the many and various conjectural explanations which the learned have furnished for us were not, and still are not, insufficient for me. Even the New English Bible's translation of St. Paul's epistles has its obscurities, but I have never been in haste to clear them up. What I know is sufficient for me, and what I don't can, as far as I am concerned, wait until the End of Days, when all truth will be revealed. Your own preference is evidently for the rabbinically minded St. Matthew, while, my early training being what it was, I confess a partiality for the Hellenic St. Luke. If you insist on taking us through a lot of 'rabbinifications' I really shall have to excuse myself, for I have other things to do. Moreover, St.

---

1. I find some points of contact with R. F. Weymouth's version. The least satisfactory is H. J. Schonfield's *Authentic New Testament* (1956, 1962) at this place.

2. G. Didier, 'Le Salaire du désintéressement (1 Cor. ix. 14–27)', *Recherches de science religieuse* 43 (1955), 228–51. A Western-rational explanation of 1 Co. 9:1–23 is provided even by D. Daube (at *Jesus and Man's Hope*, cited below, at vol. 2, 231), in spite of the fact that the vocabulary has been most illuminatingly handled in his *New Testament and Rabbinic Judaism* (also cited below), chapters 11–12.

Paul himself (if you care to look up 1 Tm. 1:4 and 6:20) warned would-be scholars not to get involved in academicism. "Avoid empty chatter and contradictions of what is called 'knowledge', for by profession of this some have missed the mark as regards the faith." Quite so! I'm afraid your delvings into rabbinical parallels and that kind of thing (fun as it obviously is for you) might lead the uninstructed into supposing that intellectual investigation of the mentality of the first century could be a substitute for faith in the Lord Jesus.'

Whew! I do see his point. 'St. Paul', however, ordered Timothy to be very particular about having the scriptures read (i.e. sung) to the church (1 Tm. 4:13). It was not his intention (so far as I can make out) that the church should not understand what was read. St. Paul's letters are intended to be read and pondered upon. There is no advantage in ignorance of the meaning—for this breeds imaginary applications, which are not only unintellectual, but, much more serious, delusions. We may err in our reconstructions, but a worse error is not to attempt to reconstruct. I quite agree that when the microscope is brought to bear on the text, and it comes into focus, the image with which we are presented is a filigree image—it is not the plain simplicity of the act of communication normally held between specimens of a young civilisation like our own. But filigree or not, it was real then: and real it must be for young people; and especially to those to whom the question is presented, 'Would you like to be recruited by a lad like young Timothy, to be a student of Jesus, to be, in fact "his faithful soldier", to "fight gallantly" in his company? That was the alternative he offered to service of the Prince of this World (which, until we are baptised, is the service we are born in).' So I shall get on with the use of my microscope, even if the result is a filigree one, 'rabbinifications' or no 'rabbinifications'.

To begin, then, at the beginning, there were in St. Paul's time two kinds of workers, free and slaves. Free workers worked for hire, after bargaining for that hire. It was their 'reward'. A highly commercial-minded nation (subject, as I have constantly repeated, to the overriding concept of solidarity) naturally used the metaphor of 'reward' to explain the motive for taboos and observances of an unseen character. Gifts to the poor produce 'heavenly rewards' (p. 152). Slaves, on the other hand, did not work for reward. Moses, you will remember, was a free man; he worked as Yahweh's emissary in expectation of a 'reward' (not merely compensation).[3] Slaves' owners, on the contrary, had already invested in them, and their labour was interest on capital. They looked to their owners to feed them and look after them, on the basis that if they did not their capital would waste away. Slaves worked under compulsion; and since they might often be negligent they could be (and often were) promised the enjoyment of a proportion of the returns on their labour. A slave could be appointed a trustee at Roman law (and also conceivably at Jewish law), and might prudently be promised and awarded by a testator or settlor of the estate to which he belonged a proportion of the income, a commission on the profits. Biblical law required even a slave to be given a parting present on his liberation.[4] The spiritual interpretation of this would be that even Yahweh's slaves could expect an ultimate 'reward' from Yahweh: but as a matter of grace, of course, not right.

Simon the Just (about 200 B.C.) showed how seriously this idea was taken. He said (so tradition assures us: Mishnah, Avot I.3), 'Be not like servants that serve the master for the sake of a reward, but be like servants that serve their master without stipulating for any reward; and let the fear of Heaven be upon you.' Even this impressive notion did not entirely satisfy the pious, some of whom read the text of the Mishnah with an ingenious variant. This would have him say, 'but be like servants that serve their master on condition of *not* receiving a reward'.[4a] The double meaning would be attractive: serving without hope of reward they prove their loyalty and entire dependence upon their Master; and, not receiving a reward *now*, they can be sure to enjoy it *hereafter* (so ibid., II.16)!

The people who entertained itinerant evangelists were naturally obliged to provide for their livelihood (not more). Workers in the vineyard might eat the grapes; the ox that threshes the corn should not be muzzled. The evangelist who worked amongst people living at subsistence level (as often in Palestine) could never confer a benefit exceeding the value of his keep. His prestige relative to his hearers would therefore be at par. It would have been quite different if he had worked for bare subsistence amongst rich people. St. Paul, characteristically sensitive on prestige matters (as all respectable people were in those days), wants to extricate himself from that dilemma. He works for his living, though he knew that reason, and

3. Heb. 11.26.                                    4. Dt. 15:12–18.
4a. See *Jewish Quart. Rev.* vol. 61 (1970), 1–2.

Jesus's own statement on the subject, entitled him to do otherwise. Fortunately his working did not interfere with his mission (did he sometimes weave and talk at the same time?), or the idea would not have worked. Thus he does not 'live by the gospel', but lives by working with his hands. His preaching is a benefit conferred *gratis* on his hearers, and his prestige (which he virtually admits is worth more to him than his life) is high: he defies anyone to deprive him of it (9:15).

How did this come about? With characteristic Jewish fussiness he analysed his position. If he had a free choice whether or not to be a preacher he would have qualified, as a free labourer, for a hire, and that, under the system Jesus had approved, amounted to living at the expense of the community he served for the time being. Now since the word 'reward', 'hire' (they are interchangeable translations of Greek *misthos* = Hebrew *sakhar*) can be used for spiritual reward, there was a splendid opportunity for a pun. Assuming that St. Paul saw himself as a slave of Jesus, as he says in so many words elsewhere,[5] he realised he could turn his imaginary slavery to good metaphorical use. One who works for Yahweh, producing a transcendental harvest, can expect a spiritual reward: indeed he earns in that sense as soon as he starts work.[6] A slave cannot expect a 'reward',[7] but he can expect a commission if he performs faithfully a trust entrusted to him. Faithfulness includes abstaining from peculation in his handling of the funds. Paul pretends that he had the option whether he would figure in the guise of a hired labourer (as he implies his fellow apostles are) or in the guise of a slave. He opts for the latter, because by that means his commission is the prestige he gains in *not* requiring his hearers to pay his expenses. This is his 'reward', a notional one perhaps, but a very real one as far as any Asian is concerned. The less he takes from them financially the more he gains, relative to them, in prestige. Against his patron or, as he would prefer to put it, 'owner', Jesus, of course he cannot boast or claim anything. He can only be grateful that he has been put into such a prestige-worthy position. And because of his prestige

5. Rm. 1:1, 1 Co. 7:21; Ga. 1:10.
6. Jn. 4:36. The harvester is already earning a reward and gathering the crop for eternal life.
7. On the word *misthos/sakhar* see Preisker at Kittel–Friedrich, ed., *Theologisches Wörterbuch*, vol. 4 (1942), 702–3 (the pagination of the English translation is almost identical).

they, the recipients of the letter (and other imagined readers), must pay attention to what he says, and render to him the respect which is his due! So the passage, which has broken the teeth of so many exegetes, should be translated like this:

> 16. It is not open to me to boast of my being an evangelist, because I am acting under compulsion. You know, it would go hard with me if I ceased being an evangelist! 17. If I were to function like this of my own free will, I should already be receiving my hire for doing it. But since I do it under constraint I am someone to whom a trust has been entrusted. 18. Now I will tell you what my 'reward' amounts to: as I preach I supply the message free of cost to the hearer, in order to take no improper advantage of my authority to preach it. 19. So I am under obligation to no one, and on that basis . . .

To give the good news without taking anything in return is of course a reward for an Asian, because he gains prestige from it. In Paul's next metaphor (9:19ff.) he pretends that he has subjected himself to others in order to make humanity itself his 'profit', profit, that is to say, not for himself, but for his master.[8] In order to subject himself for this purpose he must act voluntarily and as a free man, for a slave cannot subject himself to others. Thus St. Paul moves from one metaphor to another not wholly consistent with it. It is the series of images that counts, not their mutual consistency, and we need not be surprised that he later represents himself as a partner.

8. Some versions of 1 Co. 9:23 take the words *panta de poio dia to euangelion ina synkoinonos autou genomai* in the sense 'I do it all for the sake of the gospel, to secure my share in it.' Others (Phillips, New English Bible) take the active sense: 'to play (or bear) my part in it (proclaiming it) (properly)'. But neither is literally correct: *panta poio* means 'I do all I can'. Further, Moses was a partner with Yahweh. Parents are partners with God in procreation. The priests were partners with Yahweh (1 Co. 10:18, cf. 20: they took their meat diet at his table). So the word *synkoinonos* means literally 'partner' (as at Pap. Masp. 158. 11, cf. Rm. 11:17, 15:27). St. Paul is partner in the divine message, taking his appropriate share of the (spiritual) profits and therefore he is keen on the 'business' as only a partner is! On the verb *kerdaino* ('gain') to indicate missionary and proselytising activity see the convincing comments of D. Daube, *New Testament and Rabbinic Judaism* (London, 1956), 358–61. James, Peter, and John admitted Paul into 'partnership (*koinonia*) on condition he made collections outside Palestine for the poor Christians of Judaea (Ga. 2:9–10).

In the metaphor I consider above St. Paul is relying upon his readers' accepting that one would be quite reasonable in preferring, as one's reward, a supernatural or insubstantial entity, like a share in the spiritual gains he makes for Jesus, to the more substantial 'hire' of the community's wages, namely their supplying his necessaries. Paul makes two rather objectionable hints: firstly that his fellow apostles in taking subsistence (for themselves and their families) from their communities are somehow drawing on their earthly reward, and thus diminishing their supernatural reward (a typical Jewish notion, p. 170); and secondly that in indulging in this they are really in danger of committing a breach of trust. An 'inspired' sermon might, as it were, produce an extra melon for supper.[9] In his view an evangelist should, if possible, earn his own keep by personal labour; and then he will be a true slave of Jesus, can perform his stewardship or his guardianship faithfully, as a kind of commission on the greater number of souls gained in the process. Moreover, as he retains prestige in the community they will the more readily pay attention to what he says. Some will think this must accurately depict the psychology of Jewish communities at that period. I do not know whether it can be utilised in our world without further efforts at translation. That St. Paul was obliged at times to live upon alms from churches[10] must have been as sad a blow to his self-respect as it would be to anyone's, but fortunately, as in the passage referred to above, he felt, as Asians do, that the one who *receives* alms only *gives* the donor an opportunity to acquire merit thereby, in this case that of being in partnership with Paul in the spiritual business to which he was devoted!

One who has nothing to lose, and nothing to gain, and is interested only in the prestige which arises from a service valued for its intrinsic merit and irrespective of reciprocation, has an authority of a quite peculiar type. He does it, as it were, under compulsion, and if profit accrues it is not to him. He has not abused his trust, or taken illicit advantage of the position in which he finds himself by virtue of his service. He harps on this point embarrassingly and sarcastically at 2 Co. 11:5–15, 20. I trust I have shown why he thought it worth his while to do so.

9. St. Paul expresses this very fear at Ga. 1:10: 'If I were still seeking public approval, how could I be, as I am, a slave of Christ?' (alluding to Mt. 6:24 or its antecedent form).
10. Ph. 4:15–17.

*Note.* In case any reader should be surprised to hear that the church has failed to grasp a passage in St. Paul's writings which would have been crystal clear to a Jewish reader of his times, there is an even more dramatic example to hand. The 'Pauline Privilege' is not of much interest in the Anglican communion, but is of great practical importance in, I believe, all other churches. It has travelled overseas, and upon it are modelled statutes in South Asia enabling converts from Hinduism, or any other religion to Christianity (except converts from Islam who do not need such statutory aid) to divorce their spouses, if they were not converted at the same time and remained unwilling to live peaceably with the convert. Very recently Professor David Daube proved conclusively (in 'Pauline contributions to a pluralistic culture . . .', D. G. Miller and D. Y. Hadidian, edd., *Jesus and Man's Hope*, vol. 2 [Pittsburgh Theological Seminary, 1971], 223–45) that the relevant scriptural passage (1 Co. 7:12–16) had been completely misunderstood, St. Paul never contemplated divorce, and the Pauline Privilege is a mare's nest, as, occasionally, Anglican scholars have felt it must be.

# APPENDIX TWO

# Specific Ignorance: False Coins

At Mt. 13:52 Jesus says (and this is a passage peculiar to St. Matthew, who is fascinated by scriptural interpretation), 'So every "scribe" who has become a student of the Kingdom of Heaven is like a householder who "puts out" from his "treasure" new and old [things].' The word 'scribe' is no problem: he is a traditional expounder of the Old Testament, the bible of Jesus's world. The word for 'puts out' (*ekballei*) can have several meanings, but in the context it obviously means 'brings out', though for what purpose is obscure unless one knows what the sentence means. That meaning will also clarify what is meant by 'treasure'. To find out the meaning the English inquirer will turn to ancient commentaries and to modern, knowing that most modern commentaries make exhaustive use (and often plagiarise) the more famous French and German commentaries, themselves treasuries of exhaustive scholarly investigation. Look up this passage in Van Steen (*alias* Cornelius à Lapide) (1636), or in the summary of many more recent commentaries in our fellow Londoner, Matthaeus Polus (1669); in Wetstenius (1751); in Plummer (1909); in Jülicher on Parables (1910); in Jeremias on Parables (1962); in Peake (1962); in Fenton on Matthew (1963); in the Jerusalem Bible (1966); in Kingsbury on Parables in Matthew 13 (1969); and in A. E. Harvey's deservedly popular *Commentary on the* (New English Bible) *New Testament* (1970)—and you will be none the wiser.

The new and old things are in fact coins (the missing noun is *nomismata*),[1] the 'treasure' is the family strong-box (or pot buried

---

1. Scholars, consulting Bauer–Arndt–Gingrich, *Greek–English Lexicon* (1957), at this word will find references to Philo and Ignatius which are very suggestive. I should add a specific reference to Philo, *De Spec. Leg.* I. xix. 104 (ed. Colson, vol. 7, 161). False coinage ordinarily deceives the eye, and, for an

in the wall), and the use of *ekballein* is quite correct for paying out, 'tendering' (cf. Lk. 10:35). The same verb is used in other places specifically for tendering coins (Mt. 12:35).

The meaning of the last-cited passage will now be obvious: the dishonest man keeps a bag of false coins (like an ancient fake Ptolemaic tetradrachm I have in my study) to tender to the unwary in breach of Dt. 25:13-16, Lev. 19:11. The honest man has only a 'good' bag filled exclusively with genuine coins. But both types look exactly alike except to the expert who uses a lens to examine them, and they even weigh exactly the same.[2]

So in our simile the traditional scholar who has been trained or retrained in Jesus's school can tender words of wisdom which are equally valid, current coin, like those that were minted by Ptolemy two centuries before, by Augustus or Tiberius recently, or by the Tyrian mint a century earlier. That is to say, whether they are ancient *midrashim*, Pharisees' innovations in interpretation, or Jesus's own ingenious explanations of scripture, they are all valid. They all 'circulate', are all bound to be accepted; and none of them are 'counterfeit'.

It seems extremely likely that Jesus did use a metaphor about coins, 'coins' meaning teachings, especially teachings based (as all serious teachings had to be then) on scripture. At Mt. 13:52 he is depicted as using it with reference to interpretations of various ages (i.e. some had worn well, some were novel, inspired). At 12:35 he had already said 'A good man tenders good (coins) out of his good treasure, and the wicked man tenders bad ones from his false treasure'. If we look at the context we shall see once again that the subject-matter, as St. Matthew has conceived it, is academic jealousy and spite. His 'enemies' attack his teachings as 'fruit' of one who is in association with the Devil (12:24). Now the quality of fruit depends on the tree (v.33). If a man has counterfeit coins it is highly likely that he will tender them; he cannot, at any rate, make them into genuine ones. A good man tests his coins and nails (as we should say) the bad ones to the counter. Now we see what is meant by v.36: 'I tell you that every valueless word which men utter they will have to account for on the Day of Judgment'; and v.37: 'since it is by your words you will be acquitted, and by your

---

ancient audience, the commodity readily afforded a metaphor: Philo, *De mut. nom.* 171 (ed. Colson, vol. 5, 228).
2. Mishnah, B.M. IV. 6.

words condemned' (*J.B.*). Professor Joachim Jeremias has rightly pointed out that the Greek word for 'valueless' (*argon*) represents the Hebrew or Aramaic word *batil* (void, useless, worthless). The meaning is therefore this: all teachers who pass off worthless, valueless teachings as genuine will be condemned at the End of Days. It is hardly polite, but it is, somewhere between a warning and a curse, a direct attack upon those who impugned the quality of Jesus's own inspiration. St. Luke and St. Matthew found, at any rate, the metaphor about coins in Q. which is a source of equal authority with St. Mark; the application, by way of threat, to Jesus's 'orthodox' enemies is an interpretation, or development, by St. Matthew or his advisers.

Neither to Mt. 12:35 nor to Mt. 13:52 will you find an apposite clue in the writings of the theologians, and St. Matthew was, deservedly, and remains, the favourite and most-studied gospel.

# *Ignorance of Technique*

In this and the next two appendixes I approach difficulties due not to mere ignorance of the cultural background or the material conditions of the life of the Hebrews at the relevant period, but to the technique presupposed by the first church, which could not, at the times of the synoptic evangelists, conceive that oral elucidation of the fragments of tradition would die out. In other words the gospels themselves put us in serious difficulties, and perfectly conclusive explanations may never be forthcoming. But, shuffling as we must do, combining a sympathetic understanding of the mentality, and historical investigation of surviving Jewish literature, we creep forward unpredictably, and, though there are losses in some quarters there are equally certainly gains in others. There are, after all, hundreds of highly gifted people at work, and if no progress were to be made that would be very strange, and would be a poor return for the money spent on them.

The non-Jewish reader of the passages in which Jesus uses the text of Hos. 6:6, 'I [i.e. Yahweh] will have mercy and not sacrifice', would wonder how he could derive from it the meanings he does. He says that text means that he himself should evangelise sinners (Mt. 9:13) and that his students were entitled to pluck ears of corn on the sabbath (Mt. 12:7). At Mk. 12:33–34 Jesus approves of a scribe's deriving from that text the proposition that love of God and of one's neighbour is better than sacrificial offerings, which seems a more literal and intelligible interpretation, though not an obvious one. Are all these interpretations possible, and could any of them be wrong? It is a natural question. The answer, fortunately, is simple, because we have glosses on Hos. 6:6 by ancient Jewish scholars. They leave us in no doubt but that in their view Yahweh requires acts showing solidarity, e.g. association with the downcast, charity to the afflicted, rather than the performance of sacrificial observances in the Temple. One must read the whole of Hos. 6:6, and not only the few words quoted above (they are the catch-phrase). From the remainder of the verse it is clear that Yahweh is represented as preferring compliance with his will to those offerings, many of which had, as we have seen, a ritual, not a moral significance. When the editors of the New English Bible decided as a matter of policy not to provide the reader with the references to the Old Testament citations they made a fatal decision, such as only men indifferent to Eastern notions of scholarship would make, or men who, knowing Eastern notions, assumed that English-reading students of the scriptures could not possibly want to follow out intellectually Jesus's train of thought!

# Puzzles Created by the Synoptic Writers

We cannot know too much about the techniques of interpretation of scripture in Jesus's day. Many a puzzle created by the 'synoptics', i.e. the first three Evangelists themselves, would yield, we may be sure, to more knowledge from that quarter. A good example of our situation is Mk. 6:8–9.

'Here you go again,' said my pious acquaintance (p. 168 above), 'fiddling with details that bother nobody. Since we got rid of the friars (and that was a long time ago), I cannot conceive of anyone caring whether itinerant preachers should carry a staff or not. What on earth does it matter? In this age the symbolic significance of an evangelist's dress or equipment means absolutely nothing. The cowl never made the monk. I really don't think St. Mark paid all that attention to what the first preachers carried, and, if he was anything like a discriminating man it will have been all one to him whether they carried one staff, two staffs, or no staff at all. Surely they must have carried a knife, or a tooth-pick for that matter, and who could care, one way or the other? If all this fiddle-faddle is to be foisted on Jesus, he will turn out to be no better than the Scribes, with their pernickety ways. I am committed to the view that Jesus was the end of the Law, and as far as I am concerned most of the allusions to the Old Testament you can dig up must have been put there (if they are not figments of your imagination) by old Jewish academics of your own kidney. Don't forget, St. John said "grace and truth came by Jesus Christ", i.e. *grace and truth*, not rabbinifications!' Well, let us see what we can find out, assuming that Mk. 6:8–9 was written by a responsible person who had something important to say. My reader can make up his own mind whether the effort is worthwhile.

Specialists have pondered on the differences between this passage and its parallels at Mt. 10:9–10 and Lk. 9:3 (cf. 10:4). As has long been clear[1] two different versions circulated before the gospels were finalised and St. Matthew used the source not used by St. Mark (called 'Q') to produce his own conflation, while St. Luke uses both. The major discrepancy regarding the *staff* (see below) may be due to Q's providing only a list of negatives, having misunderstood or simplified the message (which we are about to investigate). St. Mark indicates Jesus's instructions to the Twelve, whom he sent out two by two. Mark pointedly notices this arrangement for two are needed for testimony[2] (Luke took the point up when he returned to the theme at 10:1–11). In the Marcan version the Twelve were to take nothing for their journey, except simply a staff; they were not to have any bread, nor a wallet or pouch, and not so much as a copper coin in their belt. They were to wear sandals, but not more than one shirt or under-garment. St. Luke received this version, and Q, which contained nothing but negatives, that is to say, putting both to use, he understood the instructions to be *not* to take a staff. He does not mention the sandals at 9:3 but he forbids them at 10:4. He shows Jesus forbidding the Twelve to take a wallet, bread, money, or a second under-garment. St. Matthew, too, understood the list to be entirely negative and his conflation of Mark and Q produced this result: they were to take neither gold, nor silver, nor copper coin (Matthew explains that if copper was forbidden *a fortiori* gold and silver were out of the question!) and he carries on with a series of declining importance, an anticlimax: no wallet, no second garment, no sandals, and not (even) a staff.

What was the original point? It was not, as Manson quaintly thought,[3] that they were an invading army living on the country. The preachers were to depend entirely on the community, accumulating no assets of their own. Psychologically this was entirely apt, and it fits what we know of religious history in the East. The monied monk was not authentic. St. Matthew is particularly explicit from 10:8e onwards. But did St. Mark have this point only in mind?

The first doubt is whether our text of Mark is correct: whether, after all, he too did not read the first item in the negative 'not even a staff', as Q represented it, and as St. Matthew and St. Luke also must have understood it, though the former rearranges the matter in the interests (he believes) of clarity. Wellhausen, and after him Dodd, suggested that whereas the Aramaic *'ela'* provides 'except'

1. B. H. Streeter, *Four Gospels* (1926), 248.
2. *LNT*, 160, n. 2.                    3. *Sayings of Jesus* (1949), 181.

the very similar *la'* would mean 'not' and a copyist's slip could account for the divergence. But 'not' and 'except' are so different in sense that an Aramaic speaker would be alert to such errors. Moreover, St. Mark's 'except merely a staff' could make good sense if one looks into the *midrashic* significance of the passage. Further, the parallel doubt about the *sandals* is countered by the observation that the quaint manner of Mark's 'but shod with sandals and do not wear two under-garments' certifies that we have here a genuine version of a virtually unedited Semitic original. True the American *Greek New Testament* smoothes the grammar and reads as it were, 'and that they should not wear . . .', but both the old Textus Receptus and the text of Nestlé which is followed in the New English Bible retain the quaint (and preferable) reading. Now the sandals have to be worn because they symbolise movement, not squatting in any one place and letting comfort hinder the propagation of the gospel; and they also imply purposeful activity in general exactly as at the Exodus, the first Redemption (Ex. 12:11). One who has neither sandals nor staff is obviously not a serious traveller prepared to keep moving whatever the terrain.[4] Not having spare clothing indicates poverty, dependence on one's hosts for a change of garment (in case any laundry was done), and determination to put up in a dwelling overnight—which was exactly the intended programme. I do not think the parallels that have been found in Greek literature have a close bearing on the matter, since although clothing was certainly symbolic (how Hebrews hated the characteristic Greek hat!), the symbolism in the one culture would be exactly what would *not* be used in the other.[5]

What of the staff, then? David Flusser and J. G. Kahn, struck by the fact that Jacob claimed to have obeyed Yahweh in his journey with the aid of a staff alone (Gn. 32:10), which Rashi interprets as meaning 'with no assets other than the staff', argue[6] that what St. Mark meant was that Jesus asked his disciples to carry a staff in imitation of Jacob who, in fear of his enemy (Esau), claimed to depend on Yahweh's mercy alone, with the aid of nothing but a staff—which could help him to cross a river (and by analogy to

---

4. V. Taylor, *Gospel according to St. Mark* (1963), *ad loc.*, illustrates the general lack of contact with these oriental images.
5. Diogenes Laertius VI. 13 (affectations of a philosopher); Polyaenus IV. 14 (signs of civilian status).
6. *Novum Testamentum*, 13 (1971), 45 n.

traverse any geographical obstacle). That Mark, and so conceivably Jesus himself, did have this idea is quite possible. It cannot be proved, but it cannot be disproved. St. Mark is certainly older than St. Matthew or St. Luke. The very few scholars who argue the contrary have many serious obstacles to overcome. On the basis that St. Mark was earlier it seems most likely that whatever the implications of the staff neither Matthew nor Luke valued the allusion (was it too recondite, or were they advised that it distracted the hearer?) and hence they, or their advisers, corrected their version of Mark to read a simple negative, '*not* a staff'.

My own suggestion would be much more radical than Flusser's. I think that they were to take with them a staff which was not a staff, i.e. whatever stout stick they have for their journey is not the real staff they need, and with that staff they must regard themselves as certainly being equipped. The most famous staff in Jewish history is the staff of Moses. That they cannot have, obviously, and yet they are to imagine themselves as having it. Jesus in our present story is giving *authority* to disciples *as his agents* to exercise his jurisdiction over 'unclean spirits', i.e. to be soldiers against evil— spiritual, psychological, psychosomatic, and physical. For this task a staff is needed.

Indeed one could say that there were three staffs known to us from the bible besides Jacob's, and of course the scriptural inter- preter will not have hesitated to link Jacob's with one or more of them. The first is the staff of correction, which figures in Ps. 23:4. It is the shepherd's traditional instrument (besides his sling), and it is the forerunner of the bishop's crozier. Staffs are symbolic of blessing (Gn. 47:31 [Jacob's staff] as understood in an ancient *midrash*, preserved in the Septuagint translation, and alluded to at Heb. 11:21) and of the work of the teacher-healer (Elisha's staff might have worked miracles: 2 K. 4:29-31, but failed to do so—a case of a pupil, for Elisha was Elijah's pupil, failing to effect a cure through an emissary, viz. Gehazi). The most famous shepherd's staff is Moses's. That staff or rod was called *matteh ha'elohim*, 'the rod of the Lord' (or, according to an ancient Greek version, the Septuagint, 'the rod from God') which he took out from home on his wanderings after Yahweh had shown him how he could perform wonders with it (Ex. 4:2-4, 17) and Moses and Aaron (his 'spokes- man') together had utilised those 'signs' (Ex. 4:16-17, 30). By these wonders the Hebrews were persuaded that they were about to be redeemed from Egypt, they were convinced that real freedom was theirs for the price of simple obedience to Yahweh.

With that same staff Moses performed a miracle that confounded the heathen (Ex. 7:15), and another (Ex. 7:17, 20), and another (Ex. 8:15), and another (Ex. 8:16), and yet another (Ex. 10:13) until at long last the miracles of the *two*, Moses and Aaron, overcame the scepticism of their opponents. Then with it Moses divided the Sea (Ex. 14:16), so that the whole company could cross (which reminds us of Jacob crossing the Jordan), and with the same rod got water in the desert (Nb. 20:8, 11), and that very same staff (Ex. 17:5) was the means whereby the children of Israel defeated Amalek, which signifies the evil inclination and the scourge of those that murmur against Yahweh.[7] It was appropriate enough that it should be called the 'rod of Yahweh'. This is what the evangelists had to take with them; the idea is that they need no other protection than this—and their poverty—and certainly no other weapon in order to fulfil their allotted function.[8]

The staff of Moses was eventually recognised as a prefiguration of the Cross; and with superlative irony the gospel says that this staff (cf. Mk. 10:21, Mt. 16:24, Mt. 10:38) must be the badge of every true follower of Jesus. As St. Luke puts it (Lk. 10:3), Jesus knowingly sent them 'as lambs into the midst of wolves'.

Jesus could have told them something like this: 'Take a staff, for with a staff Moses confounded the magicians and rulers of Egypt, divided the Red Sea, and defeated Amalek. That was the staff of Yahweh and it has not departed from Israel as long as there remains one without a pouch (he will be fed as Moses and Aaron were fed with manna), but with sandals on his feet, ready to go from village to village telling of what Yahweh the king demands from his subjects. Do not so much as touch a copper coin. Accept nothing from a village that will not listen to your message, and from others only what hospitality requires them to give you.'

Is this creative imagination on my part? Time will tell. Did the synoptic writers really construct their gospels with such far-fetched allusions and quaint 'silent documentation' in mind? Indeed they did if the studies in the great parables re-explained in my *Law in the New Testament* are anything to go by.[9] There is, it would seem, no superfluous word, and every turn taken by the story gives us another

7. *LNT*, 132–5.                     8. Lk. 10:19; Dt. 8:15; Ps. 91:13.
9. Perhaps ch. 9 (The Parable of the Good Samaritan) is the best example.

signpost pointing to some Old Testament story, text, or *midrash*. Fortunately, we have excellent evidence that a very early version of the instructions was consciously written with an Old Testament story in mind, and that too one which we have noticed. It is known that St. Luke found the tradition of Jesus's commissioning his 'agents' in two different pieces of composition: he used one at 9:1-5 and another at 10:1-12. The latter was more elaborate; St. Matthew also used it, and therefore it was in Q. St. Luke alone contains the command 'greet no one on the road' (10:4) which was Elisha's command to Gehazi (2 K. 4:29). This passage does *not* say that a staff must not be taken. The implication was the reverse.

St. Mark, whose tendentious use of his material is an exquisite part of his artistry, intends every hearer to understand that if he (the hearer) were to be authorised, and if *he* were to seek to proclaim to all and sundry that they must repent, and were to attempt to cure ailments by spiritual healing, *he* must likewise take that staff in hand, with nothing in his purse (or rather, no purse), and go out like Moses and Aaron went out of Egypt, with faith, and 'signs' to support them.

# A Conundrum: Violence in the Kingdom

The Kingdom of Heaven is not a commonplace expression in Hebrew writings, yet the designation of Yahweh as 'King of the Universe' is constant and ubiquitous. Hence 'Kingdom of Heaven' is potentially meaningful, and is indeed found in apocryphal writings not far removed from the era when the gospels were written. There have been so many notions of what it meant that it must be regarded as controversial; but I take it to be the concept of Yahweh as the real ruler, and Satan as the apparent ruler, and the 'coming' of Yahweh's kingdom means that his commands are actually obeyed in the area in question (p. 97). He is like an absent emperor, whose commands are set aside by disobedient and fraudulent princelings, rather as in the parable of the wicked vinedressers.[1] Difficult as it has been to pin down the concept of the Kingdom of Heaven and what is meant by its 'coming', it has proved impossible to obtain agreement as to what is meant in Mt. 11:12 and Lk. 16:16 by force being applied to the Kingdom, and men of force obtaining it. Obviously it is a paradox of some kind, and there has been considerable speculation as to the meaning, with the usual variations between the learned, and an unbounded exercise of imagination. Early writers suffered from the usual handicap, inherited from the classical education, of supposing that if a phrase means one thing it cannot mean another. On the contrary, memorable oriental sayings and maxims are cherished because they have a wealth of meaning, the same words doing duty over and over again. Hence when translated into Greek they become more precise and limited than they originally were, and translators may be virtually forced either to give two versions of the phrase consecutively, or to select for their translation one meaning which they regard as predominating. The sacrifice is

1. *LNT*, ch. 13.

one which even the most artful translator has to make at times. Puns, for example, are usually untranslatable.

Some earlier learning on this is summarised usefully by W. H. Dundas.[2] A study by W. G. Kümmel brings the literature right up to date.[3] I get the impression that the correct interpretation of the verses cited is not generally known. It will be helpful to commence with the New English Bible translation of both:

> Mt. 11:12: Ever since the coming of John the Baptist the kingdom of Heaven has been subjected to violence and violent men (*or* has been forcing its way forward and men of force) are seizing it. For all the prophets and the Law foretold things to come until John appeared . . .
>
> Lk. 16:16: Until John it was the Law and the Prophets: since then, there is good news of the kingdom of God, and everyone forces his way in.

It is clear that the translators could not make up their minds finally whether the word *biazetai* in the Matthew passage was to be taken in the middle sense, or in the passive sense, which is the one they on the whole preferred and printed in their text. Now it is obvious that unless we understand this we cannot know what Jesus (or those who report him) thought about John the Baptist, nor what was the role of the Torah and the Prophets. Was that role coming to an end, and if so why? And what is this 'force' alluded to? For some time it has been suspected that there was an Aramaic original which had been misunderstood. It is supposed that Matthew and Luke had the same original in front of them, but whereas Luke understood everyone to be forcing his way into the kingdom, or, since the word can be passive there too, to be forced into it, the other evangelist understood the kingdom itself to be subjected to force: which could amount to a contradiction.

Some have taken the view that the original saying was about violent resistance to the kingdom (e.g. on the part of the Pharisees); others that people took undue advantage of the freedom from the

2. In Hastings, *Dictionary of Christ and the Gospels*, vol. 2 (1908), 803–4.
3. ' "Das Gesetz und die Propheten gehen bis Johannes"—Lukas 16:16 im Zusammenhang der heilsgeschichtlichen Theologie der Lukasschriften', *Verborum Veritas. Festschrift . . . G. Stählin* (Wuppertal, 1970), 89–102. The latest item is P. H. Menoud, 'Le sens du verbe BIAZETAI dans Lk. 16.16', *Mélanges B. Rigaux* (Gembloux, 1970), which takes that word in a *positive* sense, with which I heartily concur.

Law which Jesus was preaching (?); others that the 'violent men' are disciples who show commendable vigour and want of caution; others that there was a misunderstanding of the implications of the Messianic Age about to commence; on the whole it was thought unlikely that Jesus could have suggested that any real entry into the Kingdom could be made by force. On the other hand it is a sensible comment to make that since Jesus and his contemporaries knew that Zealots, brigands masquerading as rebels for the sake of religion, were attempting to capture villages and districts with a mixture of psalm-singing and pillage (and occasionally succeeded until the government turned them out) there could be a beautiful irony in representing the Kingdom of Heaven as applying force of a quite different kind.

The role of conjecture being unduly high, attempts have been made to recover the original Aramaic word which could have given rise to the assumed misunderstandings. Dalman, Dundas himself, and finally, M. Black[4] searched for suitable words, and, on the basis that *oppression* is the idea to be looked for, some interesting propositions have come forward. Luke's 'there is good news', literally 'is proclaimed as Good News' (p. 96), is generally regarded as a secondary tradition and as being Luke's own word, i.e. not authentic! Black says, 'In such a notoriously *unheilbare Stelle* ["incurable passage"] as Mt. 11:12, we are thrown back on conjecture of this kind (e.g. that the "kingdom" broke violently in upon the world *in judgement*).' I do not go so far as to deny that it is an 'incurable passage' (there is something rather interesting in his putting this comment into German, for I think the Germans can be expected to find a way out of the difficulty if it can be found), but I offer an explanation which does not by any means allow that St. Luke made a mistake or introduced an erroneous idea of his own imagining. The Aramaic root for which we have been looking is not, I suggest, *PRS*, nor *'NS* but *DHQ*, which solves all the difficulties at a blow, and makes excellent sense.

The idea is of God's urgency. God has wishes, which are capable of comprehension in terms of time; the very concept of the End proves this. So God can be urgent. At Mishnah, Avot, II. 13 R. Tarfon, who was a younger contemporary of the apostles, and must have spoken their language, said 'the day is short, the task is great,

4. *An Aramaic Approach to the Gospels and Acts*, 3rd ed. (Oxford, 1967), 116, 196, 211, n. 2.

the workers are sluggish . . . and the employer urges them on (or "is urgent").' The word 'urgent' is *doheq*, which means 'presses on', 'crowds on'. P. Billerbeck[5] has already noticed the use of this root for *urgency, impatience*, but he did not see the point, since he thought it referred to hastening the days of the Messiah by the pious. The biblical Hebrew root *DHQ* means to squeeze, compress, shove aside, victimise (it occurs at Jg. 2:18 and Jl. 2:8). In Mishnaic and Talmudic Hebrew *doheq* means 'pressing', 'crowding', 'stamping'. At Bab. Tal., Ber. 64*a* we find *dahaq et ha-shaah*, 'to force time, be importunate'. To be under pressure is signified by the *niphal* form of the verb: *nidhaq*. Periphrastic forms of speech, especially passive forms, are found in Hebrew to refer to God's conduct. Like a sovereign whose taxes are in arrear God puts pressure on his kingdom. Now the Greek middle voice is very suitable for this half-and-half idea: the kingdom is under pressure and the king is the one that applied the pressure. Relevant Aramaic phrases would be: *malkhuta' de-shemayya' dehiq*, 'the Kingdom of Heaven is applying pressure, is importunate'; *m. d. midhaq*, 'the K. of H. is under pressure, or is being forced'. Let us try to translate the two passages having this root and its potential in mind.

> Mt. 11:12. But it is from the days of John the Baptist until now that the Kingdom of Heaven is under urgent pressure, and those that are forcing their way in are making booty of it. For the prophets and the Law spoke out for the time until John.
> Lk. 16:16. The Law and the prophets reigned until John. From this time onwards the Kingdom of God is proclaimed and everyone is urgently pressed into it.

Luke goes on to say (v. 17) that this does not mean that any part of the Torah is rendered obsolete or ineffective by this state of affairs. This is not an ironical comment by Jesus. What is meant is that *that* method of earning merit was still open.

I trust my readers will have been reminded of the comment made by the father of all the Hebrews, Abraham (who is an expert on merit if anyone is) to Dives at Lk. 16:29 ('They have Moses and the prophets . . .'); and also of the parable of the Great Supper,[6] where the host says to his servant (Lk. 14:23), 'Go out into the roads and walls and compel them to come in, in order that my house shall be crammed full!' I have little doubt but that the Aramaic original of

5. *Kommentar* on Mt. 11:12, p. 599.                6. *LNT*, ch. 6.

'compel' was *DHQ*.⁷ The idea was that the Torah and the prophets gave the Hebrews a way of earning merit, preparing themselves for the World to Come. If they followed that method faithfully they would certainly share in it (and still may, needless to say). But when John the Baptist came, who was thought to be a prophet, but was really greater than a prophet (Mt. 11:9, Lk. 16:26), a new dispensation started, a new offer, as it were, a new means of qualifying for the World to Come, in effect by enlisting as a member of the (real) kingdom, to react effectively to the announcement, the 'good news', preached by John and those who were baptised by him and were therefore in the line of his authority and teaching. Thus the rag, tag, and bobtail of society, those who had no knowledge of the Torah, and no long life of good works to their credit, could still, if they repented and were baptised, claim membership of the kingdom, and since they had not paid for it in the traditional way they could well be visualised as crowding in, taking all at one snatch what others had worked for laboriously.

For long it must have been suspected that the words could not really be a condemnation; indeed they are not. God is in a hurry. He has, to use a most inappropriate, but still expressive metaphor, 'put the steam on'. Life is hurrying to a close, and the legal niceties of the past age were not good enough. Now those who were previously disqualified are qualified under a new scheme, and they look, and perhaps feel, no better than robbers. Thus the exact 'voice' of the word *biazetai*, whether it be middle or passive, is not so important. The idea is not of violence to the kingdom, but of para-legal, mass, hurried claims to be members of it. I cannot believe that this brilliant idea can have been without Old Testament textual authority, but it remains to be traced. Is. 8:3 may have some relevance.

7. As for the vocabulary, the Greek term for the Hebraic habit of forcing people to accept hospitality is *parabiazomai*. Ac. 16:15 is a good example, and at Lk. 24:29 we find the procedure applied, as it were, to Jesus himself. This kind of urging one to do something supposedly in one's own interest is evidenced at 1 S. 28:23; 2 K. 5:16. In ordinary Greek one finds, at Plutarch, *Brut.* 993 D (quoted by Wetstenius) *liparein kai biazesthai epi deipnon*, 'to be importunate in pressing someone to come to dinner'.

# The Last Words of Jesus according to St. Luke

## Law and the Resurrection

It does not do to suppose that the great events of the Jesus-story are so removed from real life that it would be unprofitable to draw closer to them. The notion that ignorance about the New Testament text is excusable or immaterial was natural enough in my imaginary uncommitted youthful reader; but I hope he has another view of the position by this time.

The death of Jesus has a great bearing upon the nature of the Resurrection, and, though this great puzzle must await further light, we are not precluded from looking into the vocabulary. St. Luke had available to him (and so of course had others) sources other than St. Mark's gospel, which he possessed in the form in which we have it, or something very similar to it. In the light of those sources he was not content with St. Mark's description of the last cry or cries of Jesus: yet there were features in St. Mark's account to which he adheres strictly. In St. Luke's view Jesus made only one great cry (23:46). St. Matthew understands Jesus to have cried out twice. The first time occurred with the quotation from the twenty-second psalm, which is most inappropriately called the Cry of Dereliction. In actual fact the point which is being made is that the role of Israel depicted in that psalm (the agony psalm) is announced by Jesus to be lived out in him. It was *as if* Jesus *were* at that moment the character or hero of Ps. 22; and it is obvious that Ps. 22 neither was, nor could be held to be, a psalm of dereliction, since its point is that Yahweh will deliver, and *as if* has already delivered, rescued, and redeemed his people (as is plain from Ps. 22:21–22ff.).

The second cry mentioned by St. Matthew is simply described as 'crying (or shouting) again with a great voice'. We are not told whether he said anything. It is evident that Matthew follows Mark closely, yet when we turn to Mark's text we do not find exactly this arrangement. No doubt Matthew's understanding of Mark is logical, reasonable, and plausible. St. Mark gives the quotation from Ps. 22, in a slightly different form, and the concentration on the Aramaic (presumably targumic) version in what was intended to be an exact phonetic representation of the original sounds strongly suggests that St. Mark understood the words to be Jesus's last words, charged with supernatural power. But a close investigation of Mark as it stands now suggests a doubt of great interest. It omits the word 'again', i.e. that was an addition by St. Matthew, and relates that Jesus 'expired' after letting forth a great voice. It would be possible to read this as meaning that the great voice, with which he quoted the psalm, was virtually the prelude to his expiring. We are *not* by any means certain that St. Luke had St. Mark's work in the form in which we have it, and it is quite possible that he was shown an Aramaic version, with its ambiguous and ambivalent tense structure, which might have led him to think that St. Mark himself knew only of one cry and not two.

This is a conjecture, but it is a reasonable one, because St. Luke omits the so-called cry of dereliction. The loss in point of reference to Ps. 22 is enormous. There cannot be any doubt but that the first church searched minutely to see 'references' to that psalm in the crucifixion story and that of the trial that preceded it.[1] To those to whom the Resurrection was a reality that very psalm was relevant and important. It easily bears a Messianic and resurrection interpretation. Why, then, did St. Luke abandon it? I suggest two explanations, both good. He wanted to substitute for it something better. And he did not believe that Jesus in fact quoted that psalm.

In other words the tradition available to him was that the doubt expressed at Mk. 15: 35-36, Mt. 27:47, 49 could, and must, be resolved in another way.

The actual sound the bystanders heard, when they compared notes, may well have been (as we shall see confirmed below) '*el* followed by an indeterminate vowel which might have been *i* or *e*. I repudiate the suggestion of sceptics that since the synoptists are not agreed we cannot believe that Jesus gave forth any sound at all (!). With consummate irony (for Elijah, as it were, had already come)

1. *LNT*, 404 n. 2, 435.

St. Mark relates how some thought Jesus was calling for Elijah. Others, with insight born of meditation and research, identified the word as the first word, the catch-phrase, of the twenty-second psalm, whose appropriateness we are bound to note as they did. It was not at all a bad guess (if I am right) because *'eli* can be the catch-phrase of only this passage. If Jesus repeated it, *'eli*, *'eli* (in whatever form, whether indeed Hebrew, or Aramaic in whatever dialect of that language), then the connection with Ps. 22 was obvious, as no other *'eli 'eli* occurs in the Hebrew bible. But St. Luke was able to adopt another, and, he thought, better reconstruction of what Jesus said. It is commonly said that he was offended by the 'cry of dereliction', but if he was he must have been singularly ill-informed, as I have shown.

Lk. 23:46 should be translated as follows: 'Jesus cried out with a great voice and said, "Father, into thy hands I commit my spirit." And when he had said that he expired.' First of all we must concentrate on the rather unpromising word 'expired'. This is taken over from St. Mark. It is high-flown Greek, a fancy word, seemingly out of keeping with Mark's Hebraic style. In Euripides we can parallel St. Matthew's substitute, 'he gave up his spirit', and in Sophocles and Plutarch we find 'expired' as a decorative word for 'died'. *Ekpneein* is by no means so common in this sense as its Latin equivalent *exspirare*. We are so used to the term that it does not occur to us that it is by no means the first word we should choose to express the idea that is surely desperately wanted here, if anywhere, namely that Jesus did really die. It was not a matter of going into a coma, whether deliberately adopted (as an Asian holy man might readily do) or unintentional: the circulation stopped and clinical death occurred (the question of the possibility of resuscitation being left open). St. Mark rubs it in: at Mk. 15:39 the same word is repeated, unnoticed by St. Matthew or St. Luke. To Mark it is important that the act of dying was an 'expiring'. And of course in Hebrew idiom this is correct. A man conceived of as willingly dying, would give up his spirit, expel it: what to Hellenes is a physical act of breathing out (the normal and expected meaning of *ekpneein*) is to the Hebrew the severing of spirit and body, leaving open the question whether they will be reunited (as we shall see presently). Now we know why, though death is common enough in the New Testament, only Jesus does the act described by Mark and Luke as *exepneuse*, 'he expired'. *Ekpneein* is not used of death in the Septua-

gint, nor in the contemporary language of the papyri. It was not
merely a peculiar word for death; it was tolerable here chiefly
because of its Hebraic meaning and overtones.

I wonder if it was the word *exepneuse* which put St. Luke on to
his reconstruction of what Jesus actually said? I think this would
be difficult to prove, since the ambience of the whole discussion is
Hebraic, and the information he must have been given would have
been Aramaic in thought and diction, even if translated to him in
Palestinian Greek. He had medical material in front of him, and he
is often credited with knowledge as a physician. He will have
weighed up as best he could what must have happened. Long before
those matters were explained to him he must have considered the
Resurrection in all its aspects. The words descriptive of Jesus's
death must have been weighed by him minutely. The tradition was
that Jesus *gave up the spirit*, and the implication of the whole story,
as all four gospels confirm, was that Jesus died *prematurely*, i.e.
much sooner than any skilled person would have expected, indeed
so much sooner that suspicions were aroused that all was not above
board. The implication with which all four evangelists leave us is
that Jesus determined when to die, master of the situation to the last.

Now let us turn to the words St. Luke says Jesus used, not—it
would appear—just an inarticulate, or doubtful cry, but an intelligible sentence. However, this does not conclude the matter. The
as-if technique does not allow us to assume that St. Luke himself
believed that a perfectly articulated sentence was uttered, any more
than was the case with St. Mark's quotation, adopted without
hesitation by St. Matthew. It was *as if* he said these words. Let us,
however, see what the words mean. A knowledge of law and legal
history will be found useful here. Had my predecessors (saving one
forgotten theologian called Lucas Brugensis)[2] thought of this, the
theological knowledge of St. Luke would have been appreciated
differently. Here again 'Billerbeck' gives half the story[3] and in such
a form as not to indicate the significance of what he had found: the

2. Franciscus Lucas Brugensis, *In Sacrosancta Quatuor Iesu Christi Evangelia*
(Antwerp, 1606), 883–4 (following Theophylact [11th cent.] on Matthew).
It is remarkable that J. Cocceius (*Opera*, vol. 2 [1701], psalm., p. 109), having
rendered '*afqiyd* correctly by *depono*, still did not see what was meant.
3. Strack–Billerbeck, *Kommentar*, vol. 2, 269. It is most disappointing that A.
Edersheim, who was a Talmudic scholar, did not see the point (*Life and
Times of Jesus the Messiah* [1906], vol. 2, 609). J. Klausner did not either
(*Jesus of Nazareth* [1959], 354). Nor did G. F. Moore in his *Judaism*.

legal point escaped him entirely. Here the *Midrash on Psalms*, which is replete with references of the greatest interest to Christians, curiously, and rather pointedly disappoints us by not including a comment on Ps. 31:6.

Ps. 31:6 in the Hebrew bible, which is Ps. 30:6 in the Greek translation, the Septuagint, deserves close scrutiny. The whole psalm is a psalm of appeal to Yahweh for redemption from fear, grief, and shame; and it ends, like Ps. 22, with recognition and gratitude that Yahweh has answered the prayer. The whole is set, in ancient and characteristic Hebrew idiom, in the metaphor of a member of a faction temporarily at a disadvantage in feuding—this being a concept which seems to have been (and still is?) a continuum in the culture. The New English Bible renders vv. 4-5 (vv. 5-6 in the Hebrew) in this way, 'Set me free from the net men have hidden for me; thou art my refuge, into thy keeping I commit my spirit. Thou hast redeemed me, O Lord thou God of truth.' The Hebrew of v. 6 reads literally, 'In thy hand I entrust my spirit. Thou hast redeemed me, Yahweh, lord of truth (i.e. truthful lord).' The word for 'entrust', namely the root *PQD*, means exactly to commit in the sense of a deposit. Taking the psalm at large the meaning is plainly simply that the safety of the individual (i.e. Israel) depends on Yahweh, whose dependant he (i.e. they) must be; therefore it is 'up to Yahweh' as it were, to see that the safety of the suppliant is secured. But this was not the only way in which that verse was taken in Jesus's time. Quite the contrary.

The Septuagint read the same verse similarly to the Masoretes. They seem to have read the word for 'hand' in the plural, which makes perfect sense, especially in the West, where the unpropitious connotations of the left hand (p. 130 above) were unknown. Instead of the present tense, 'commit', they read the verb as future, 'I shall commit', and the verb used, *paratithemi*, in the middle voice, is exactly that of committing or entrusting a deposit. The word for spirit is *pneuma*. The Targum which we have reads 'hand' in the singular, and the verb for 'entrust' in the future; the Syriac places the verb in the past, 'I have entrusted'. Altogether these variations are of very slight importance, except that the LXX version does explain how it was that the so-called Western text of Luke, a revision of the original work of St. Luke, substituted the LXX reading of the psalm for the words of Jesus which originally placed the verb in the present tense, as in the Hebrew.

The phrase 'In thy hand I entrust my spirit. Thou hast redeemed me, Yahweh, lord of truth' was used as a prayer before sleeping. It still is.[4] Adults and children may now, and might then, be habituated to longer or shorter prayers, more or less elaborate formulas for dispelling the Evil One, and calling upon the Lord to restore the spirit at waking. But the central and constant core of the prayer was these words,[5] ending with the phrase *'el 'emet*. This is a significant phrase, which everyone would know. Just as, if one says suddenly 'For ever and ever' numbers of people will sleepily and automatically say 'Amen', so then if the head of the household said *'el 'emet* the remainder of the household would automatically say *amin*, and no further talking would be allowed. Asians can drop off to sleep like a light going out. The words *'el 'emet* occur nowhere else in the Hebrew bible. It is a commonplace that Yahweh is truthful, i.e. faithful (cf. Dt. 32:4). Faithfulness is shown, amongst other ways, by restoring a deposit unharmed, unworn, as fresh as it was delivered or committed. The idea behind the use of Ps. 31:6 as a prayer before sleeping is simply this, that the spirit leaves the body at sleep as it does in comas or other forms of unconsciousness, and returns at waking or being revived. Yahweh restores new every morning the spirit which the individual has left in his hands the night before.

In the ancient world deposit of valuables was very common indeed. Since it was difficult to prove the exact condition of any valuable which was not deposited in a sealed container, and since in any case lawsuits were expensive and problematical, it must often have happened that people deposited goods with little hope that they would recover them intact. In consequence ancient laws went, with a particularity for which the modern world has little use, into the details of the tacit or imputed terms of the contract of deposit, including the gratuitous bailment which most deposits amongst friends were. The Jewish law does not allow a depositary to use the deposit (except, obviously, coins deposited with a money-changer or banker); and it holds him liable for negligence. He must keep the deposit exactly as he keeps property of his own of the same sort. And if he uses the deposit, or allows others to use it, he owes the depositor the difference between the value when deposited and the value when restored. In a vast number of cases the depositary will

4. S. Singer, *Authorised Daily Prayer Book* (London, 1962), 393, 440.
5. Bab. Tal., Ber. 5*a*. Tanhuma and the Midrash Rabba on Numbers are cited to the same effect by Billerbeck, where cited above.

have used the article and not given the owner anything for that use, upon the basis that the latter was lucky to have it looked after gratuitously. But a 'faithful' man would confess that he had obtained valuable use from it, and would do his best to make it up to the owner unless the latter, with a generosity which the fussy Jewish law does not explicitly anticipate (it did not need to do so), waived his rights. The rabbis explain that whereas a human being restores a deposit at demand the worse for wear, or at the very least decaying through lapse of time, Yahweh restores the spirit in the morning the better for its change of possessor!

The use of words for 'sleep' as a euphemism for 'death' is notorious (p. 133). The likeness between the two went back to primitive times. Death is a sleep from which the dead appear not to wake up: but there is no knowing whether they wake up elsewhere! Consequently the rabbis took Ps. 31:6 as a further proof of the popular belief that Yahweh will restore the spirit after death. If he restores the spirit of man, which was his own gift, each morning in life, how much more will he restore it afresh, bright and new, in the world to come, at the general resurrection![6] The lord of truth, i.e. faithful lord of the Hebrews, when he had a soul committed to him (and he took it, *ergo* death occurred: cf. Ws. 3:1), would surely return it none the worse for its adventure.

Thus with the words *'el 'emet*, which I think St. Luke was told were really the words Jesus uttered as his last speech prior to his Resurrection, Jesus was made to say three things: (1) he gave up his spirit of his own will; (2) to his mind the experience he faced was that of sleep (cf. Mt. 9:24, 27:52; Jn. 11:11–12); (3) he knew Yahweh would restore his spirit and that he would rise again. Jesus died with a promise of the resurrection upon his lips.

I hope my readers will agree with me that this secret, virtually unknown to scholars for eighteen centuries, was worth recovering, and that a general knowledge of oriental laws is helpful for the purpose. And if they have doubts as to whether I have correctly understood St. Luke's meaning they may check the facts by considering three points: firstly that the word *paratithemi*, and the noun *paratheke*, are constantly used in the New Testament for a (legal) deposit, often, without the slightest hesitation, metaphorically, with an emphasis on the nature of the trust, and the obligation imposed

6. *Midrash on Psalms*, Ps. 25, § 2 (trans. W. Braude, New Haven [1959], vol. 1 p. 347). Cf. the speech of Eleazar at Masada, Jos., *BJ*, vii. 349.

upon the depositary when he accepted the deposit—and the soul is certainly a deposit from God in the first place;[7] secondly that the stalwart Essenes who gave up their lives under torture at the hands of Pilate's compatriots 'resigned their souls on the basis that they would receive them back again (in the World to Come)', to follow Josephus's way of putting it (*BJ*, ii. 153), Josephus, whose life overlapped with those of the younger of the apostles; and thirdly that St. John, to whom we can be sure a version of the synoptic tradition (possibly St. Mark or even St. Luke himself) was available, expresses what I have been attempting to convey in so many words: 'It is for this reason that the Father loves me, that I lay down my soul in order that I may take it up again. No one takes it from me, but I lay it down voluntarily. I have permission to lay it down, and I have permission to take it again. That commandment I obtained from my Father' (Jn. 10: 17–18). Why does Jesus, in St. John's view, lay down his life (i.e. place it at risk, enable it to pass from him)? This was already expressed at v. 15: 'I lay down my soul on behalf of the "sheep".'

7. For *paratheke* see 1 Tm. 6:20 (cf. 14), 2 Tm. 1:12, 14. For *paratithemi* Lk. 12:48; Ac. 14:23, 20:32; 1 Tm. 1:18; 2 Tm. 2:2. Especially note 1 P. 4:19, which, in so many words, utilises the idea I explain in this appendix. That this is genuinely Jewish is to be seen from *Pesiqta Rabbati*, 43, § 6 (trans. W. Braude [New Haven and London, 1968], vol. 2, 763–5: Yahweh is the faithful trustee of deposits, in fact in respect of deposits of *nefashot*, souls or spirits). Josephus has no difficulty in speaking of the soul as a deposit *from* God when he deals with the (by no means irrelevant) subject of suicide: *BJ*, iii. 372. For secular learning concerning deposits see *LNT*, 30, n. 1.

The ancient world was puzzled as to what happens when a person is awakened, and takes a short while to 'come to'. Prettily, the rabbis said that the *soul* never sleeps (it is only the body that does so); the soul is pure and during sleep, goes on a visit to see Him who neither slumbers nor sleeps (Ps. 121:4). See *Midrash Rabbah*, Lev. iv. 8 (Soncino Press trans., 58–9).

# APPENDIX SEVEN

# Cutting off the Hand that Causes Offence

If anyone has tired of my somewhat theatrical displays of what the theologians do not know, he may care for a final example. Turn to Mk. 9:43–45: 'And if your hand causes you to stumble, chop it off: it is better for you to enter into life with a stump (literally "deformed") than to have both hands and pass on to Gehenna, to the unquenchable fire. And if your foot causes you to stumble, chop it off; it is better for you to enter into life lame, than to have both feet and be flung into Gehenna.' 'Stumble' is an obvious metaphor for 'succumb to temptation', 'fall'. The theologians, in print, refer to this passage and its syncopated version at Mt. 18:8 as 'very strongly worded advice to tame the natural desires and passions at all costs' (cf. 1 Cor. 9:27), or as showing how nothing is too high a price to pay for entry into the Kingdom (T. W. Manson), or as emphasising that Sin is man's greatest disaster, no price too high if Sin (and the 'destination' to which it sends the sinner) can be avoided (P. Gaechter). If you ask any of them privately what the passage means he will add, as like as not, that this is oriental exaggeration of a kind similar to that of the Asian carpet-dealer who swears that he paid not less than a thousand pounds for the carpet you covet, and strangely allows you to carry it away for a hundred and fifty. Or he may point to surgical operations and point to the patient's willingness to lose a leg rather than die of gangrene. But Jesus speaks of the member's causing, or being involved in, temptation, sin, and this is quite specific. It is possible to get much closer to his idea.

The passage sounds rather different if you know that, irrespective of what the bible said on the subject of punishment, and irrespective of what the Pharisees considerately taught as the right way to discourage crime, chopping off a hand was actually used in Palestine

201

as a punishment for robbery or sedition. It was regarded as more humane than the Roman penalty, crucifixion. It was part of Jewish customary practice, and it never found its way into textbooks, because it was part of what happened, but since it had no scholarly authority it was politely forgotten when norms were spoken about. Jesus refers to what actually used to take place. Old textbooks on eastern law reveal (as travellers in the Ottoman Empire and in India up to the first decades of the nineteenth century saw often enough for themselves) that first one hand, then both, and if that did not work, then a foot were amputated as successive punishments for crimes against property. In ancient times[1] there was some tension between the abhorrence which all primitive societies feel against theft (it is pathological when one can beg from one's mates) an abhorrence which led (e.g. in ancient Babylonia) to a death penalty for thieving—and a more humane doubt whether the protection of *A*'s property really justified *B*'s death. Fines often took the place of physical punishment, and there seem to have been fluctuations throughout ancient times between corporal and pecuniary punishment. The public found amputation congenial (and it must have been known and understood in the Yemen and Saudi Arabia in quite modern times) because at the moment of his crime, snatching with the hand, climbing up with his foot, the thief or robber could associate the chances of profit with the chance of losing for ever the opportunity of repeating the offence: the hand is stretched out and he wonders, is the prize worth the hand itself? A Pakistani judge, attending a conference in Australia within the last decade, recommended that such punishments (orthodox in Islam) should be introduced throughout the world: that was his contribution to penology!

In the time of Jesus wherever biblical rules yielded to customary practices and where Pharisees had not enough power to stop it, *humane* authorities chopped off hands (as an alternative to capital

1. The customary penalty (like the execution of John the Baptist) finds no mention in books on the Jewish law. For a comparative legal history on the subject one can consult the very thorough treatment at Bernard S. Jackson, *Theft in Early Jewish Law* (Oxford, 1972), chs. 7 and 8; and see especially p. 153. The book law knew nothing, either, of *drowning* as a punitive or retributive measure (cf. Mk. 9:42)—but it happened (Jos., *Ant.*, xiv. 450), a fact which is known to the theologians (V. Taylor, *Gospel acc. to St. Mark*, 410).

punishment) to discourage offences against property. I have referred to this above (p. 99). Josephus says 'I reminded Justus that before I arrived from Jerusalem the Galilaeans had cut off his brother's hands on a charge of forging letters before the war began'. At the most relevant place, in his *Life*, Josephus tells how the people of Tiberias revolted from the Jewish government represented by Josephus himself and declared for Herod, who had Roman support; Josephus goes to Tiberias, the citizens change their minds, and surrender ten ring-leaders. The author of the 'sedition' a 'rash and headstrong youth named Cleitus' was informed against by the Tiberians. 'I ordered,' says Josephus, 'one of my bodyguard, called Levi, to step forward and cut off one of his hands'. In an account of what followed which has been thought to be somewhat garbled, Josephus said to Cleitus, 'For such base ingratitude to me you deserve to lose both hands.' Cleitus urged to be spared one hand, and cut off his own left hand with a sword held in his right. Josephus says he did it 'gladly'. He preserved his life at the cost of one hand, for if he had lost both he would have been reduced to beggary amongst fellow-townsmen who were only too ready to repudiate him. In another account of the incident Cleitus begs to be allowed to keep one hand on condition that he cut off the other himself. This took place in A.D. 66 or a little before.

I need hardly add, to complete the picture, that blinding a person was a punishment known in practice in the East in ancient and even relatively modern times, the notion being that those who had the power to inflict this could be credited with humanity in not killing their victim—and secretly they could gloat over the continuing grief of the wretched object of their 'kindness'. Jesus knew that his audience would *not* hear his words as 'oriental exaggeration'. The balance between a limb, or an organ, and life was one they were familiar with. It was obvious that life was worth more than the limb with which one had been tempted into crime. The thought that the profits of crime might not be adequate to compensate for the loss of a limb was familiar to them. Jesus merely transferred the idea from the realm of crime to that of sin. In a society which did not distinguish crime from sin on any intrinsic basis, but only on the level of the chances of being caught and punished by a legally constituted court or by some lynching party, any interchange between sin and crime would be so easy as to escape notice. Even if a skilled jurist could point out the difference, the populace could not. It is better to avoid thieving if the cost will be your hand or your foot; it is better not to defy the earthly king if the cost of unsuccessful defiance is the loss of your hand; it is better to avoid the means of sinning (thereby defying the heavenly king) if the cost is your soul. Only Jesus has said it much more aptly.

Blinding as a punishment was, as I have said, known in general, but in the first century it was notoriously associated with adultery. The famous legislator, Zaleucus of Locri (*c.* 650 B.C.) ordained that adulterers should lose one or both eyes, as it was the eye that led them into sin. From Aelian (*V.H.* xiii. 24) and Valerius Maximus (vi. 5) it was widely believed that when Zaleucus's own son was convicted of this offence the father gave one of his own eyes to save the son from losing both (on the story see Pauly-Wissowa, *R.E.*[2] xviii, 1967, 2299–2300). The link between this story, our Mt. 5:29, Job 31:1, and 25:11 was correctly made as long ago as Antonius Matthaeus, *De Criminibus* (Amsterdam, 1661), 75.

# Bibliographical Note

The professional or experienced student of theology has no need of any help I can give him here, and I address myself to my ideal 'curious' reader, who is in danger, once his curiosity is really excited, of flying off on what I should call a 'one-man heresy'. The original sources are first and foremost the New Testament itself. Translations differ surprisingly, and no one translation will ever meet specialists' approval. The New English Bible and the Jerusalem Bible, now widely used, are not prepared with liturgical use in mind, and they are often banal and unsuitable when read out in church, but as accurate reproductions of the meanings of the original authors of the biblical books they are in advance of their competitors.

The New English Bible has a perfectly splendid translation of the Apocrypha. But both the Old Testament and the New Testament in that version suffer from a defect inescapable in our age. One finds ripe scholarship only in the elderly; but in other ages, particularly when the Authorised Version, the Revised Version, and the Revised Standard Version were made, that age-group did not suffer from self-assurance to quite the degree that is notorious in our half of this century. As we have seen, the New Testament contains a great many puzzles, and passages which are obvious on the surface, but contain hidden meanings, allusions, and puns, which defy translators, unless they are modestly, humbly, and conservatively *literal*. The Old Testament is worse: it is full of problems, linguistic and intellectual, and there are numerous corruptions and places where the original text can be recovered only by conjecture. Former translators were aware of this, and, knowing that it would be many centuries before the truth would be arrived at, if ever, they translated literally, and left the rest to God. The workers on the New English Bible, and to a lesser degree the Jerusalem Bible, feeling, as it were, compelled to come down, once and for all, have taken the other approach. They have gone on attacking the text until it yielded, to their satisfaction, a meaning which could be pinned down, and they have translated accordingly. They have been clever, and many impressive reconstructions of what the original authors might have meant (many centuries before Christ) have occurred to the translators of the Old Testament. There, and in the New Testament, we gain immensely where they are right; but where they may be wrong all possibility of divining the true meaning is gone, unless one has sufficient scholarship to have been worthy to join the translators themselves. And the reader has no means of finding out for himself where they are right, and where perhaps not. So for purposes of study the Jerusalem Bible should be used at first reading; for deep, careful, watchful comparative work the man who does not have the sacred languages could safely use the Revised Standard Version. No version, however, gives or can give a translation similar to Jesus's audience's understandings of the Hebrew bible.

The Jerusalem Bible has the advantage of being provided with cross-references as between the two Testaments (which are essential); the edition of that version which contains a commentary is a marvel of assistance to the unlearned, Without testing his patience, it saves him from errors which a bare reading of the text might involve. The publishers of the New English Bible, with surprising lack of forethought, have left out the references, so that the new life which the Old Testament has in the New is almost completely obscured, and, as we have seen, there are places where this fact reduces the New Testament text almost to gibberish.

To savour the atmosphere of the New Testament world the original works of Josephus and Philo are helpful. The first is never hard going as his racy, though tendentious, writings carry one along at a good pace. If one cannot spare the time for Josephus himself, E. Bevan's *Jerusalem under the High Priests* (1904 but still in print) will be rewarding. But there is nothing to equal Yigael Yadin's *Masada: Herod's Fortress and the Zealots' Last Stand* (London, Sphere, 1971) as a means of taking the reader actually into the dilemmas and the psychology of the religious patriots of the first century. The Israel official tourist guides are the best in the world, and the best of them are over middle age. I wish my reader (especially if he is about 18 to 20) to go through Yadin's unbearably poignant story (the archaeological sensation of all time), to go to Masada and stand and listen to the guide telling him that there, at his feet, were found the lots drawn by the last defenders to select the one who should despatch them, their wives and children, and then kill himself, while the Romans burst through the breach beside them. The story is at Josephus, *BJ*, vii. 304–406, but how different the tale looks when, rhetoric apart, the actual surviving testimony can be seen! At that moment my reader should say to himself, 'Those things happened in the year 73. Jesus recruited youngsters of about my age. And when those men and women died up here, convinced, it seems, that they would take up their lives again in a better world, those same students of Jesus will have been about the age of that guide over there. There was so short a distance of time between the events. What will *they*, or the survivors of them, have thought of the story of Masada?' I do not know whether that is a question which the official guide, for all his knowledge and charming style of communication, would be able to answer.

Philo, too, was a contemporary of the apostles, and his style and notions have a closer bearing on their thought world than is usually appreciated. But since he is attempting to restate Judaism in a style attractive to pagan Hellenes and lapsed Jews in Egypt, subtle sophistications creep in constantly and unpredictably, and the student must proceed warily; he will find the Loeb edition the most handy, since C. D. Yonge's translation is imperfect.

Other near-contemporary Jewish sources must be looked into, perhaps rather than the mishmash of them that one finds in the otherwise excellent and constantly praised *Judaism* of G. F. Moore (1927, often reprinted). A flood of light on the bible as Jesus and his students knew it is thrown by the Palestinian Targum on the Pentateuch. The translation of Etheridge is by far the most handy, and, it appears, it will not be superseded when Diez Macho's edition of the Neofiti Targum is completed, since, most unfortunately, the 'Neofiti' version of the Aramaic Targum of the Five Books of Moses is not the fullest example of the tradition: not that I would decry that magnificent publishing venture, of which I have seen the *Gen.* and *Ex.* volumes. Nor are the Targums to the Pentateuch the only early evidences of the way in which Jesus and the apostles heard the Hebrew scriptures explained in their childhood, Sabbath by Sabbath, in the synagogue; the Targum (called that of Jonathan) to the Prophets is full of evidence that it, or, in some passages, versions once equally up-to-date, but of an earlier period, made far more of an impression on the public than the obscure and ambiguous oracles of the ancient Hebrew seers in what passed for their original words. My present reader cannot be expected to read through the most valuable work of P. Churgin (1927), a glance at which would repel him, nor the more charming, but equally shapeless work of P. Kahle: but a flip through both works would convince him that the bare Old Testament text, translated by our experts of today as best they can, was not the bible with which Jesus and his students worked—a discovery pregnant with more gain than loss, I believe.

Targumic studies are now à la mode. R. Le Déaut's *Introduction à la littérature targumique* (Rome, 1966) is valuable, also his article 'Les Etudes targumiques. Etat de la recherche . . .' in H. Cazelles, ed., *De Mari à Qumrân* (Festschrift for J. Coppens, I) (Gembloux/Paris, 1969), 302–31. A breathless survey of targumic and midrashic studies with an enormous bibliography in various languages is provided by Merrill P. Miller, 'Targum, Midrash, and the Use of the Old Testament in the New Testament', *Journal for the Study of Judaism*, vol. 2, no. 1 (1971), 29–82. An example of the more coherent contributions is M. McNamara's *New Testament and the Palestinian Targum to the Pentateuch* (Rome, 1966). The weight of instances of midrashic allusion in the New Testament, both in the gospels and the epistles, has accumulated to such an extent that the burden of proof that it is a waste of time to investigate the techniques lies upon him who asserts it (pp. 163–4 above).

Alongside the Targum one must consult the ancient *midrashim*, many of which go back, in essence if not in precise form, to the pre-A.D. 70 period, and they thus breathe the spirit of Judaism as Jesus knew it. It was, after all, that Judaism which he intended to represent and re-present in a guise of his own choosing, and we cannot know what he was intending to teach unless we know the ideas commonly circulating in his day. The collection known as Midrash Rabbah, or 'the Great *midrash*' on the books of the Pentateuch, and other collections on many of the Hebrew scriptures, is fortunately available in an English translation published by the Soncino Press (London).

The Dead Sea Scrolls have caused great excitement, and provided an abundant literature. It is invidious to select one author as most reliable for the general reader. However, I should recommend the two works of G. Vermes, his translation of A. Dupont-Sommer's classic (the original title was *Les Ecrits Esséniens découverts près de la*

*Mer Morte*, 3rd ed., Paris, 1968), and his own *The Dead Sea Scrolls in English* (London, Pelican Series A.551, 1966). The little composite volume edited by M. Black, *The Scrolls and Christianity* (London, 1969) gives an up-to-date bibliography for the use of the reader whom I contemplate, and should put to rest any alarms he might suffer after going through the Dead Sea texts in Vermes. After those sources we come to the Mishnah. This, in H. Danby's translation (1933), is a mine of detailed information, much of which goes back to the pre-A.D. 70 period *in principle* though the rabbis quoted are mostly from later, and even much later periods. The Mishnah introduces the reader to the fussiness, and legalistic particularity of the rabbinical mind, essential for understanding the gospels and the epistles of St. Paul. But the tractates Sanhedrin and Makkot have been compiled, many years after the Crucifixion, to give an ideal picture of what the Pharisees thought ought to be the law, at a period when they were seldom able to put their views into practice; the law only occasionally represents what actually was enforced when Sadducees were in command.

Since I have used the Babylonian Talmud extensively in the past, and often with striking success, the reader will ask why I do not recommend the enthusiastic student to plunge into that quagmire of law, religious speculation, philosophy, medicine, and whatever topic interested the ancient world? Granted that it is not in its entirety traceable to within several centuries of the time of Christ, the fact that it illuminates my sort of inquiry at every turn should urge me to urge others to take the heavy volumes in hand and pore over them. Why not? The caution that one must use when reading Philo would have to be redoubled in handling so unsystematic a work, professedly embodying traditions (many of them discordant) which grew out of social and political conditions that arose after the middle of the second century, and often well after that date. On the other hand the traditions found in the Talmuds concerning the early Pharisees, and especially the *dicta* of teachers contemporary with Jesus and with the apostles, must have a great value if they are isolated from the other material and considered critically. The whole question of transmission of didactic quotations (which Professor B. Gerhardsson has pursued so helpfully) can only be pursued if the material is assembled systematically, and without distraction from the immediate contexts. A very substantial beginning has been made in two works of Jacob Neusner, *Development of a Legend, Studies on the Traditions Concerning Yohanan ben Zakkai* (Leiden, Brill, 1970) and *The Rabbinic Traditions about the Pharisees before 70 A.D.* (Leiden, Brill, 1971), the last in three large volumes. Such a collection illustrates more favourably than does the Mishnah the scope of ideas and modes of intentionally memorable self-expression used by the great teachers.

I do not think modern books on Judaism, e.g. Morris Joseph's rather sanctimonious *Judaism as Creed and Life* (London, 1920), or *Judaism* by I. Epstein, are really helpful for the student of the first century. Apart from the apologetic aspect, which is a fault from which so many Christian books also suffer, Judaism itself has been through several stages since then. Christianity has influenced it, and Phariseeism has purified and refined it, and made it into something new. It will be noticed that few books purporting to explain Judaism as a religion go into the details of Jewish practices, superstitious usages, and conventions, which are quite another matter. Reading through a work of the genre of G. Friedlander's *Laws and Customs of Israel* (London, 1921) would be an eye-opener, provided one remembers that individual rules cannot be traced accurately back to the first century. The style is illuminating. And the same can be said with confidence of the *Code* of Moses ben Maimun, *alias* Maimonides, which is being translated into English in the Yale Judaica Series, and which makes Jewish law pleasurable and instructive reading. Maimonides lived far from the Land of Israel, centuries after Jesus, and many of his propositions existed only in embryo then, and a few not at all: but the cultural continuity of this unique people has placed a mark of almost unqualified approval on his work, and that argues a certain identity with the remoter past which is greatly to the modern student's advantage. Strictures on modern Jewish productions, on the basis that they do not represent ancient Judaism entire, ought not to be cast indiscriminately over medieval works, and Ibn Paquda's *Duties of the Heart* is most rewarding.

For the general history E. Schürer's *History of the Jewish People*, available in an English translation (1886–90), is still an authentic and valuable work. A new edition is awaited with eagerness; it will, no doubt, bring up to date its magnificent bibliography.

I must mention reference works, avoiding the great continental standard encyclopedias. *Peake's Commentary on the Bible* (1962) is a handy work, and so is the very similarly styled *Catholic Commentary on Holy Scripture*, of which there are two editions, both valuable. Every book of the bible has its individual commentary in many series, of which the *International Critical Commentary* is perhaps the most solid. A. E. Harvey's *Companion* to the New Testament portion of the New English Bible (1970) carries a huge weight of learning in a simple, direct, and attractive style. It is a true companion. The rival encyclopedias of an earlier age, the *Encyclopedia Biblica* and Hastings's two monoliths, *Dictionary of the Bible* and *Dictionary of Christ and the Gospels*, have articles filled with detailed information, the first from what it called an 'advanced critical' angle, while the second pair took the broad middle of the road, as was seemly in a typical British publication. But no specialist will quarrel with me when I say that the results, in point of interpretation, do not reflect the present age or mood. Were it not for the handy collections of information which they provide I should recommend them no more heartily than I could any theological work, which is always presumed to be tendentious and directed towards the needs of Christians who, for any reason, stand in a defensive or apologetic position.

This Note makes it plain that I think no entry to the New Testament is satisfactory if it is not Jewishly orientated. If any think otherwise they should go to Tokyo to study Shakespeare, or to Göttingen to study Handel or Locke. I have not the least doubt but that such studies could be pursued with very great profit in those places; but the nuances of any topic can best be picked up in an ideal environment, and it is there that we must go. Jesus belongs to the Hebrews, and anyone who is keen to describe him and his intentions in terms of what would please any class of society in England (or elsewhere in the British Isles) is not an academic—I do not know what he is. For that reason I recommend, though it is not light reading, David Daube's *New Testament and Rabbinic Judaism* (1956). It does not concentrate on the first century, and it is a book of ideas rather than 'hard grit', but it shows, at every turn, how the outlook of New Testament writers can be illuminated from Jewish literature. My own *Law in the New Testament* (1970) is hardly to be mentioned in the same breath, but it proves, with exhaustive studies of specific passages, that Jesus's parables were models of Jewish biblical scholarship, and that Jewish ideas and attitudes explain a great deal that (to the Western reader) is quite obscure: for his inquiring glance is often reflected from the mere surface of the biblical texts, and if not is more often refracted within them.

One who dips into the Targumim, and acquaints himself with *midrashim* tends to get intoxicated. Except for some works in Hebrew which remain to be translated, there are no comprehensive explanations of the *content* of haggadic *midrashim*, or their rationale. The work of Max Kadushin, *The Rabbinic Mind* (2nd ed., 1965) is the first of its kind, attempting to explain what themes were uppermost, and how easily they made themselves felt in exegesis of any and every text. Apart from the indigestible style of the work, it was a pioneering effort, and disciplined successors have not been forthcoming. It is all too easy for Christian scholars to dip their bucket in the sea of *midrash*, to fish up some glorious similarity with a gospel passage, and to run off laughing with joy. But this does not take them to the heart of the Hebrew mentality, nor enable one to predicate (as is needed) what exegesis of scripture was available to Jesus and his audience on a systematic basis. Britain has not led in this field of study, nor has Germany. The very competent lecture given in Oxford by the late A. Guillaume, 'The Midrash and the Gospels', as far back as January 1926 (printed in the *Expository Times* for 1925–6, 392–8) seems to have called forth no response whatever, even though I. Abrahams and G. H. Box, two very competent scholars, had made striking contributions in A. S. Peake's *The People and the Book* (Oxford, 1925).

Readers of French are in a much better position. The pro-Christian bias of Fr. R. Le Déaut, whose recent works (illustrated above) and reviews in this field are fascinating, will be taken in their stride; and they have an even more satisfactory guide in Renée Bloch, whose untimely death deprived us of fine objective research in this field. Her article 'Midrash' in *Dictionnaire de la Bible*, Suppl. 5 (Paris, 1957), 1263–81, is an excellent starting-point. Nevertheless, I continue to repeat, the best expositor of Haggadah and Midrash will always be a Jew from an oriental or traditional environment.

But I would not wish to be thought ungrateful for two illuminating, and if I may say so with respect, extremely useful publications in Britain in recent years. P. R. Ackroyd and C. F. Evans edited the first volume of the *Cambridge History of the Bible* (Cambridge, 1970), in which there appear articles by S. Talmon, G. Vermes, C. K. Barrett, and R. P. C. Hanson, all of which (quite apart from the remainder of the volume) bear directly on the search which I hope I have stimulated in my own reader's mind. J. Bowker's *Targums and Rabbinic Literature* (Cambridge, 1969) pleased me, and will please those who have been engaged on a quest like mine; it illustrates abundantly how the Hebrew commentator, untouched by modern and occidental notions of scholarship, understood the Hebrew bible in the light of itself, in all its variety, and in the light of the golden legend that is coeval with it. A mind prepared with a study of the *Cambridge History* and with Bowker's abundant illustrations can safely approach the strange propositions of Aileen Guilding in her *Fourth Gospel and Jewish Worship* (Oxford, 1960). The learned author of that celebrated but over-enthusiastic treatise uncovered striking coincidences, raising the presumption that St. John wrote to provide a lectionary in keeping with the Hebrew ritual-liturgical year, the implications of which remain to be digested by the theologians, many of whom (I gather) have been forced to suspend judgment for the present.

Further study will confirm the central position which Law had, along with Eschatology, in the mental furniture of Jesus's audience, whose psychology we must know if we are to make anything even of haggadic *midrash*. A reader who wishes to see how far, and in what respects Jewish law differed from its contemporaries in the world's legal systems may do so readily in Derrett, ed., *Introduction to Legal Systems* (London, Sweet & Maxwell, 1968), where the succinct chapter on Jewish law is from the pen of Professor Z. W. Falk of Jerusalem and Tel Aviv. *Eschatology*, alias *A Critical History of the Doctrine of a Future Life in Israel, in Judaism and in Christianity* by R. K. Charles (2nd. ed., 1913), which the Dead Sea finds have richly illustrated (and, had its eminent author survived till their discovery, would have necessitated a new edition from him) is still an important guide to an easily-forgotten aspect of Judaism.[1]

I shall be accused of over-reacting, and depriving the untutored reader of access to Hellenic sources which have so long (far too long) ruled the roost in New Testament studies. Now that I imagine him truly inoculated against the evil effects of commencing in an Hellenic mental environment I should by no means hesitate to recommend C. H. Dodd's *The Bible and the Greeks* (London, 1935) or the now somewhat antiquated works of William Fairweather, *Jesus and the Greeks* (Edinburgh, 1924) and *The Background of the Gospels* (Edinburgh, 1911). I should *not* recommend G. Friedlander's *Hellenism and Christianity* (London, 1912) as this is virtually an

1. Now see D. S. Russell, *The Method and Message of Jewish Apocalyptic* (1964).

anti-Christian work tinged with the *Golden Bough* style of 'critical scholarship' much favoured in the first quarter of this century, which was (for example) very pleased to have 'discovered' that the traditional Nativity stories were a version of an Adonis myth! They were not (see *Studia Evangelica VI*, Berlin, forthcoming, pp. 94–102), but that is another story. G. H. C. Macgregor and A. C. Purdy, *Jew and Greek: Tutors unto Christ. The Jewish and Hellenistic Background of the New Testament* (Edinburgh, 1936) was produced in a new edition in 1959, and has an excellent bibliography.

The discovery of the Dead Sea scrolls, as also the Murabba'at manuscripts (see Y. Yadin, *Bar-Kokhba*, London, 1971), rendered all the classical treatments of the Hellenistic Eastern Mediterranean significantly out-of-date at almost one blow. Yet readers whose library facilities are restricted can still gain much information from the *Cambridge Ancient History*, vols. 10 and 12; readers of French will find pleasant (if a little too pious) material in Daniel-Rops' *La vie quotidienne en Palestine au temps de Jésus* (Paris, Hachette, 1961), and a splendid bibliography in M. Simon and A. Benoit, *Le Judaïsme et le Christianisme antique* (Paris, Presses Universitaires, 1968). J. Dauvillier's, *Les Temps Apostoliques. 1er Siècle.* (Paris, Sirey, 1970) is devoted to legal ideas, but its bibliographies are massive and versatile. W. O. E. Oesterley, *The Jews and Judaism during the Greek Period* (London, 1941) retains a good deal of its value. C. K. Barrett, ed., *The New Testament Background: Selected Documents* (London, S.P.C.K., 1956), though dry at first sight, is most useful provided the individual immediate relevance of the materials is beyond doubt. J. Finegan's *Light from the Ancient Past* (Princeton, 1946), pp. 209–253, is useful. The collected essays of A. D. Nock, of which I have made some use in this book, cannot easily be recommended to anyone but a classical scholar, to whom he needs no recommendation from me, any more than does the work of F. Cumont on oriental religions in Roman paganism, happily available in English.

The Roman side of the New Testament story is told in A. N. Sherwin-White's *Roman Society and Roman Law in the New Testament* (Oxford, 1963). His incidental contribution to the question of the historicity of the gospel accounts is valuable, coming, as it does, from a historian of another culture. But, in the East, myth can invade factual tradition much more readily than it may in the West. 'As if' is far from unknown in the West, but Asia is its home.

I hope that this book will come into the hands of some people who have no scholarly pretentions, but who (in keeping with the times) see no reason why this should preclude them from getting to grips with abstract questions. There are many beautiful books on Roman History (e.g. by J. P. V. D. Balsdon) which a good librarian will recommend, but for one who can plan his day and is not likely to be tired of instances of the superstition, the craftiness, and the heroism of the ancient world there is nothing to compare with Plutarch's *Lives*. John Dryden's translation of the 'Lives of the Noble Grecians and Romans', as revised by Arthur Hugh Clough, is readily available in many editions, and is compulsive reading. Our scale of values is different from that which obtained before the Second World War, and we are not so clear about the exact challenge and contribution of Christianity in the wretched world in which, and for which, Plutarch wrote, but T. R. Glover's *Influence of Christ in the Ancient World* (Cambridge, 1929) still has value.

# INDEX OF CITATIONS OF BIBLICAL AND
# APOCRYPHAL SOURCES

(For the order of books, and the places where they may be found, see pp. 29–30 above.)

# INDEX OF NAMES AND TOPICS

Jacob, 46, 60
Jeremias, Joachim, 20 n., 177
Jerusalem, 58, 59
*Jerusalem Bible*, 206
Jesus, his courage, 13; as a teacher of law, 13–14; as a 'Man for all seasons', 22; grandnephews of, 36 n.,; and 'sinners', 62; his Passion, 94; and 'as if', 103; riding the donkey, 104; and the Messianic Age, 144; last words of, 193 ff.
'Jesus is God', 13
Jews and New Testament studies, 24
Jews, modern non-oriental, 23
John the Baptist, 103, 105, 191
John, St., the evangelist, 15
joint living, 36
jokes, 68
Josephus, Flavius, 22, 25, 27, 47 n., 50, 67, 87, 88, 92 n., 106, 122, 135–6, 146, 203
*Against Apion*, 27, 50 n.
*Ant.* 33 n., 39 n., 58 n., 60 n., 64 n., 69 n., 71 n., 79 n., 82 n., 85 n., 88 n., 92 n., 97 n., 99 n., 117 n., 118 n., 121 n., 124 n., 132 n., 142 n., 159 n.
*BJ.* 31 n., 33 n., 34 nn., 37 nn., 39 n., 41 n., 43 n., 44 nn., 46 n., 48 n., 51 nn., 52 nn., 54 nn., 55 n., 56 n., 58 n., 59 n., 60 nn., 64 n., 69 n., 70 nn., 74 nn., 75 n., 76 n., 78 nn., 79 nn., 82 n., 85 nn., 85 nn., 88 n., 90 nn., 92 nn., 95 n., 96 n., 98 n., 99 n., 107 n., 115 n., 117 n., 118 n., 120 n., 121 n., 132 n., 133 n., 134 n., 140 n., 142 n., 150 n., 207
*Life* 19 n., 47 n., 55 n., 99 n., 134 nn., 142 n., 146 n
joy, 68, 71
Jubilee, 78
judges, 57, 65, 88
Judith, 34
justice, 42

Kadushin, M., 212
Kalisch, M. M., 24 n.

Kee, H. C., 21 n.
ketubah, 33, 38
kingdom, secular, 75, 96
kings, 87, 94–5
kinsmen, 38
kiss, 69
Klausner, J., 196
Kümmel, W. G., 188

labourers, 76–7
Lamsa, G. M., 18 n.
law, 98 n.
Law, the, 56, 64, 65, 82, 109, 110, 111 ff., 143, 150, 151
'Lazarus', 78 n.
Le Déaut, R., 208
leadership, 40
'leaven', 137, 142
left hand, 42, 130
legislation, 97–8
Léon-Dufour, X., 10 n.
Levites, 46
Levison, N., 21 n.
life, 103
Lightfoot, J., 25
literacy and illiteracy, 32
*LNT*, 34 n., 35 nn., 40 n., 41 n., 46 n., 47 n., 55 n., 63 nn., 64 nn., 76 n., 95 n., 98 n., 99 n., 103 n., 113 n., 114 n., 153 nn., 163 n., 185, 187 n., 190 n., 211
Longenecker, R. N., 20 n.
loyalty, 97
lynching, 90

Macho Diez, 207
magic, 49, 112, 115 f., 122, 125
Maimonides, 82 n., 210
mammon, 64, 74, 131
man, 156
marriage, offers of, 31; arranged, 33, 36
Marsh, J., 104
Martha, 127
martyrdom, 92 n.
Masada, 51 n., 199 n., 206
maxims, 113, 143
McKenzie, J. L., 20 n.